Population, Resources and Development

Second Edition

Jane Chrispin

Community Development Worker, North East Derbyshire

Francis Jegede

Lecturer in Geography (with special interests in developing countries, international relations and population studies), University of Derby

LANDMARK GEOGRAPHY

Collins Educational

An Imprint of HarperCollinsPublishers

Contents

1 Growth, wealth and happiness

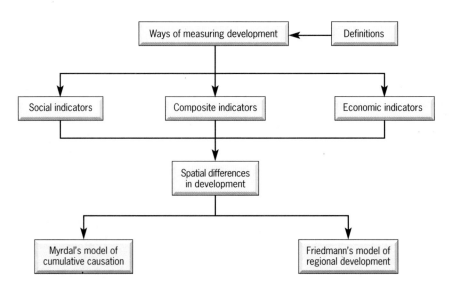

?

1 Study Figure 1.1. The aim of the Peters projection is to show the correct size of continents in relation to each other.
a Compare Figure 1.1 with map projections used in an atlas. State how the Peters projection is different.
b Explain why the Peters projection has been used here to show the North-South divide.

2 Look at Figures 1.2–1.4.
a Would you say that the people shown are happy or unhappy in their situations?
b In your opinion, is there anything that they are lacking or have, that affects their happiness?
c Using one image, write a letter expressing how you would feel in a similar situation.

3a Identify those areas in your country which may be regarded as either 'rich' or 'poor'. Describe the main features of these areas which make you classify them in this way.
b On a smaller scale (such as your local government area or nearest city), identify the places which could be regarded as rich or poor. Suggest reasons for the differences.

1.1 Introduction

Wealth is not evenly distributed among countries and people throughout the world. We live in a world where inequality is a fact of life. In spite of the advances in technology, which have made many rich countries even richer, the vast majority of the world's population still lives in poverty.

Inequalities exist at different scales. On a global scale, the rich countries of Western Europe, North America, Australasia and Japan are often grouped together and referred to as the **developed countries**. The term the rich 'North' is also used to describe them because most of these countries, except those in Australasia, are in the northern hemisphere (Fig. 1.1). Other countries, located mainly in the southern hemisphere, are generally poorer and are often referred to as the poor 'South'. The term **developing countries** has been used to describe these countries that are relatively poor. The **North-South divide** is also used to express the spatial patterns of inequalities on this global scale.

More recently, the terms **Majority** and **Minority Worlds** are used to describe the poorer and richer nations, respectively. These terms are considered, by some, as politically correct, given that the majority of the world's population remain relatively poor and that a minority continues to accumulate wealth. However, controversy surrounding the use of these and other terms remains. For the purposes of this book, the terms developed and developing countries are preferred.

Irrespective of the terms used, within each country, whether more developed or less developed, some areas or regions are wealthier than others. This inequality of wealth within a country can be just as extreme as the inequality that exists between different nations, particularly so for the developing countries. Here, the poor regions tend to be so lacking in resources that it is highly unlikely that they could ever attract any development or investment without active government policies aimed at diverting resources to such areas. The poor areas therefore tend to become even poorer, while the comparably wealthier areas become richer (see section 1.4). Even at the local level in any country, there exists an uneven distribution of wealth and resources (Figs 1.2–1.4).

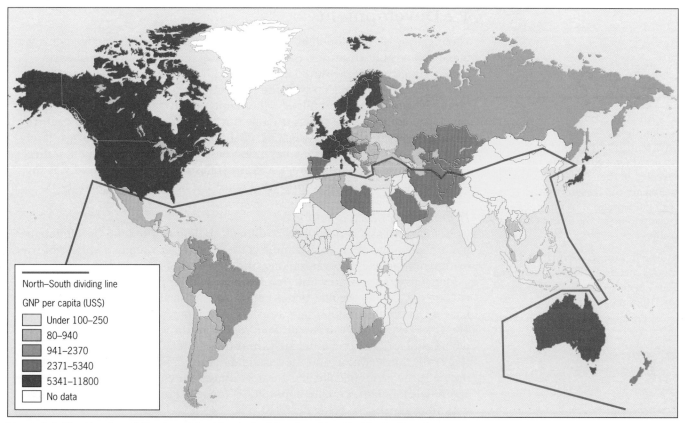

Figure 1.1 The 'developed' North and the 'developing' South as identified in the Brandt report, 17 December 1979, with the global distribution of GDP, 1992 (*Source: World Factbook*, CIA)

Legend:

North–South dividing line

GNP per capita (US$)
- Under 100–250
- 80–940
- 941–2370
- 2371–5340
- 5341–11800
- No data

Figure 1.2 Homeless, London

Figure 1.3 Waiting for food distribution, southern Sudan

Figure 1.4 Ladakh village school, Kashmir, India

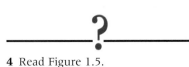

4 Read Figure 1.5.
a Identify the ways in which environmental damage has occurred on a global scale, as revealed in the *Living Planet Report*.
b Explain the reasons for the regional variations in the consumption of the world's natural resources.

5 Search through newspapers for articles that deal with environmental issues in development. Summarise the issues involved.

1.2 Development

The meaning of 'development' changes according to the value judgements we make about other countries. Early examples of terms used to describe the poorer countries (as measured by the strength of their economies and the nature of their relationship with the rich countries) include 'colony', 'underdeveloped' and 'primitive', all of which imply that economically developed countries are superior while the economically developing countries are inferior. Similarly, terms such as 'First World' and 'Third World' are rarely used now, as they stem from a definition based on political alignment – the First World was the USA, Europe and Australasia, the Second World was the Communist bloc, and the Third World consisted of the non-aligned states.

Definitions of development

'Development' as a concept is very difficult to define. The term development' has a wide range of meanings and has therefore been used in a variety of ways, by different people or organisations, at different times.

Many geographers now link development with improvements in human welfare e.g. greater wealth, better education and health. Environmental issues have also become an important aspect of development throughout the world. The UN Earth Summit in Rio de Janeiro, during June 1992, examined the whole issue of environmental **sustainability** in relation to development (Fig. 1.5). Conservation and the sustainable use of the environment, rather than just the economic factors, are now important considerations in all debates about development. Equally important is the concern over the rate at which natural resources are being depleted (Fig. 1.6).

A planet in crisis – our assault on the natural world

Humans have destroyed more than 30 per cent of the natural world since 1970 with serious depletion of the forest, freshwater and marine systems on which life depends.

Consumption pressure from increasing affluence has doubled in the past 25 years and continues to accelerate, according to a ground breaking report from the World Wide Fund for Nature, the New Economics Foundation, and the World Conservation Monitoring Centre at Cambridge. *The Living Planet* Report says that the acceleration in environmental destruction shows that politicians who have been paying lip service to the idea of sustainable development have done little to promote it. "Time is running out for us to change the way we live if we are to leave future generations a living planet," Nick Mabey, WWF's economic policy officer, said at the launch of the report in London yesterday. "We knew it was bad but until we did this report we did not realise how bad."

One of the most serious problems revealed for the first time is the depletion of freshwater resources with half of the accessible supplies being used by humans – double the amount of 1960. The rate of decline of freshwater eco-systems is running at 6 per cent a year, threatening to dry up many wetlands, and push the species of those habitats to extinction.

The report says that governments should increase the efficiency of their water use, and stop wasteful irrigation schemes where water losses are highest.

Carbon dioxide emissions have doubled in the same period, and, being far in excess of the natural world's ability to absorb them, are accelerating global warming.

Wood and paper consumption has increased by two thirds, worldwide, and most forests are managed unsustainably. In the same period, marine fish consumption has also more than doubled and most of the world's fish resources are either fully exploited or in decline.

Although western countries have high consumption rates, some of the developing countries are depleting their natural resources at an alarming rate. The people of Taiwan, the United States and Singapore are singled out as the world's most voracious consumers, responsible for depleting the earth's resources faster than other countries. The United Kingdom comes 41st in the list of more than 130 countries.

The report says that while governments are failing to take action to protect croplands and resources, every individual bears a responsibility for being careless with the world's resources.

Dr Norman Myers, from Oxford, said: "As the world becomes economically richer, it becomes environmentally poorer. Many people have known this for a long time but they have sometimes lacked evidence of a comprehensive and compelling sort. More power then to WWF for documenting our declining prospect in such fine grain detail."

Although the report says that increasing population is part of the problem, it is increasing individual consumption that has been the main problem. The average North American or Japanese consumes 10 times as much as the average Bangladeshi.

Japan and Bangladesh have the same populations but have a vastly different effect on the world's eco-systems, particularly in timber and fish consumption.

The average North American resident consumes five times as much as an African and three times as much as an Asian. However, in total Asia takes more of the earth's resources because there are 3.2 billion of them compared with only 0.3 billion in North America.

Figure 1.5 Development and the depletion of natural resources (*Source*: Paul Brown, *The Guardian*, 2 October 1998)

We shall use the term 'development' to mean improvement in people's quality of life and general well-being. It is essential to note that economic growth both leads to, and results from, an increase in output or income of a nation – but economic growth does not necessarily mean that the country is developing. It is possible therefore to have economic growth without development. In other words, development needs economic growth, but economic growth does not necessarily lead to development.

1.3 How do we measure development?

There are several methods of measuring development – some focus on economic indicators, others on the quality of life. The common indices of development and the problems associated with the use of each of these indices are discussed below.

Economic indicators of development: GNP and GDP

Gross National Product (GNP) and **Gross Domestic Product (GDP)** are the most widely used economic measures (indices) of development. GNP may be defined as the total value, or output, of goods and services which become available during a period of time (usually a year) for consumption or saving within a country, plus income from foreign investments. This is usually expressed per head of population (per capita), i.e. the value of GNP divided by the total population. GNP/capita is therefore a measure of average national income.

GNP, as an indicator of development, does have its weaknesses. First, it is often very difficult to obtain accurate information about the economy of a country. Second, what is actually produced in many economically developing countries does not always have a monetary value, so in this respect GNP could be very misleading. For example, **subsistence agriculture** is still extremely important in developing countries. Most of this agricultural produce is used for domestic consumption, and does not count towards the GNP. Third, GNP and GDP are always given in US dollars, so there is a problem of currency conversion – some countries have artificially high or low currencies. Fourth, apart from showing the monetary value of goods and services produced in a country, the GNP alone tells us nothing about the quality of life experienced by the majority of the population (Table 1.1). Fifth, although an increase in GNP is necessary for improvements in living standards to occur, it does not always follow that economic growth automatically produces better living conditions. GNP does not show the *actual* distribution of wealth or the levels of inequality.

Another economic indicator of development is GDP. Gross domestic product is defined as the total monetary value of all goods and services produced by a nation during a year (excluding any income from foreign investments).

The major weakness of GNP and GDP as indices of development is that they define a country's economy (rather than its well-being) in monetary terms. They are quantitative rather than qualitative measures and therefore give no indication of the distribution of wealth in each country. Although it is easy to assess the growth of the economy through the GNP figures, GNP does not show if the increase in wealth has been used to improve living standards across the population as a whole.

Social indicators of development

Other non-monetary indicators have been used to measure the levels of social development and standards of living for different countries. Many of these, unlike the strictly economic measures, reveal information about general living standards in each country. Some of these social and demographic indices emphasise quality of life and include measures, or a combination of measures, such as those shown in Table 1.2. We can use a selection of these social indicators to show differences in levels of development between countries (Table 1.3).

Figure 1.6 The Earth Summit, Rio de Janeiro, 7 June 1992: children sign a giant quilt called the Earth Flag supporting pro-environmental measures. At the same time, 178 UN member states agree to a commission on sustainable development to oversee nations' efforts to develop without harming the environment.

Table 1.1 GNP for selected countries, 1992, 1997 (*Source:* World Development Report, 1992, 1999)

Country	Per capita GNP (US$) 1992	Per capita GNP (US$) 1997
Brazil	2 770	4 720
The Gambia	390	240
Italy	20 510	20 120
Nigeria	320	260
USA	23 120	28 740
Japan	28 220	37 850

6a Describe the global variations in levels of GDP per capita in Figure 1.1.
b Say, giving reasons, whether you agree with the division between the rich North and the poor South.

7a Research the GDP figures for ten countries, from both developed and developing worlds, over the last 30 years.
b Using an appropriate technique, illustrate the rates of change over the 30-year period.
c Suggest reasons for the changes identified.

In recent years, some of these individual social indicators have been combined and used as composite measures of development. Generally, the latter examples below recognise that economic, social and demographic indicators are closely interrelated.

Table 1.2 Social indicators of development

- Labour force in agriculture (%)
- Literacy rates (%)
- Life expectancy (years)
- School enrolments as a percentage of the relevant age group
- Infant mortality (deaths per 1000)
- Number of people per doctor
- Calorie supply (per capita)
- Energy consumption (kJ per capita)
- Ownership of consumer durables e.g. washing machines (per capita)
- Ownership of telephones (per capita)
- Quantity of letters sent (per capita)
- Real income (per capita)
- Growth of labour force (%)
- Urban population growth (%)

Table 1.3 Social indicators of development for selected countries (*Source*: Human Development Report 1998)

Country	Adult literacy (% of total population >15 yrs), 1995	Life expectancy at birth (average year, M and F), 1996	Number of doctors per 100 000 population, 1993	Telephone main lines per 1000 persons 1995	Total calories per capita per day, 1995	Human Development Index (HDI) 1995
Brazil	83.3	66.6	134	75	2 824	0.809
The Gambia	38.6	46.0	2	17	2 122	0.291
Italy	98.1	78.0	42.4	434	3 157*	0.922
Nigeria	57.1	51.4	21	4	2 254	0.391
USA	99.0	76.4	245	626	3 157*	0.943
Japan	99.0	79.9	177	488	3 157*	0.940

* Average value for developed countries

8a Study Figure 1.1 and Tables 1.1 and 1.3. For those countries listed, compare the levels of GNP per capita with the other indicators of development.
b Which of the indicators best reflect the level of development of the countries selected? Give reasons for your answer.

9a For 15 selected countries, find the GNP per capita, the energy consumption per capita, and the average annual population growth rate.
b Using Table 1.4, calculate the Spearman's rank correlation (see Appendix A 1) between: • GNP per capita and energy consumption,
• GNP per capita and average annual population growth.
c Comment on the level of significance of your results.

Human Development Index

In 1990, the United Nations Development Programme (UNDP) argued that income growth alone was not a good indication of development and that human development should lead to greater and more sustainable economic growth.

This is a reflection of the current emphasis on human welfare in development, as against the economic priorities of the 1950s and the 1960s. Consequently, the UNDP devised the Human Development Index (HDI) in an attempt to measure development.

The HDI consists of three aspects of development:

- real income per capita, i.e. taking into account what a person is actually able to buy with a given income;
- adult literacy combined with the mean number of years of schooling, which gives a measure of educational attainment;
- life expectancy at birth.

The HDI is expressed as a value between 0 and 1. The closer to 1 the score is, the higher the level of human development.

Development indices and women

The recent recognition that women can play a vital role in development (see section 6.5) has led to new indices of development. These include the gender-related development index (GDI) and the gender empowerment measure (GEM).

The GDI is the HDI adjusted downward for gender inequality. This index uses the same HDI variables but the GDI focuses on inequalities in achievement between women and men. The greater the gender disparity in

10a For all the countries in West Africa, collect the most recent data for • life expectancy at birth • adult literacy rate • GDP per capita • Human Development Index.
b Using an appropriate graphical technique, compare life expectancy at birth with levels of adult literacy for the selected countries.
c Comment on your results.

11 Study Tables 1.4 and 1.5.
a Why is it important to use different methods of measuring human poverty for the developed and developing countries?
b Apart from the indicators used to measure levels of human poverty, identify other important aspects of daily life, which reflect social deprivation. Justify your choice of indicators.

basic human development, the lower a country's GDI compared with its HDI. The four variables included in the calculation of GDI are:

• female and male life expectancy at birth;
• female and male adult literacy rates;
• female and male combined enrolment ratio;
• female and male share of earned income.

The gender empowerment measure GEM, indicates whether or not women take active part in economic and political life. It concentrates on female participation and decision-making in a country's economic and political activities. Unlike the GDI it exposes gender inequality in opportunities in selected areas.

The following variables are used in the calculation of GEM:

• % of seats in parliament held by women;
• % of female administrators and managers;
• % of female professional and technical workers;
• % of women's share of earned income;
• weighted share of females and males based on % of total population.

The New Human Poverty Index
In 1997, a new Human Poverty Index (HPI) was introduced to measure different dimensions of deprivation. As an aggregate measure, the HPI focuses on the prevalence of poverty in a country and concentrates on three essential elements of human life already reflected in the HDI. These are life expectancy, knowledge and decent living standards.

The difference between the HPI and HDI is that while the HDI measures progress in a country as a whole, the HPI highlights the extent of deprivation, i.e. the proportion of people in the country who are excluded from progress. There are two sets of measurements used to calculate the HPI. HPI-1 is used for developing countries and HPI-2 for developed countries.

The following measures are used to calculate the HPI-1 (for developing countries):

• % of people not expected to survive to the age of 40;
• % of adults who are illiterate;
• % of people without access to safe water;
• % of people without access to health services;
• % of moderately or severely underweight children under 5.

Table 1.4 Human Poverty Index (HPI-1) for selected developing countries (*Source:* Human Development Report 1998)

Country	People not expected to survive to age 40 (% of total population)	Adult illiteracy rates (%)	Population without access to safe water (%)	Population without access to health services (%)	Underweight children under age 5 (%)	HPI-1 Rank
Chile	4	4.8	5	3	1	2
Jamaica	5	15	14	10	10	10
Mauritius	4	17.1	2	0	16	12
United Arab Emirates	3	20.8	5	1	6	14
Dominican Republic	9	17.9	35	22	6	18
Sri Lanka	6	9.8	43	7	38	22
Iran	10	31	10	12	16	26
Tunisia	8	33.3	2	10	9	28
Lesotho	23	28.7	38	20	16	30
Nicaragua	12	34.3	39	17	12	32
Kenya	27	21.9	47	23	23	35
Myanmar	19	16.9	40	40	31	36
Guatemala	14	35	23	43	27	39
Nigeria	31	42.9	50	49	36	54
Ethiopia	34	64.5	75	54	48	74

Table 1.5 Human Poverty Index (HPI-2) for selected developed countries (*Source:* Human Development Report 1998).

Countries	Deprivation in survival (% of people not expected to survive to age 60)	Deprivation in knowledge (% of people aged 16–65 who are functionally illiterate)	Deprivation in income (% of population below the income poverty line)	Social exclusion (% of total labour force in long-term unemployment)	HPI-2 rank
Sweden	8	7.5	6.7	1.5	1
Netherlands	9	10.5	6.7	3.2	2
Germany	11	14.4	5.9	4.0	3
Canada	9	16.6	11.7	1.3	10
Belgium	10	18.4	5.5	6.2	11
Australia	9	17.0	12.9	2.6	12
New Zealand	10	18.4	9.2	1.3	13
UK	9	21.8	13.5	3.8	15
USA	13	20.7	19.1	0.5	17

The HPI-2 is used as a comparative measure of human poverty in developed countries. The following are used to calculate the HPI-2:

• % of people not expected to survive to the age of 60;
• % of people functionally illiterate;
• % of people living below the income poverty line set at 50% of the median disposable personal income;
• rate of long-term unemployment (12 months or more).

HPI-2 and poverty in the developed countries

The Human Poverty Index, as an aggregate measure, highlights aspects of development not normally expressed in economic terms alone. For example, the HPI-2 shows that 7–17% of the population in developed countries is poor. This suggests that high average levels of national income do not always reflect low levels of poverty. A case in point is the USA, with the highest average national income, which also has the highest percentage of population experiencing human poverty in the developed world. Also, countries with similar per capita incomes can have very different levels of human poverty. For example, the Netherlands and the UK have HPI-2 values of 8% and 15% respectively, despite having similar income levels.

Unlike many other measures of development, the HPI-2 shows that human deprivation is not just a problem in the developing world. The Human Development Report 1998 shows that more than 100 million people in rich countries suffer a similar fate. Nearly 200 million people are not expected to survive to age 60. More than 100 million people are homeless and at least 37 million are without jobs and often experiencing a state of social exclusion.

UK National Quality of Life indicators

During the 1990s, both Conservative and Labour governments in the UK pressed for new measures of development, which would reflect the social aspects of sustainable development. As part of this strategy, the New Labour government published its model of sustainable development based on the following objectives in 1998:

• maintenance of high and stable levels of economic growth and employment;
• social progress, which recognises the needs of everyone;
• effective protection of the environment;
• prudent use of natural resources.

?

12 For the countries listed in each of Tables 1.4 and 1.5, find the most recent GDP figures.
a Calculate the Spearmans' rank correlation between the HPI-1 rank and GDP.
b Calculate the Spearmans' rank correlation between the HPI-2 rank and GDP.
c Comment on your results.

Using the following indicators, the UK government proposes to measure progress towards these objectives as follows:

'Maintenance of high and stable levels of economic growth and employment'
- gross domestic product;
- total investment in public assets (transport, hospitals, schools, etc.);
- people of working age who are in work.

The objective would be to see and increase in each of these each year.

'Social progress, which recognises the needs of everyone'
- expected years of healthy life;
- qualifications at age 19;
- homes judged fit to live in.

The objective would be to see an increase in all of the above.

'Effective protection of the environment'
- emmissions of greenhouse gases (measured in tonnes of carbon equivalent);
- days of air pollution;
- road traffic;
- rivers of fair or good quality;
- populations of wild birds;
- new homes built on previously developed land.

The objective would be to reduce the first three measures and increase the latter three.

'Prudent use of natural resources'
- measured by amount of waste and waste disposal measures.

General problems with indicators of social development

There are other social indicators of development, some of which are under constant review as definitions and concepts of the term 'development' change. Certain aspects of daily life, such as freedom of speech, the right to vote, freedom from discrimination and from subservience to others, the role of women in society and a nation's level of debt are some of the issues which are considered important in measures of development.

   Whichever index you choose, many social indicators of development unfortunately do not reflect inequalities in income distribution. This is in spite of education, health care, and infant mortality being commonly associated with income patterns. Another problem is the lack of agreement for a universal system of measuring social aspects of development.

1.4 Spatial aspects of development

Great contrasts in development often exist between different parts of a country, and it is these contrasts which give rise to what are called 'regional problems'.

Core and periphery

Wealth is never spread evenly through a country, but tends to be concentrated in certain areas. These areas are known as the **core** and have a concentration of population, wealth and resources. In contrast, the **periphery** consists of sparsely populated areas which are less developed than the core. They tend to lack both wealth and resources, or their resources are drained by the core (known as **backwash effect**, see Myrdal's model). Where such differences of wealth occur, governments may attempt to spread development more evenly throughout a country. Such efforts are referred to as regional development policies (Chapter 9).

   The concept of core and periphery can be applied at all scales: global, continental, national and regional.

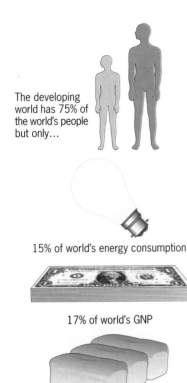

The developing world has 75% of the world's people but only...

15% of world's energy consumption

17% of world's GNP

30% of world's food grains

18% of world's export earnings

11% of world education spending

6% of world's health expenditure

5% of world science and technology

Figure 1.7 A world divided

Global scale: North-South divide

On a world scale, the developed countries constitute the global core, whereas the developing countries make up the periphery (see Fig. 1.1). Figure 1.8 illustrates the development gap between the economically developed core (rich North) and the economically developing countries of the periphery (poor South).

Continental scale: Western Europe

The west European core (Fig. 1.8) is more attractive to industries than its periphery. This is because the core:

• is near to a large wealthy market;
• has skilled labour available;
• has higher-quality infrastructures;
• has facilities for research and development.

In contrast, the peripheral areas are a long way from the largest industrial markets and the other advantages of the core.

A significant proportion of the UK lies outside the main European core. However, the opening of the Channel Tunnel, a fixed all-weather link between Great Britain and Europe, has reduced Great Britain's geographical peripherality. On the other hand, the creation of the single European market at the beginning of 1993 has given greater freedom to industry to invest anywhere in Europe and therefore, the core is more likely to attract even more capital at the expense of the periphery. One of the main responsibilities of the European Commission is to formulate policies that aim at restricting industrial growth in the core areas and diverting it towards more peripheral areas, which might otherwise suffer from continuing decline and rising unemployment.

National scale: Nigeria

Nigeria is a typical example of a country which has wide regional variations in development. Like so many countries in the world, Nigeria is characterised by wide spatial and social inequalities that in some cases have increased in recent years. According to the 1991 census, the official population figure for Nigeria then stood at 88.5 million. The 1991 census gives the mainly Muslim (Hausa-Fulani) northern states a 5 million majority over the southern (mainly Ibo and Yoruba dominated) states. The population throughout the whole of Nigeria is unevenly distributed (Fig. 1.9).

?

13 What economic advantages could the UK and Ireland derive from developing transport and communication links with the European core?

14a Refer to Figure 1.9 and identify three countries that are within the European core and three countries within the periphery.
b For the three countries in the periphery, explain how their locations relative to the core may affect the future development of each country.

15 What problems may result from a growing concentration of wealth, population and resources in the core area of Europe?

16 Investigate what steps have been, or could be, taken by the European Union (EU) in order to reduce the concentration of wealth in the core and spread it more evenly throughout the member states of the EU.

Figure 1.8 The core and peripheral areas of Western Europe. Even within the core, wealth is not spread evenly: some areas will attract more investment than others and these wealthier areas are known as the inner core. Areas with a lower concentration of wealth are known as the outer core.

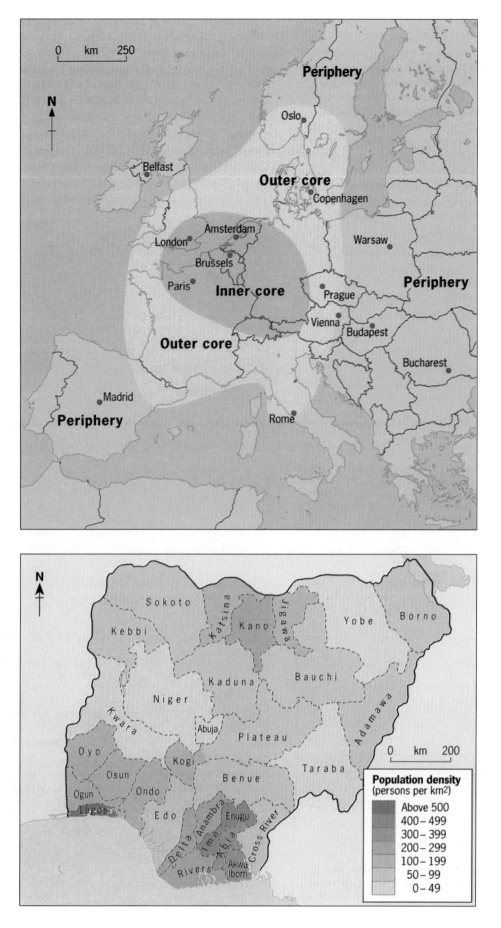

Figure 1.9 Nigeria: population density, 1991 (*Source:* Binns, *Teaching Geography*, vol. 18, no. 2, 1993)

?

17 Study Figures 1.9–1.11.
a Suggest where Nigeria's core and the peripheral areas might be, and give reasons for your answer.
b The new capital city of Abuja was given planning approval in 1979, and building for Phase 1 of the plan was complete by 1993 (see Figure 3.1). Do you think that the construction of Abuja will help the Nigerian authorities to reduce these spatial inequalities of development? Give reasons for your answer.

18 Describe the problems facing those developing countries, such as Nigeria, which have wide regional disparities of wealth.

Although Nigeria is now largely a one-product economy (oil production and export), for many years the economy was geared towards agricultural production and the export of a range of cash crops (Fig. 1.10). The rapid development of the oil industry has had widespread repercussions throughout the Nigerian economy and society (see section 7.5). There has been investment in basic infrastructure concentrated in a few urban centres, such as Lagos, Kano, Kaduna and Port Harcourt. Consequently, the output of manufacturing industry increased fourfold between 1970 and 1980. The regional concentration of investment resulted in a steady population drift away from the rural areas to the growing urban centres (Fig. 1.12, see section 4.6). The rural-urban migration has led to the decline of agricultural output. This pattern of development has created greater spatial inequalities of wealth throughout Nigeria.

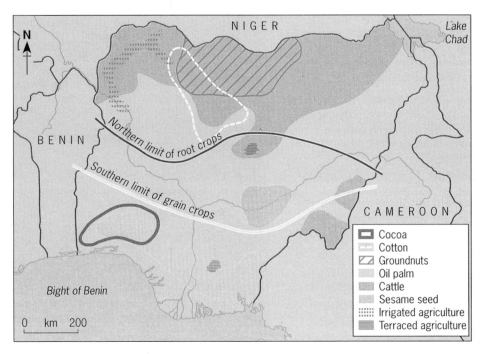

Figure 1.10 Nigeria: main agricultural regions. Before independence from the UK in 1960, the export of cash crops accounted for more than 75% of export earnings and the country was generally self-sufficient in basic foodstuffs.

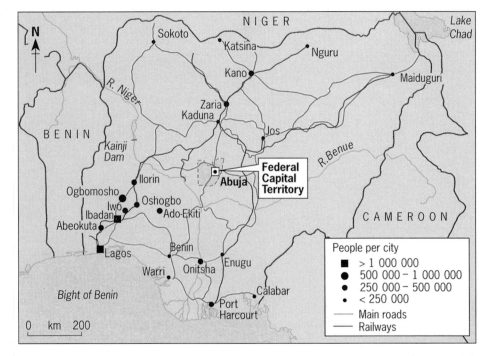

Figure 1.11 Nigeria: cities and communications (*Source:* Binns, in *Teaching Geography*, Vol. 18, no. 2, 1993)

Figure 1.12 London's Docklands: In 1980 the Docklands were among the most run-down parts of the capital. Within 10 years, public and private investment had transformed the economy and physical environment of this core region; 1981–90 saw the location of more than 600 new companies and employment boosted from 27 000 to 42 500.

Myrdal's model of cumulative causation

Within individual countries, economic development is likely to take place more rapidly in some areas than in others (Fig. 1.13). The processes which lead to this uneven spread of development were first outlined in a model by Gunnar Myrdal in 1956. This is now known as the model of **cumulative causation** (Fig. 1.13). Essentially, this spatial model attempts to explain why some areas become more economically developed than others. Myrdal's model sets out the following main stages of regional development.

Stage 1

Early economic growth takes place where there are natural advantages. This may be a sheltered coastline where a natural harbour could lead to the development of a major port. Similarly, industries may develop where there is an abundance of natural resources, such as coal mining or iron and steel. Once growth in a region is under way, the area develops more rapidly than its surroundings as the process of cumulative causation takes place. Gradually, acquired advantages, such as skilled labour, improved infrastructure, more efficient services and sizeable markets, reinforce the natural advantages. This area, with both natural and acquired advantages, constitutes the core. As job opportunities arise within the core, people continue to migrate from the periphery. Original industries prosper and the demand for labour increases as further industrial growth occurs. This is the **multiplier effect** which takes place as linked industries become established. As the original growth area continues to develop, this then becomes a **growth pole** (see section 9.3). A chain reaction is set in motion producing self-sustaining economic growth.

Stage 2

The concentration of economic activity leads to a backwash effect as the core region develops at the expense of the periphery. **Downward spirals** in the periphery then occur as people leave in order to find work in the core. Growth in the core is therefore sustained by a constant supply of labour, as well as resources, from the periphery. The loss of valuable labour and resources seriously reduces further industrial development in the periphery.

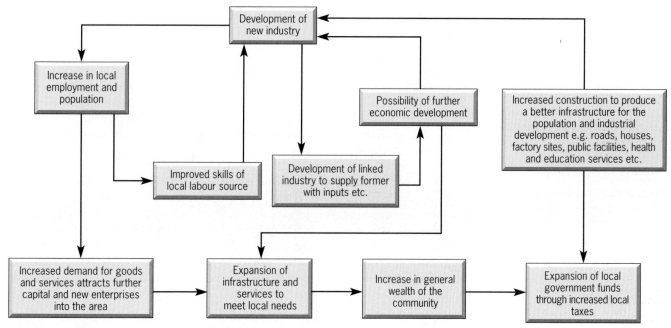

Figure 1.13 Myrdal's model of cumulative causation

Stage 3

As core areas flood the periphery with cheap products, the poor areas have little necessity to develop any industry. The result is the industrially expanding region of the core on the one hand, and the stagnating or declining periphery on the other.

In theory, once the process of cumulative causation is under way, it becomes self-sustaining and the core region continues to grow. This process may also work in reverse, however. A factory may close as happened in many parts of Britain during the **de-industrialisation** of the 1980s and 1990s. This creates an overall regional depression, since other industries dependent on the factory will also close. A downward spiral in the core is therefore established, and it may only be possible to reverse this trend through government intervention.

Using Myrdal's model

The cumulative causation model helps to explain the regional variations in the UK's industrial development and the government policies aimed at promoting economic growth in the depressed peripheral areas (Fig. 1.14).

In the UK, both Labour and Conservative governments have used regional development policies to address the problem of regional inequalities – with varying degrees of success. It is important to note that each of the main political parties has its own view on the long-term effectiveness of regional development policies.

The free market viewpoint

One political viewpoint is that inequalities of wealth and development will eventually disappear as a matter of course. According to this view, **spread effects** (opposite to backwash effects) will eventually lead to the spread of wealth throughout the periphery, often along growth poles or along growth axes. This spread of wealth will result from an increasing demand from the core for the raw materials found in the periphery, in order to help sustain the growth of the core. Increased activities in the periphery will lead to an increase in wealth so expansion of industries in this area is eventually made possible.

This view suggests that in a free market, imbalances of wealth are temporary and will ultimately be reduced by the market forces. The Conservative governments of the UK, since 1979, have followed this school of thought: their policies assume that growth will eventually happen even in peripheral areas, without much need for government intervention.

The interventionist viewpoint

Another political viewpoint is that government policies are needed to stimulate economic development in the otherwise peripheral areas. In post-war Britain, successive Labour governments introduced strong regional policies in the form of tax incentives or infrastructure provision to encourage companies to locate in areas of high unemployment. These policies are intended to stimulate economic growth in the periphery, and so increase the likelihood of future industrial investment in these areas. More recently, the new Labour government elected in 1997 has adopted a different regional development strategy. With development funds coming from a variety of sources other than central government, the new focus is on encouraging local community groups to form partnerships with private and public organisations. These new partnerships can then apply for money to develop their areas according to their own priority needs (see chapter 9).

Whichever political viewpoint is followed, continuing regional imbalances in economic development will have an effect on human development, especially in the periphery. For example, prolonged unemployment in the periphery may have a demoralising effect on the local community. Young people may move away in search of employment elsewhere and leave an ageing population.

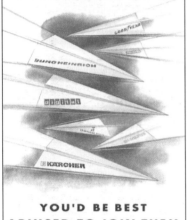

Figure 1.14 Local government advertisement designed to attract investment into an area in England's North-West. This was part of a core region in the late l9th century, but suffered from a downward spiral during de-industrialisation.

19 Using the example of Nigeria, produce a flow diagram similar to Myrdal's model (Figure 1.13) for:
a the development of the oil industry (page 128),
b the creation of the Federal Capital Territory of Abuja.

20a Draw an annotated diagram to show how a cycle of decline can affect the periphery.
b Around your diagram list the possible responses to regional decline.
c What range of values and attitudes have influenced these?

There is then often a shortage of service provision, as industries moving out, or closing down, result in lower tax revenues to pay for services. The productivity of the periphery declines as a result of the loss of the bright and best educated members of the community who may not wish to return to the area.

Friedmann's model of regional development

A more complex model or theory of regional development was proposed by a regional planner, John Friedmann, in 1963. This model is evolutionary, because it shows that spatial inequalities change over time. It is also a spatial model: Friedmann identified four types of areas, each at different stage of development (Fig. 1.15).

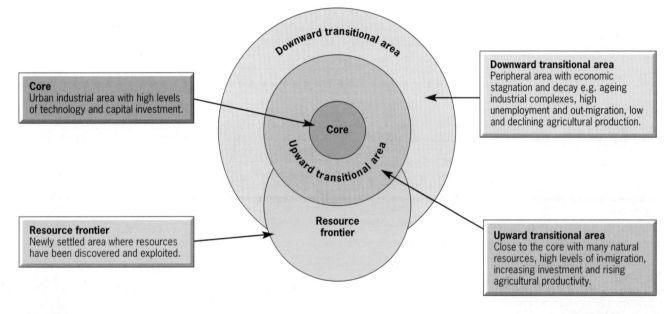

Core
Urban industrial area with high levels of technology and capital investment.

Resource frontier
Newly settled area where resources have been discovered and exploited.

Downward transitional area
Peripheral area with economic stagnation and decay e.g. ageing industrial complexes, high unemployment and out-migration, low and declining agricultural production.

Upward transitional area
Close to the core with many natural resources, high levels of in-migration, increasing investment and rising agricultural productivity.

Figure 1.15 Friedmann's model of regional development

Figure 1.16 Cambridge Science Park: High-tech activities tend to cluster in areas where they can recruit and keep highly-skilled researchers and technicians. The enterprises need suppliers and services and so reinforce existing centres of production. This then attracts other industries.

The core regions

Core regions are concentrated metropolitan economies with a high potential for economic growth and innovation. These are the centres of the national or international markets with large-scale industry, commercial services and high levels of technology. The core regions present a positive image, and have a concentration of resources, professional and highly skilled workers and a well-developed infrastructure. The growth of the core is often at the expense of the periphery because labour and resources from the periphery move to the core to sustain economic growth. In this respect, the core may be described as parasitic in relation to the rest of the country.

On a national level, we can see this pattern in the urban hierarchy with the country's capital as the national metropolis and other large cities as secondary cores. On an international level, metropolitan areas such as the Paris-London-Amsterdam-Berlin cluster constitute the European core (see Fig. 1.8).

Upward transitional areas

These are growth regions within the periphery and are relatively close to the core. In these areas, the availability of natural resources promotes greatly intensified use of these resources. They are characterised by high immigration rates and industrial and economic growth (Fig. 1.16). These areas also benefit from high levels of investment in industry as well as in agriculture.

21 Essay:
a With reference to any one named country, identify those areas which may be regarded as
• core areas, • resource frontiers and • peripheral areas.
b Describe why and how the economic circumstances of these areas might change in the future.

Downward transitional areas

These are peripheral areas characterised by declining or stagnant economies, often with low agricultural productivity or the loss of a primary resource base, caused by a reduction in the demand for minerals such as coal. These areas may also have old and declining industries, a negative image, and be unfavourably located in relation to the core. Other characteristics of such areas are low rates of innovation, low productivity and an inability to adapt to new economic circumstances due partly to an ageing population as a result of young people moving out of the area. Usually, labour and resources are drained from this area by the core.

Resource frontiers

These areas also lie outside the core regions. They are zones where new development is taking place, for example as a result of newly discovered mineral resources. Other examples of resource frontiers include mountains, deserts and island areas which could be used for recreational purposes. Along with the core regions, these areas perform a major role in generating economic growth throughout the nation.

'Development will never be, and can never be defined to universal satisfaction. It refers, broadly speaking, to desirable social and economic progress, and people will always have different views about what is desirable. Certainly, development must mean improvement in living conditions, for which economic growth and industrialisation are essential. But if there is no attention to the quality of growth and to the social change one cannot speak of development.'

Brandt Report, 1980

'A country, or a village, or a community, cannot be developed: it can only develop itself. For real development means the development of people. Every country in Africa can show examples of modern facilities which have been provided for the people – and which are now rotting unused. If real development is to take place, the people have to be involved ... Roads, buildings, increase in crop output ... are not development; they are only the tools of development.'

Julius Nyerere, 1973

'Development is not only a fundamental right but a basic human need, which fulfils the aspirations of all people to achieve the greatest possible freedom and dignity both as individuals and as members of the societies in which they live.'
The Oxfam Handbook of Development and relief, Volume 1 (Deborah Eade and Suzanne Williams)

'Development is a human issue, a concern with the capacity of individuals to realise their inherent potential and to cope with the changing circumstances of their lives'.
Marxian/Socialist's concept of development

Figure 1.17 Selected definitions of development

22 Read Figure 1.17.
a Which of the definitions do you agree with most? Explain why.
b Write your own definition of development.

Summary

- The concept of development has changed over the years, and so have the methods of measuring levels of development.
- Economic development is often expressed in terms of GDP and GNP, which are indicators of national wealth.
- There is a wide 'development gap' between countries mostly in the northern hemisphere and those mostly in the southern hemisphere, a situation often described as the North-South divide.
- Increasingly, development is becoming associated with improvements in human welfare rather than just economic gain.
- Concern for the environment has become a major issue in matters of development.
- Some regions develop more rapidly than others, leading to spatial inequalities in the distribution of resources and wealth.
- Regional development policies are aimed at reducing such variations in levels of development.
- Myrdal's model of cumulative causation and Friedmann's model of regional development help to explain how regional inequalities occur.

2 Colonialism, dependency and aid

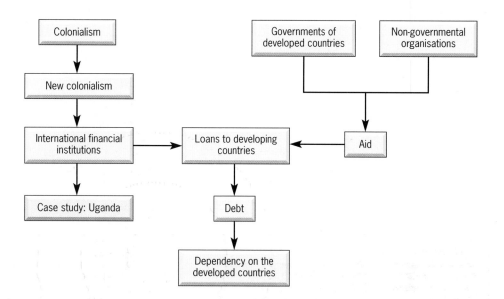

2.1 Introduction

We have to understand the nature and influence of colonialism before we can understand the inequalities which exist between the rich and the poor nations today. Although many countries have gained independence from their colonisers, they have now become dependent on such international financial institutions as the World Bank and the International Monetary Fund (IMF). Increasing amounts of aid given to the **developing countries** by the rich nations and high interest rates on loan repayments have plunged many of the poorer countries into a debt crisis. This in itself is a form of dependency. This chapter focuses on some of the economic, social and political consequences of past colonial control and looks at attempts to ease dependency through aid.

2.2 Colonialism and development

From the mid-fifteenth century onwards, and particularly after about AD1500, powerful European countries began to explore, and expand, into the rest of the world. There were three main motives behind this expansion. First was the exploration motive, the desire to discover places and peoples that were unknown to the explorers. Second was the desire to take Christianity to other people across the world. Third was exploitation: the craving to gain wealth and/or territory through trade or possession.

Europeans 'discovered' new lands in Asia, Africa and the Americas and settled, traded and took possession of them either by treaty or by force (Fig. 2.1). By the end of the nineteenth century, much of the world was controlled by the European countries either directly, as part of their empires, or indirectly through the power held by colonial settlers from the home nations (Fig. 2.2). In the twentieth century, **neo-colonialism**, or economic control, over some former colonies still exists through **transnational corporations (TNCs)** (see section 6.8).

Figure 2.1 Spaniards in Peru force Indians to carry their loot, *circa* 1532

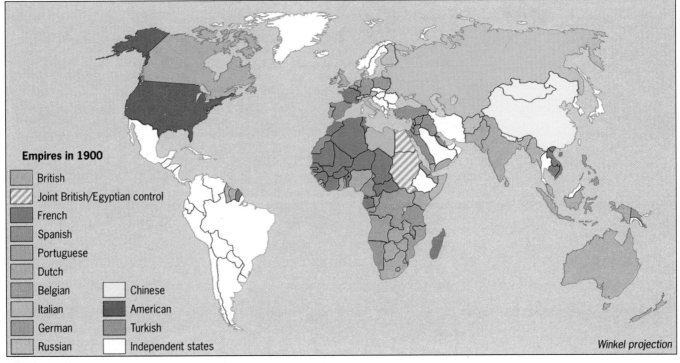

Empires in 1900

- British
- Joint British/Egyptian control
- French
- Spanish
- Portuguese
- Dutch
- Belgian
- Italian
- German
- Russian
- Chinese
- American
- Turkish
- Independent states

Winkel projection

Figure 2.2 European control of the world, 1900

Colonialism in South America

After Christopher Columbus had 'discovered' the 'New World' in 1492, other Spanish and Portuguese sailors set out to claim land for their countries and to spread the Christian faith. At the Treaty of Tordesillas, in 1494, the two colonising nations agreed to the 'Pope's line', which was a boundary between the Portuguese dominated eastern part of South America and the Spanish controlled regions to the west (Fig. 2.3).

The Spanish moved into Mexico during the 1520s and began exploring the west coast of South America. The indigenous people known as the Incas controlled a huge area, including part of the Andes, and stretching from what is now known as Ecuador to as far as northern Chile. Inca society was very complex and organised. The people were cared for by the state when ill, as well as when they reached old age. Most occupations were hereditary, with important skills passed down from one generation to another. The Incas governed a large empire but did not over-exploit it. They needed the resources of their mountain environment to live on, so they **sustained** those resources as best they could within the limits of the farming practices and technology of the time.

Led by Francisco Pizarro, the Spanish army landed on the South American coast in January 1530. During the following two years, the army slaughtered thousands of indigenous people, took possession of large areas of land, and finally executed the Inca leader for refusing to become a Christian. Huge sums of gold, collected as ransom, were sent back to Spain. Between 1500 and 1650, 180–200 tonnes of American gold were added to the European treasury, worth an estimated US$2.8 billion in today's terms.

Most Spanish and Portuguese colonies had gained their independence by the year 1900 (Fig. 2.2). However, it was not until many decades later that the majority of countries in Africa and Asia became independent from European rule. Although some countries show certain gains from foreign domination, such as the institution of democratic government systems, others still suffer from their colonial experience. This is because their economies and political administrations had mainly served not their own needs, but the needs of the colonising power.

Figure 2.3 South America's colonial heritage: countries, their dominant languages and religions

?

1 Select five developing countries and carry out a library search to find out:
a whether these countries were ever colonised,
b who the colonisers were,
c the duration of the colonial period,
d some of the gains and losses resulting from the colonial experience.

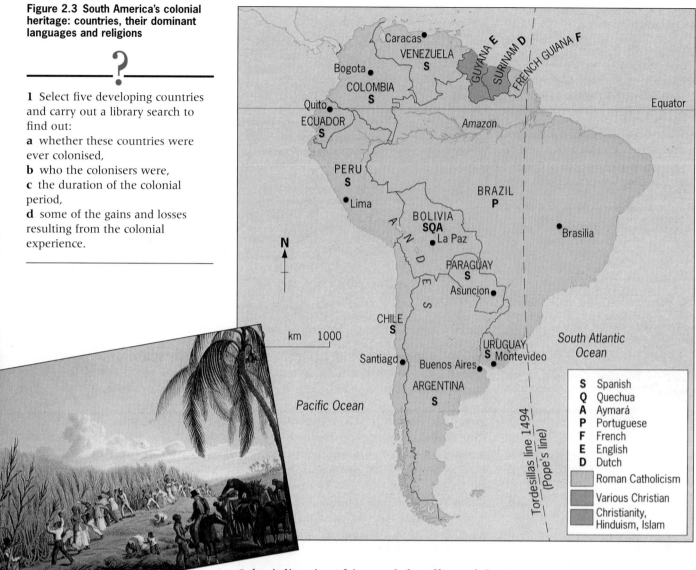

Figure 2.4 African slaves felling ripe sugar cane, Antigua, 1823

Colonialism in Africa and the effects of slavery

During the time of the Spanish and Portuguese colonisation of South America, other Europeans were exploring the western coast of Africa and making the first contacts with the well-developed settlements along the west African coast.

With the extension of their influence in Africa by the mid-sixteenth century, Europeans began forcefully taking West Africans across the Atlantic. They then sold them as slaves to work on the new sugar and cotton plantations of South and Central America and the Caribbean (Fig. 2.4). Although trading in slaves was not new (the Greeks and Romans had done it, and Arab traders had for centuries traded in African slaves), the European slave trade was more systematic and on a greater scale than had ever been seen before (Fig. 2.5).

It was usually the most able men and women, often well-skilled in local crafts, who were taken as slaves. Although impossible to calculate, it has been estimated that traders shipped over 12 million slaves from Africa to the Americas between about 1650 and 1850. It is unknown how many millions of these died, as a result of ill treatment or disease, either in Africa or on the appalling 'middle passage' journey on the slave ships. The impact of this on Africa had disastrous and long-term effects: the export of slaves, combined with the many lives lost in the slave wars, meant that the size of the African population probably remained static for over two centuries. Many people believe that one of the reasons why most African countries are poor today is

Figure 2.5 The 'triangular trade' of the eighteenth century

European ship owners, African chiefs, slave and goods merchants and plantation owners all increased their wealth

The growth of ports such as Bristol and Liverpool was based on the slave trade

Raw goods e.g. sugar, cotton, ginger transported for sale in European markets

Slaves sold at auction to work on plantations, in mines and as domestic servants

Manufactured goods e.g. cloth and guns transported for purchasing Africans

Able men and women, 'sold' by African chiefs, transported on 'middle' passage

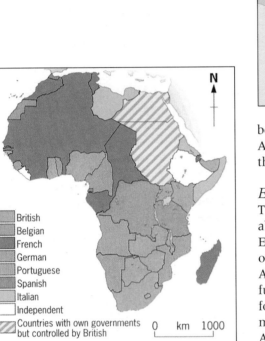

British
Belgian
French
German
Portuguese
Spanish
Italian
Independent
Countries with own governments but controlled by British

0   km   1000

Figure 2.6 Sharing out the wealth: Africa in 1914, after partition by the European powers

2 Use library resources and select three former British colonies in Africa.
a List the different ways in which the African continent was exploited by the British.
b Assess the impact this exploitation has had on the present-day economic situation in Africa.

because of this massive displacement of the continent's human resources. Some African political leaders are now requesting reparations from the rich nations that were heavily involved in the African slave trade.

European domination and control in Africa
The UK abolished the slave trade in 1807 and slavery in 1833 (the Danes had abolished slavery in 1804), and over the next twenty years the USA and most European powers did the same. The decline in trade as a result of the abolition of the slave trade, missionary zeal, and optimism regarding the riches of the African continent all combined to encourage the European powers to explore further into the African interior in the mid-nineteenth century. The 'scramble for Africa' began in about 1870, and at the Conference of Berlin in 1884–5 the major European powers decided among themselves how they would divide Africa up (no representatives from Africa were invited to the conference). So effective was the partition of Africa that, by 1914, only Liberia and Ethiopia remained independent (Fig. 2.6).

The European powers controlled these artificially created African countries by military force. Their motives for such control were mainly political (reflecting the struggle for power and influence between the European countries) and economic (colonies provided a source of raw materials and a market for manufactured goods, see section 8.2). A great deal of European wealth originates from this time in colonial history.

Different people have viewed the European colonial influence in Africa in different ways. One view is that, as a result of European involvement in Africa, many social and economic improvements were made. These included commercial farms, large-scale plantations, mines, roads and railways. Another view, held by most Africans, is that Africa and its people lost far more than they gained from this period of European domination.

2.3 International financial institutions

Western influence on the developing countries is not just limited to the period of colonisation. Even after their independence, many poor countries still depend on financial aid, credits and support from their ex-colonisers and political allies to help with their development programmes.

Such reliance on foreign capital has consequently increased the economic dependency, and the debt burden of the poor countries on the rich. This is sometimes referred to as neo-colonialism. Several international financial institutions, such as the World Bank and the International Monetary Fund (IMF), now play a key role in the development process of the developing countries.

Zaire debt 'shame'

The World Bank has suspended its existing projects in Zaire until the country settles the $25 m arrears it owes. Reliable sources say the deadline for the payment had been set for November 15. They added that if this deadline was not met various projects being funded by the World Bank, which amount to a total of $175 m could be cancelled outright.

Zaire had apparently been notified for the past six months that its should pay its arrears. The World Bank had been funding more than 10 projects in Zaire, mostly in road and social sectors and in the Water and Power Distribution Administration, a public company which supplies drinking water to Kinshasa and other towns in the interior.

Meanwhile, the Zairean government has decided to put in circulation new currency notes and is urging those in possession of old Zaire notes to deposit them in their bank accounts or simply exchange them for new notes. 'Those who are unfortunate enough still to be in possession of the old notes on November 23 can only blame themselves,' said Luwowo Ngongo, Zaire's Communications Minister.

Figure 2.7 Unable to pay for World Bank 'support' (*Source: West Africa, 29 Nov.–5 Dec. 1993)*

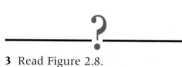

?

3 Read Figure 2.8.
a Identify arguments for and against the Arun III dam project.
b What is the long-term benefit of this project to Nepal?

World Bank and the International Monetary Fund

The World Bank and the IMF are two international financial institutions that were set up following the Bretton Woods Conference of 1944. Their original aim was to help rebuild the economies of Europe devastated by World War 2 and the effects of recession. The conference members believed that global economic problems could be solved if international trade were encouraged. This meant greater economic co-operation among countries, free movement of capital and goods and the establishment of the US dollar as the international currency. Consequently, the World Bank aims to assist countries developing their economies by providing aid. This takes the form of loans and technical assistance. In turn, the IMF promotes the expansion of international trade by, e.g. providing borrowing facilities and easing exchange rate controls.

Part of this overall strategy to solve global economic problems included the General Agreement on Tariffs and Trade (GATT). This was established to encourage **free trade** and commerce between countries (see section 8.5).

The Marshall Plan and the rebuilding of Europe

After World War 2, European countries lacked the resources for reconstruction. They needed to use World Bank and IMF facilities but refused to accept the strict conditions imposed by these international financial institutions. Had they done so, such measures could have resulted in the European countries losing control over their own economies and thus their sovereignty.

As a result of the European rejection of IMF conditions, the much looser and less stringent Marshall Plan was established. The Marshall Plan aimed at providing finance to Europe through grants rather than loans (though the then Soviet Union and its satellites refused to participate in the Plan).

Unlike the European nations, which receive concessions from the IMF and the World Bank when using their loan facilities, the developing countries are obliged to follow strictly the Bank's conditions (Fig. 2.7). For example, the developing countries are obliged to keep their economies completely 'open' to international market forces. To use the World Bank facilities, therefore, these countries must also import foreign goods, capital and services. Each borrowing country then has to pay for its imports through increased exports.

The World Bank's economic principles

Until recently the World Bank has followed these five major economic principles:

1 Poor countries need cash to develop their economies. To get this, they have to borrow money, mostly from Western creditors and international financial institutions.

2 For their economies to be competitive, the poor countries need to buy technology from the rich nations. With the technology they can produce goods and services which they could sell back to the rich nations to generate the foreign exchange necessary for development and help pay back their debts. According to the World Bank, this is one way in which the developing countries can be integrated into the global market.

3 Government spending on social services, such as health, education, transport, etc., needs to be cut to save money, and more money needs to be earned through exports so as to make the economy 'efficient' and competitive.

World Bank test of credibility

World Bank president Lewis Preston recently replied to each of 26 congressmen who signed a letter condemning the Arun III dam in Nepal project as an example of 'uneconomic, massive, destructive engineering investment.' Mr Preston has also lobbied to defuse American opposition to Arun.

Joseph Wood, the Bank's vice-president for South Asia, spelled out what was at stake. If the Bank failed to win approval of the project he said, 'We will lack credibility as a financing partner for controversial power and infrastructure projects.'

Bank officials say they have bent over backwards to make sure that the project is environmentally and economically sound, but the Bank will be tried anew today when the United States presents its misgivings to bank officials.

Only 155 families are affected by the project in Arun, a remote valley 200 kilometres east of Katmandu inhabited by endangered species such as the Asiatic black bear, the clouded leopard and the Annamese macaque.

Arun, estimated to cost at least $1 billion over eight years, would provide more than 400 megawatts for a country in desperate need for electricity. So far, Nepal has developed only 241 megawatts of hydro-electric power, accessible to barely 10 per cent of the population.

The Bank would provide a loan of $140.7 million through its soft loan arm, the International Development Association, $473 million would come from countries such as Japan and France, and Nepal would put up $473 million.

Arun has been criticised by a coalition of local groups as unnecessarily large and expensive, diverting resources away from social programmes like health and education. The coalition favours small- and medium-scale projects that would not gobble up so much of the Nepalese budget.

Nepalese groups have accused the Bank of failing to follow its policies on environment, indigenous people and energy and for not honouring requests for information, in violation of the Bank's new policy of openness.

Figure 2.8 World Bank under question (*Source:* Mark Tran, *The Guardian,* 7 Nov. 1994)

4 Efficiency in the economy can only be achieved through the adoption of what the Bank regards as the policy of **structural adjustment** (see below).
5 Poor countries should strive to compete with the rich nations on the world market and embrace the philosophy of a free market. This aims to be characterised by completely deregulated trade and a free flow of foreign investments.

In recent times there has been an admission by the World Bank and development experts that these economic principles have not worked.

World Bank projects

Since their foundation, the World Bank and the IMF have played a leading role in the development of the developing countries. The World Bank has provided long-term loan facilities to the poor countries in order to finance development projects such as building dams, road construction, hydro-electric power schemes and water supply, among many others. Up until 1995, these projects were usually large scale (called mega-projects) and mostly aimed at bringing about the economic development of the nations concerned.

Examples of World Bank assistance include US$304 million lent to Brazil in 1980 to build an iron mine at Carajas, an 890-km railway to transport the ore and a deep-water port at Ponte de Madeira. In 1985, US$156 million was lent to Indonesia for the Kedung Ombo Dam in central Java. In the early 1980s, India received a loan of nearly US$200 million for **social forestry**. Many other countries have received funds at one stage or another from the World Bank's loan facility for development. This has resulted in many countries building up considerable debt burdens, which the national economies cannot support (Table 2.1).

By 1995, many large-scale development projects were wholly or partly financed by the World Bank and other Western creditors. This has given the international financial institutions and the rich Western creditors greater control over the economies of these poor nations.

Table 2.1 External debts (millions US$) of selected developing countries (*Source:* World Development Report, 1994, 1998/99).

	Total external debt (1980)	Total external debt (1992)	Total external debt (1996)	Debt as per cent of GNP (1996)
Tanzania	2 476	6 715	7 412	114
Bangladesh	4 053	13 189	16 083	30
India	20 582	76 983	89 827	22
Kenya	3 394	6 367	6 893	64
Pakistan	9 936	24 072	29 901	39
Ghana	1 407	4 275	6 202	56
Sudan	5 163	16 193	17 600	—
Philippines	17 417	32 498	41 214	51
Mexico	57 378	113 378	157 125	44

Impacts of World Bank projects

Investments in large-scale projects financed by World Bank loans are not always completely beneficial to the poor nations. In fact, critics of the Bank believe that many World Bank sponsored projects in the developing countries are unsuccessful. This is because, while such projects may help to increase the **Gross Domestic Product (GDP)** through more exports, the majority of the people in the developing countries do not receive the benefits of this increased wealth. More often than not, these mega-projects financed by the World Bank result in the displacement of indigenous poor people and can cause serious damage to the environment (Figs. 2.8–2.11).

?

4 Study Figures 2.9–2.11 and decide whether each of the mega-projects was a success or a failure. Justify your decisions.

Figure 2.9 Sudan: Gezira Agricultural Project

El Gezira: The Sudan's prime cotton-producing area covering 2 million ha, accounting for most of the nation's export earnings.
Project: From 1952–62, over 16 000 km of canals were built to control the White Nile and supply irrigation for cotton production. Project aimed to modernise production and reverse falling yields and low productivity.
Costs and donors: World Bank lent Sudan US$50 m to purchase pesticides and herbicides for one season. The Bank of Sudan contributed many more dollars for heavy machinery and fuel.
Winners: Multinational chemical companies won the contracts to supply the pesticides and herbicides. (Some of these products were selling poorly on the international market because of health risks.) Farmers in Gezira had at least a temporary boost to their cotton production.
Losers: The government's schemes for alternative pest management were undermined by the heavy promotion of pesticides by the chemical industry. Farmers spent 25–30 per cent of total production costs buying chemical inputs, and have become increasingly dependent on these. The DDT and Malathion dropped on cotton fields by aircraft has drifted into mosquito-breeding habitats, creating strains of malaria-carrying mosquitoes resistant to conventional treatment.

Figure 2.10 Sri Lanka: Mahaveli Irrigation Programme

River Mahaveli: 300 km long river in Sri Lanka
Project: 1978 irrigation scheme to supply power; increase food self-sufficiency by modernising agriculture and manufacturing; provide homes; provide a livelihood for 50 000 people. Involved building 3 dams and constructing power stations to triple the country's energy-generating capacity and irrigate 120 000 hectares of new land.
Costs and donors: 60 per cent financed mainly by foreign aid: UK, Sweden and Germany (giving US$100 million each). Sri Lanka also had to borrow large sums on 'soft' commercial terms. However, the budget doubled to nearly US$14 billion, so Sri Lanka had to raise taxes and cut food subsidies to meet the spiralling costs.
Winners: Most construction contracts were awarded to companies in the donor countries who employed expensive foreign personnel and machinery. Most of the newly-irrigated land was leased to foreign companies using imported machinery.
Losers: Little Sri Lankan labour was used. 1.5 million people had to be resettled on small plots of forested land 90 km away from their homelands. To meet expenses, the government had to cut compensation for lost crops, cost of land-clearing and new houses. Habitat of rare animals threatened. Frequent repairs to the dams.

Figure 2.11 India: Narmada River Project

Narmada River valley: Interstate (Gujarat, Maharashtra and Rajasthan) valley following the 700 km course of the River Narmada in northern India.
Project: To flood much of the valley using 30 major dams, canals and water from the Narmada River and provide 1450 MW of electricity power, drinking water for 131 urban centres and 4720 villages, irrigation across 1.8 bn ha in a drought-prone area.
Costs and donors: The Narmada Project receives World Bank assistance under two credit/loan agreements of US$450 m; machinery, cement, equipment and training supplied by multinationals.
Winners: Water supplied to millions of people suffering from a steady decline in available water; people protected against floods in Gujarat; 700 000 workers employed during and post-construction; increased food production.
Losers: 70 000 people displaced; up to 100 000 ha of land submerged including 40 000 ha of forest, rare wildlife and heritage sites. Irrigation on such a vast scale will cause waterlogging and a build-up of salt in some of the soils. Dams easily become silted and will then be useless.

Structural Adjustment Programmes

Another major criticism of the Bank is the terms and conditions under which poor countries can benefit from the Bank's credit facilities, alongside the requirements for the repayment of loans. These are the Bank's policies of Structural Adjustment Programmes (SAPs) imposed on the poor countries and which have been a major issue raised by the Bank's critics.

The World Bank holds the view that the governments of poor countries have mismanaged their economies. As a result, they are not producing sufficient goods to sell or export in order to pay for their expenditure on imports and social services. The Bank's idea, therefore, is that poor countries should adjust their spending in order to pay back their debts. Such SAPs involve cutting back on government spending, especially on 'unproductive' social services, privatising public-sector enterprises (Fig. 2.12) and devaluing currencies so that imports are expensive and exports are cheap. According to the Bank, all these measures will promote domestic investment and increase export earnings for poor countries.

Although the World Bank realises that this process of adjustment might be difficult in the short term, it expects that in the long term SAPs will help the economies of the poor nations. The Bank sees such adjustment as being unavoidable. In fact, millions of people in over 70 countries of the world have been affected by the SAPs and the economic policies of the World Bank and the IMF.

To reduce the hardship initially caused by the SAPs, the World Bank and IMF promises relatively low-interest loans to those countries agreeing to accept the Bank's terms. Loans from other sources, especially from rich Western governments and private banks, have increasingly been made conditional upon the acceptance of the World Bank's SAPs. Poor countries in Africa, Asia and Latin America are the most widely affected by the World Bank's economic policies.

Structural Adjustment Programmes in Africa

The SAP's adverse effects are clearly evident throughout most of Africa. In fact, the effect and influence of the World Bank is extensive. Countries such as Nigeria, Ghana, Mozambique, Liberia, Zimbabwe and Sierra Leone, among others, have adopted the World Bank's imposed SAPs. In Mozambique this led to rising unemployment, which reached 50 per cent in 1992. Reduced government spending, which is part of the SAPs, resulted in fewer jobs in the public formal sector.

There is growing evidence that SAPs are adversely affecting people's lives as well as the economies of developing nations. In fact, many observers blame SAPs for the increasing number of protests and civil disturbances in many African countries. We can see these, in part, as a result of rising unemployment and a drastic reduction in government spending on social services, such as education and health. According to the UN Economic Commission for Africa, expenditures on health in countries where the World Bank has imposed SAPs have declined. Similarly, we can also associate the implementation of SAPs with tribal and regional conflicts in many parts of Africa, together with the spread of disease and growing poverty. If anything, Africa is the World Bank's failure with more poverty than in any other region of the world (see Fig. 1.1, Table 1.4). All these difficulties have led to a progressive weakening of governments' ability to govern. In fact, we need to consider whether people are actually becoming poorer as a result of the Bank's economic policies.

?

5 Read Figure 2.12. Discuss the view that the imposition of SAPs could be detrimental to individuals in developing countries in the long term.

6 Review the information on SAPs and evaluate how they are affecting development in the countries mentioned.

Effects of structural adjustment in Uganda

In 1987 a structural adjustment programme started in Uganda (Fig. 2.12). In previous years, a series of Ugandan presidents adopted economic policies that had serious consequences for the nation's economy. During the 1970s President Idi Amin, expelled the majority of Asian entrepreneurs then living in Uganda. Until that time the Asians had been in control of the most profitable sectors of the economy. As a result of this expulsion, the GDP plummeted to a fraction of what it had been during the period of independence in 1962.

Idi Amin's successor, Milton Obote, presided during a period in which the GDP per capita stagnated and inflation threatened to run out of control. Later in 1986, Yoweri Moseveni became president and inherited a situation in which inflation was accelerating and economic growth was virtually absent.

Since Uganda was struggling to repay its growing debts, the imposition of a SAP was considered necessary. Some observers believe that in economic terms, the SAP in Uganda has been relatively successful, whereas others would disagree. By 1997 inflation was under control and the GDP per capita was growing at rates similar to those experienced then by the Asian Tiger economies (see section 6.7). GDP had also reached a level comparable with the earlier peak of 1969 (Table 2.3).

Some of this growth was a direct consequence of the authorities taking a less interventionist approach in the market for coffee, which still remains Uganda's main export crop (Fig. 2.13). Until the imposition of the SAP, the small Ugandan farmers sold coffee to just one main buyer. This system known as a **monopsony**, is similar to a monopoly in that the buyer has considerable market power. The single buyer in this case was the Ugandan Marketing Board which, until privatisation under the SAP, dominated the national economy.

The purchasing of coffee is now in the private sector with the effect that some farmers receive a better price for their crop following the competition between buyers. However, those who consider the SAP in Uganda a failure would argue that small farmers in remote areas do not always benefit from this system. These rural producers, farming on marginal land, do not have up-to-date information about prices and the market. Also, the remoteness of some of these village producers often precludes their involvement in main commodity trading activities.

The progress made in Uganda towards economic diversification, an essential part of any SAP, has been limited. Coffee still dominates Uganda's export trade (Fig. 2.13).

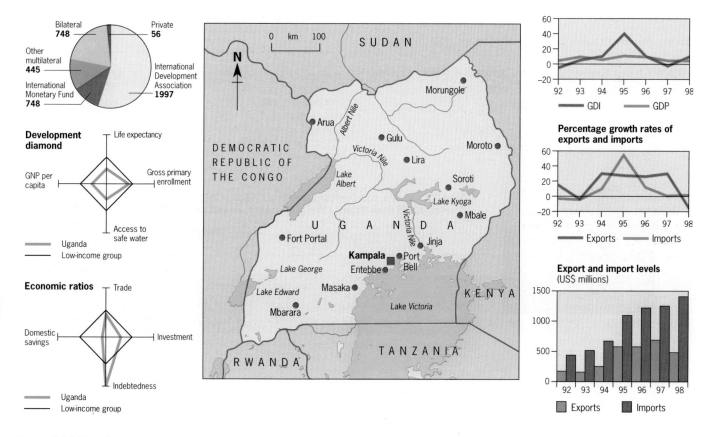

Figure 2.12 Uganda at a glance (*Source:* World Bank Group: World Development Indicators (1999), www.worldbank.org/data/wdi/people.html)

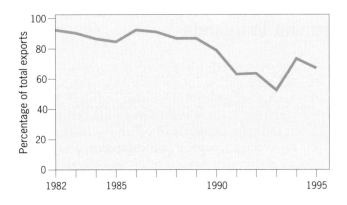

Figure 2.13 Exports of coffee (*Source:* P. Smith, Poverty in Rural Uganda, *Economic Review* vol. 16 no. 4, April 1999)

Human development and SAP in Uganda

Although Uganda has followed a structural adjustment programme for more than a decade, economic success has not trickled down to all members of society. In 1998, Uganda ranked 160 out of 174 countries according to the Human Development Index. Life expectancy at birth was only 40.5 years. At least half of the country's population was said to be living below the United Nations Development Programme (UNDP) poverty line of $1 (purchasing power parity) per day (Table 2.3).

Considerable regional variations in development also exist throughout the country. For example, in 1995 the HDI for Kampala (the capital) was estimated at 0.627. If the whole country had reached that level, Uganda would have been ranked 110 instead of 160 on the HDI Index. In the northern region of Moroto, where there has been much civil unrest in recent years, the literacy rate is 11 per cent whereas in Kampala it is 89 per cent. Similar statistics on access to health care reflect other regional variations (Fig. 2.14).

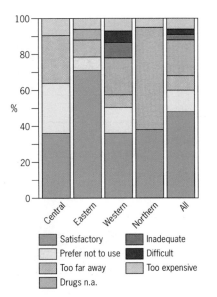

Figure 2.14 Access to health care (*Source:* P. Smith, Poverty in Rural Uganda, *Economic Review* vol. 16 no. 4, April 1999)

Even if economic growth in Uganda has been achieved by the adoption of a SAP, as some suggest, it is apparent that not every one in the country has benefited. Development efforts need to be geared towards alleviating poverty throughout the whole country. By the social indicators used by the World Bank, Uganda still remains one of the poorest countries in Africa (Table 2.3). Because people living in remote rural areas suffer from a lack of access to information, resources and to the main urban centres, better roads and communication facilities are needed. In addition, improved marketing services are required, if the benefits of SAPs are to 'trickle down'.

Similarly, if general improvements to health care are to be made, more attention needs to be focused on the provision of better sanitation systems. As only 3 per cent of households in Uganda have access to electricity, improvements to the general infrastructure would further enhance the quality of life in the country.

Efforts to improve the human capital (through health care and education) and social capital (through better access to markets and information), would require huge financial resources. However, it is difficult to see how the political leaders in Uganda could face this challenge given the size of the country's debt burden. In Uganda in 1999, £2 per person is spent on healthcare, compared with £11.50 per person on debt repayments (Table 2.2).

Table 2.2 Uganda – Economic trends. (*Source:* World Bank Group – World Development Indicators, 1999)

	1987	1997	1998
GDP (US$ billions)	6.3	6.3	6.8
Total exports (US$ millions)	384	671	466
Total imports (US$ millions)	514	1246	1393
Total debt (per cent of GDP)	30.6	58.1	53.6
Interest payments (% of GDP)	0.4	0.6	0.6
Total debt service (% of exports)	39.4	19.4	25.4
Present value of debt (% of GDP)	—	28.5	26.7
Present value of debt (% of exports)	—	208.0	265.1

Table 2.3 Uganda and Sub-Saharan Africa – Social Indicators (1998) (*Source:* World Bank Group – World Development Indicators, 1999)

	Uganda	Sub-Saharan Africa	Low-income countries
Population, mid-year (millions)	20.9	628	3515
GNP per capita (US$)	320	480	520
Average annual population growth (1992–98)	3.0	2.6	1.7
Percentage of population below national poverty line	46	—	—
Urban population (per cent of total population)	11	33	31
Life expectancy at birth (years)	42	51	63
Infant mortality (per 1000 live births)	97	91	69
Child malnutrition (% of children under 5)	26	—	—
Access to safe water (% of population)	41	47	74
Illiteracy (% of population age 15+)	36	42	32
Gross primary enrolment (% of school-age population)	91	77	108

?

7 Read Table 2.2.

a Choose an appropriate graphical technique to illustrate Uganda's position, in relation to Sub-Saharan Africa and other low-income countries, with respect to the listed social indicators.

b Research the same social indicators for the country where you live. Comment on the differences between Uganda's level of development and that of your own country.

2.4 The beginning of the debt crisis

By the late 1960s, some developing countries had experienced moderately high growth rates in their economies (Table 2.4). This was partly due to the boom in the price of primary commodities, particularly oil. Much of the money earned through oil exports was invested in western banks to generate further income. In turn, these banks lent vast amounts of this money ('petrodollars') at low interest to the poorer non-oil producing countries.

Table 2.4 GDP growth rates (%) for selected developing countries, 1965–1997 (*Source:* World Development Report, 1979, 1994, and 1998/99)

	1965–73	1973–83	1980–92	1990–1997
Oman	21.9	6.5	7.7	6.0
Libya	7.7	3.0	—	—
Saudi Arabia	11.2	6.9	0.4	1.7
Kuwait	5.1	1.4	—	—
Nigeria	9.7	1.2	2.3	2.7
Morocco	5.7	4.7	4.0	2.0
Venezuela	5.1	2.5	1.9	1.9
Argentina	4.3	0.4	0.4	4.5
Chile	3.4	2.9	4.8	7.2
Ecuador	7.2	5.2	2.3	3.1

The low interest rates and high inflation of the 1970s therefore made borrowing attractive to many developing countries. Between 1973 and 1982, the total external debt of the non-oil-producing developing countries increased five-fold, reaching the US$612 billion mark. Many poor nations had been desperate to take out more loans to finance their desired 'Western' style of development, agricultural development and the green revolution (see section 5.5). However, the world economic situation was changing and as OPEC forced a rise in oil prices (see Fig. 7.13), so banks were forced to raise interest rates during the mid-1980s – with disastrous results for the developing countries.

The knock-on effect of this rise in interest rates on the debtor developing countries was a substantial rise in the interest paid on their external debts. This also created the problem of a balance of payments deficit for these countries. (The balance of payments is the difference between what a country pays and what it receives through its international transactions.)

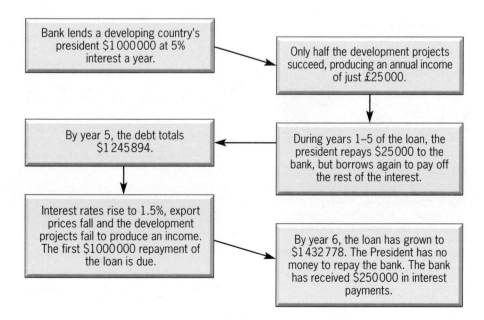

Figure 2.15 The slide into debt

'Corrupt' council

The Accra Metropolitan Authority (AMA) has been accused of corruption and inefficiency. For example, in fraudulent deals involving 40 individual officers, the AMA lost C170m through falsification of accounts, misappropriation of revenue and other shady dealings, such as financial records going missing, between May 1991 and May 1993. One area accountant is said to have misappropriated over C81m while two others stole C29 m and C26 m respectively.

Figure 2.16 Lost finances (*Source: West Africa*, 15–21 Nov. 1993)

As a result, the value of exports from developing countries fell as governments of the importing (developed) countries imposed **tariffs** to protect their own industries. With less income from exports, higher interest rates and an increase in the cost of imports, it became more and more difficult for developing countries to finance their debts. Some countries even found it difficult to pay the interest on their loans, let alone the capital. In 1982, for instance, Mexico suffered from this problem, and so it defaulted. To avoid this trap of not being able to pay their interest, many countries receiving loans use a high percentage of their export income to pay off their debt interest.

All this marked the beginning of the debt crisis for many developing countries (Fig. 2.15). The total debt owed by the poor nations in the South rose from US$751 billion in 1985 to US$1355 billion in 1990. Ironically, most of the money borrowed by the developing countries ended up being spent on mega-projects that were sometimes ill-considered and irrelevant to local needs (see Figs. 2.9–2.11). Some development experts have suggested that the high level of corruption, especially by the powerful elite and rulers of some of these countries, could mean that some of the loan money ended up in personal accounts, sometimes in the same banks that made the original loan (Fig. 2.16).

Although the World Bank often tries to underplay the growing debt crisis in the developing countries, there is now sufficient evidence to suggest that the debt burden of the poor nations is hindering the very economic development it was originally supposed to be helping.

Budget and trade deficits now afflict most poor countries in the world, and the debt load on these nations has crippled their capacity to meet all the needs of their citizens (Fig. 2.17). Many of these countries still have to find money to pay off their debts and at the same time find the resources to develop. It is now generally believed by development observers that there is a greater flow of money *from* the poorer *to* the richer nations today as a result of the debt situation (Fig. 2.16). In fact, the World Development Movement states that 'for every pound the British public gives for overseas aid, British banks take back eleven pounds in debt repayment'. This has created a 'wealth gap' on a global scale where the rich nations continue to get richer and the poor become ever poorer. However, it should be stressed that both the developed and developing countries are adversely affected by the growing debt crisis (Fig. 2.18).

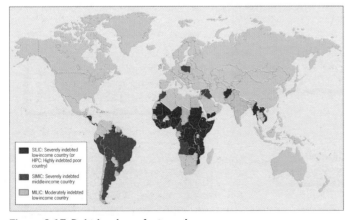

Figure 2.17 Debt burden – facts and figures (*Source:* Jubilee 2000 Coalition, *A Silent War. The devastating impact of debt on the poor.* www.oneword.org/jubilee2000/silent.html

- Each year developing countries pay the West nine times more in debt repayments than they receive in grants.
- The UK Charity Comic Relief raised £26 million in 1997. Africa paid this back in debt service in just over a day.
- Each person in the developing countries owes about £250 to the West – much more than a year's wage for many.
- Of the 32 countries classified as severely indebted low-income countries, 25 are in sub-Saharan Africa.
- Africa spends four times as much on debt repayment as she does on healthcare.
- In 1960, the income of the wealthiest 20 per cent of the world's population was 30 times greater than that of the poorest 20 per cent. In 1999, it is over 60 times greater.
- For a billion people, development is being thrown into reverse. After decades of steady economic advance, large areas of the world are sliding back into poverty.

?

8 Use Figure 2.18 to assess the extent to which the developed countries 'suffer' as a result of the growing debt problem.

?

9 In what ways can growing debt in the developing countries hinder economic and social development?

10 You work for a current affairs magazine and have to investigate the policies of the international financial institutions. Write a report assessing the aims and programmes of these institutions and give your own view as to their success.

Table 2.5 Net official development assistance (ODA) disbursed from members of the Organisation for Economic Co-operation and Development (OECD), 1994, 1996 (*Source*: Overseas Development Administration)

	Per cent of GNP 1994	Per cent of GNP 1996
Australia	0.38	0.30
Austria	0.29	0.24
Belgium	0.30	0.34
Canada	0.42	0.32
Denmark	1.03	1.04
Finland	0.31	0.34
France	0.64	0.48
Germany	0.33	0.33
Ireland	0.24	0.31
Italy	0.20	0.20
Japan	0.29	0.20
Luxembourg	0.40	0.44
Netherlands	0.76	0.81
New Zealand	0.24	0.21
Norway	1.05	0.85
Portugal	(0.28)	0.21
Spain	0.26	0.22
Sweden	0.90	0.84
Switzerland	0.36	0.34
UK	0.31	0.27
USA	0.15	0.12

?

11a Rank the OECD countries according to the percentage of aid they contributed in 1996 (Table 2.5) **b** Consider reasons why some countries give more aid towards development than others.

The six boomerangs

ENVIRONMENT Debt-induced poverty causes people in developing countries to exploit natural resources in the most profitable and least sustainable way. This causes an increase in global warming and a depletion of genetic bio-diversity. This ultimately harms the North too.

DRUGS The illegal drugs trade is the major earner for heavily indebted countries like Peru, Bolivia and Colombia. The social and economic costs of the drug-consuming boom in the North is phenomenal - $60 billion a year in the US alone.

UNEMPLOYMENT Exports from rich countries to the developing countries would be much higher if those countries were not strapped by debt. This would stimulate manufacturing and employment in the North. The loss of jobs due to 'lost exports' is estimated to account for one fifth of total US unemployment.

TAXES Governments in the North have used their tax-payers' money to give banks tax concessions so that they can write off so-called 'bad debts' from developing countries. But in most cases this has not reduced the actual debts of poor countries. By 1991 UK banks had gained from tax credits for more than half their exposure. The eventual total relief will amount to £8.5 billion.

IMMIGRATION The International Labour Organization estimates that there are about 100 million legal or illegal immigrants and refugees in the world today. Many go to the richer countries in the North to flee poverty and the effects of IMF-imposed economic policies.

CONFLICT Debt creates social unrest and war. Iraq invaded Kuwait in 1990 largely in retaliation for the latter's insistence that Saddam's regime repay a $12 billion loan.

Figure 2.18 The impact of debt boomerangs back to the developed countries (*Source: New Internationalist*, May 1993)

Solutions to the debt problem

To solve the growing debt crisis in developing countries development experts have suggested four major solutions. These are outlined as follows:

Rescheduling Debt rescheduling is the traditional method of debt management. Both the capital and repayment interests are rescheduled to a time agreed between the creditor and debtor nations.

Debt-for-nature swaps This is an arrangement whereby a country agrees to preserve an area of rainforest or nature reserve in exchange for a cancellation of debt. There is no immediate advantage to the creditors and it is unlikely that many creditors will be keen to accept this solution.

Debt-for-equity swaps Debt is 'sold' at a discount in order to raise local currency for multinational investors who may be interested in local projects in the debtor nation. Under this arrangement, debt is acquired as a substitute for local currency and then used to make local investments. The proceeds from such investment are used to pay off the country's original debt. Once the debt has been paid off, any further proceeds will be the investor's profits. In economic terms, this is known as debt equity conversion.

Debt forgiveness or cancellation This is the idea of 'writing off' the debts owed by poor countries. While debt cancellation may be a practical and compassionate solution to the debt problem in the developing countries, many creditors may be unwilling to do this.

In 1996 the IMF and the World Bank produced a debt relief initiative (the Highly Indebted Poor Country Initiative – HIPC), which considered the cancellation of debts owed to them. The World Bank has established a Trust Fund to finance the initiative. So far, the IMF has refused to commit resources to this Trust Fund. As an alternative, the IMF will offer cheaper loans to pay off expensive loans. As of 1999, Uganda was the first to receive debt relief. The effects of HIPC have been very limited with only few countries likely to see any benefit in the short term.

Table 2.6 Countries needing current debt cancellation plus extra aid required (1999) (*Source*: Jubilee 2000 Coalition, *The Silent War, The devastating impact of debt on the poor*)

	Extra aid required (US$ million)
Bangladesh	197
Burkina Faso	102
Burundi	59
Cambodia	56
Chad	30
Congo DR (Kin)	1170
Ethiopia	1293
Gambia	11
Haiti	53
India	4597
Kenya	368
Lesotho	12
Madagascar	269
Malawi	132
Mali	142
Mozambique	161
Nepal	234
Niger	164
Nigeria	1021
Rwanda	2
Sierra Leone	87
Somalia	160
Sudan	366
Tanzania	461
Togo	25
Uganda	124
Vietnam	153
Yemen	339

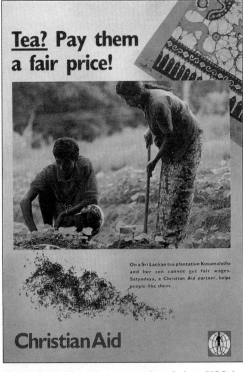

Figure 2.19 Changing your point of view: NGOs' supply of information for humanitarian purposes

2.5 Non-governmental organisations and debt cancellation campaigns

We only need to look at the media to see that governments and other official aid agencies have not succeeded in eradicating poverty, hunger and destitution in many developing countries. This probably explains why many **non-governmental organisations (NGOs)** are now actively involved in the development programmes of the poor countries. NGOs are non-profit-making organisations, mainly run as charities.

The World Bank defines NGOs as 'groups and institutions that are entirely or largely independent of government and characterised primarily by humanitarian or co-operative, rather than commercial, objectives'. We tend to use the term NGO to describe private organisations that actively try to relieve suffering, promote the interests of the poor, protect the environment or undertake community development. There are NGOs based both in the rich nations in the North and in the poor countries in the South which provide a variety of functions and support in the developing countries. Some of these are involved in grassroots work through funding, technical advice and education programmes. Most of the finances for the work done by NGOs comes both directly from governments and from fund-raising activities.

Growth of the NGOs
During the 1950s and 1960s people in both the developed and developing countries became dissatisfied with the development progress of the poorer nations. This encouraged the growth of the NGOs. The role of the NGOs became apparent as the established official development agencies, such as the World Bank and the United Nations Organisations, seemed to be failing many poor nations. These international institutions concentrated most of their efforts on promoting 'economic growth', rather than responding to the basic needs of people. Consequently, the NGOs became a major instrument for development and the 1980s was known as 'the decade of NGOs'. The hope that the NGOs would provide alternative solutions to the problem of under-development in the poorer countries was based on the fact that NGOs have a particular ability to reduce poverty and to pursue sustainable development. They achieve this through their grass-roots involvement, by their ability to reach remote communities, by working more cost effectively than bureaucratic government and commercial institutions, and by remaining flexible and innovative. NGOs are popular with the receiving countries for their use of local resources, their promotion of self-help and self-reliance (Fig. 2.19).

Jubilee 2000 – a debt-free start for the developing countries by the year 2000
Jubilee 2000 is a coalition of NGOs including charities, trade unions and religious groups campaigning for the cancellation of unpayable debts owed by the world's poorest countries. This global movement, with a campaign being promoted in over 120 countries, believes that the debts are unjust, unpayable and are responsible for the growing poverty and destitution in developing countries.

It is estimated that the debt burden of the poorest countries is 93 per cent of their total national income. In Zimbabwe, for example, if the country's debt was shared equally amongst the population, every citizen would owe the country's creditors $790. This is more than twice the average annual income for the country. In order to repay their debts, developing countries have to divert already scarce resources away from health, education and sanitation.

In the UK, Jubilee 2000, a coalition of over 80 organisations, is calling for a one-off cancellation of the unpayable debts of the world's poorest countries (Table 2.6). The target for this is the year 2000 and the organisations involved are calling for this process of cancellation to be fair and transparent.

In May 1998, about 70 000 people formed a human chain around the Summit of the eight most powerful leaders. Key national and international figures such as Muhammad Ali, Desmond Tutu and the Dalai Lama, amongst others, are known to publicly support the 'Drop the Debt' campaign.

2.6 Aid and dependency

Aid is the giving of resources from one country to another. When aid is given directly from one country to another, it is called **bilateral aid**. An example of this is the UK's £4.5 million aid package to Angola in June 1995, to support the country's immediate needs and rehabilitation efforts after civil war. Contrastingly, aid is frequently given by and through international organisations, such as the World Bank, which then redistribute the finances to a number of countries. This is known as **multilateral aid**. Funds of about £5 billion for the Narmarda River Project, in northern India, were supplied by the World Bank between 1987 and 1996 (see Fig. 2.11).

Project aid is the term used to refer to aid given by a donor country for special developments, such as road building, water supplies or health and school facilities. In this case, the donor country has some control over the use of the money and some knowledge of the progress of the project.

Governments tend to be the main contributors towards development aid, although the contributions made by non-governmental organisations (NGOs) are also vital (see section 2.5). The United Nations has suggested that each developed country should aim to give 0.7 per cent of its GNP towards helping the development process in the developing countries (Table 2.5). Whether they actually do this is questionable.

?

12 Read Figure 2.20 and identify five major ways in which food aid could be harmful to the local economy of the recipient nation.

EU aid 'damaging' Eastern Europe

THE European Union has been dumping food surpluses in Eastern Europe in the form of food aid, disrupting Eastern Europe's fledgling market economies, according to a report from the EU's financial watchdog.

EU aid to Eastern Europe has in some cases actually hindered reform. Assistance has been poorly administered, poorly thought out and sometimes harmed the people it was intended to help.

In Latvia, for instance, the EU sent rye as food aid from its grain mountains. This led to saturation of the local market, drastically reducing prices and 'sparking off discontent among farmers'. In November 1992 Latvia raised the problem with the EU and in January 1993 asked that the aid

either be stopped or converted to a different crop. But a further 32 500 tons were sent in April. After this the government threatened to return food shipments. By December 1993 40 000 tons of rye were still in storage.

The quality of food aid was often poor: five-year-old wheat was sent to Lithuania and substandard meat was sent to Albania. And, in Albania, all the available warehouses in the main port were requisitioned for storage of EU aid. 'There was, in the autumn of 1993, no further capacity for private business', the report says.

It says that EU assistance is 'indispensible' but adds that it is 'sometimes counter productive for the reform process, especially for the newly developing private sector'. In addition to criticism of food aid,

the report targets the Phare and Tacis programmes of technical assistance, saying 'no clear strategy' for assistance is apparent and the programme 'still fails sufficiently to take national priorities into consideration'.

The report raises many problems with the use of outside consultants and experts and says that co-ordination of assistance is poor. 'This task should not, in future, be substantially delegated to a group of experts, low-level employees or supply companies.

In some programmes there has been abuse of internal financial controls, slow implementation, overlapping programmes and irregular charging of expenditure. In some cases, national officials in Eastern Europe were paid directly out of EU funds.

Figure 2.20 Helpful solutions for EU surplus? (*Source*: Andrew Marshall, *The Independent*, 10 Oct. 1994)

?

13 Research one recent development project by an NGO and one by an official agency.
a Analyse their strategies for development.
b Assess the success of each of these projects according to their original aims.

14 There are now a large number of international NGOs covering wide areas of development in the poor countries. Construct a questionnaire to examine public awareness of NGOs (see Appendix A2). You could include questions about:
a which NGOs are most well-known
b the type of aid they supply
c which NGOs are most deserving of support.

15 Carry out further research into debt cancellation campaigns and prepare a report to convince the public to support Jubilee 2000's initiative.

Motives for aid

There is a certain amount of controversy surrounding aid, especially when it is 'tied' aid. Donor countries often prefer aid to be 'tied' as this is the type of arrangement which offers the developed countries most benefits. Tied aid means that any goods and services needed during the spending of the aid must be obtained from the donor country. For example, the building of a dam will require construction workers and materials, etc., and these will be acquired from the country providing the money. It is therefore the donor country which benefits in terms of employment and sales of goods.

Some of the aid sent to developing countries, especially during a period of emergency and environmental or natural disaster, such as war, drought, or epidemic, has gone a long way to reducing the suffering and misery of people in those countries. However, a long-term reliance on aid from the rich nations is seen by some development experts as being counter-productive. In some cases, not only has aid discouraged local investment, but it has also caused more harm than good to the recipient nation, as the European Union's aid to some Eastern European countries proves (Fig. 2.20).

It is also sometimes the case that aid is given to countries which share the same political or religious views. In such situations, the giving of aid becomes highly controversial, particularly when linked with the provision of military hardware. A prime example of this is the military aid that was given to Cuba by the former Soviet Union, 1961–62.

?

16 To what extent do you think the NGOs could provide solutions to the growing problems of poverty in the developing countries?

17 What are the potential problems NGOs face today in raising funds in your country?

18 Essay: Discuss the view that the developing countries have become increasingly reliant on the developed countries since the end of colonialism.

Summary

- Many development problems facing the developing countries have their roots in the colonial past.
- The political and economic relationships between the rich and the poor nations reinforce dependency of the developing countries on the developed countries.
- The modern international capitalist system gave birth to such institutions as the World Bank and the IMF. These institutions try to influence development in the developing countries through loans and mega-projects.
- The World Bank notion that international trade and competition could result in growth, and so benefit everyone, has not materialised.
- Capitalism tends to increase poverty and inequality in the developing countries.
- Aid, in all its forms, may do more harm than good in the long term. Some development experts have suggested that aid is another form of dependency.
- NGOs play an increasingly important role in providing aid to the developing countries at a more grassroots level.
- NGOs provide information about the developing countries and help foster a humanitarian attitude towards the predicaments of the poor nations.
- Jubilee 2000 is a coalition of NGOs campaigning for debt cancellation in the world's poorest nations.

3 Population dynamics and structure

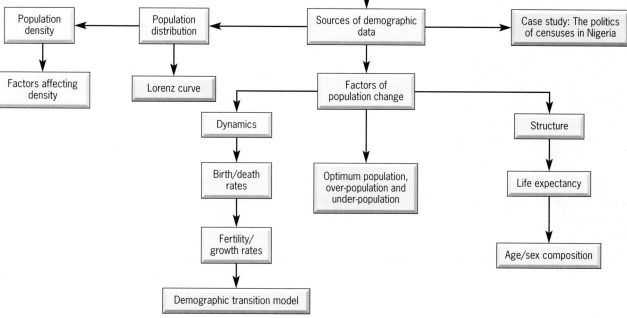

3.1 Introduction

This chapter examines various aspects of population in relation to development. We will firstly consider data collection and the sources of information about population. With such information, we can look at **population distribution**, or the arrangement of people over a geographical area, and population density, the number of people per unit of area. We will then analyse population structure, involving the numbers of people in different age and sex groups, together with the changes in population characteristics over time.

3.2 Sources of demographic data

Census information

Statistics about the population of any region or country are essential for planners if any development is to go ahead (Fig. 3.1). **Demography** is the scientific study of the various aspects of population, such as gender, age, birth and death rates, and information about the population is usually obtained through a census. This is a statistical survey which the United Nations define as 'the total process of collecting, compiling and publishing demographic, economic and social data pertaining, at a specified time or times, to all persons in a country or delineated territory'.

The United Nations recommends that a census is carried out every ten years, although it prefers censuses to take place every five years. In **developed countries**, the census requires heads of households to complete a form answering questions about all members of their household. The questions are related to age, sex, marital status, birthplace, ethnic background, education and

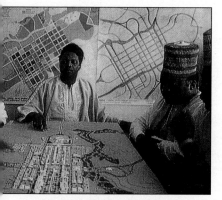

Figure 3.1 Inspecting the plans for the Nigerian Federal Capital, Abuja. The city planners, including experts from Milton Keynes had to construct buildings and an infrastructure to cater for an increasing population.

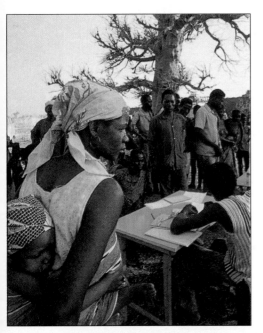

Figure 3.2 Collecting data for the 1991 census, Burkina Faso. The enumerator is responsible for collecting data in a particular district and must make sure that all census questions are answered. When individuals are unable to read or write, the enumerator has to interview them.

?

1 List as many likely uses of vital registration and census data as you can think of for planners at a local, regional and national scale.

2 Select an appropriate sampling technique and explain how you would carry out a survey to determine the average size of households in your local community.

3 Suggest some likely problems caused by using unreliable census data for planning purposes in the areas of:
a health
b education
c employment.

economic activities. Other questions might be included relating to household structure, housing tenure, amenities and transport. Governments make the process of conducting a census easier by dividing the country or region into areas known as 'enumeration districts' (Fig. 3.2).

Vital registration

In developed countries, and in some **developing countries**, there is a legal requirement for people to register significant events such as births, deaths and marriages. People usually go to the local register office for this. In the UK, vital registration statistics are regularly used to update a previous census.

Special surveys

Special surveys are often used to supplement insufficient or poor-quality data provided by the census or vital registration. For example, in the UK, the General Housing Survey (GHS) is an annual sample survey carried out by the Office of Population Censuses and Surveys (OPCS). Different topics, such as leisure and/or smoking are covered every two to three years, or whenever the government may need specific information.

The World Fertility Survey

At an international scale, the World Fertility Survey (WFS) aims to assess the state of human fertility throughout the world. The first pilot study was carried out in 1973. Women were then asked about the history of their pregnancies, duration of marriage and their use of contraception, etc.

The WFS came about as a result of the poor quality of demographic data available for the developing world and the need for better population data – both for scientific study and for policy applications. The Survey was funded by a number of international and national agencies, mainly the United Nations Fund for Population Activities (UNFPA) and the United States Agency for International Development (USAID). The WFS provided a wealth of information which has helped to clarify some of the relationships between population change, economics and development. From such data, governments were able to formulate national population policies. For example, a great deal of detailed WFS information about fertility in Asia, South America and the Middle East helped to determine levels, trends and factors influencing infant and child mortality in these locations.

3.3 Problems of data collection in developing countries

In some developing countries the census may be the only national survey which ever takes place. In fact, some countries, like Ethiopia, Sudan and Afghanistan, have had very few census surveys. This is usually due to government instability, a weak infrastructure or disruption caused by war. Additionally, vital registration in most of the developing countries is inadequate and those people who do register may not be representative of the whole population. Often, they are better educated, wealthier and they understand the need and procedures for vital registration. Conversely, people who live in the more remote areas are often under-represented because they are less accessible. This inadequacy of data collection is a problem for demographers (people specialising in the study of population) who depend on using accurate and trustworthy information. Overall, though, we know that wide demographic variations exist between the relatively better-off urban dwellers and the poorer rural inhabitants. Even in developed countries, people may refuse to fill in their census forms. This occurred in the UK when individuals tried to avoid paying the new community charge, 'poll tax', introduced by the Conservative government in April 1990. As a result, the 1991 census returns were perhaps the least reliable since World War 2. However, in most developing countries there are many other factors which may distort the accuracy of census data (Table 3.1).

Table 3.1 Selected reasons for unreliable census data

• Households may be omitted due to incomplete mapping of enumeration areas.	• Language barriers, e.g. in Cameroon there are 30 major language groups.
• Lack of trained staff to administer the census.	• In areas where there are low literacy levels, some people have difficulty filling in the forms.
• Nomads and the homeless may be difficult to record.	• Age misreporting: a person may not have a birth certificate and in some cases the enumerator may have to guess ages; people may describe themselves as being younger or older than they actually are, e.g. teenage girls and older women shift their ages into the fertile age band; where status is associated with age, people may give an older age.
• Transport difficulties in remote rural areas (often made worse by seasonal weather patterns, e.g. monsoon).	
• In northern India and the Middle East, male enumerators are not allowed to interview women.	

The politics of census surveys in Nigeria

Nigeria has the largest total population in Africa, with an estimated 108 million people in 1994 (see Fig. 1.9). The first attempts to enumerate the population were in 1863, and since then there have been 10 censuses. These Nigerian census surveys illustrate how unreliable government statistics can be.

Official estimates

The 1991 census involved 500 000 staff covering 225 000 enumeration districts over three days. In 1989 the government's official population estimate for 1991 was 109.2 million (Fig. 3.3) while the 1991 census revealed a total of only 88.5 million.

Inaccuracies

The population estimates were based on the census of 1963, which was considered the most accurate of all Nigerian censuses. However, the then western and eastern regions accused the northern region of inflating its figures so that it could keep political control of the country. The response from the northern region was to accuse the others of also over-inflating their population totals in order to receive an unfair share of the government's revenue. This tribal rivalry escalated into the Biafran war (1967–70) when eastern Nigeria (Biafra) claimed independence but was then defeated by the Nigerian government forces. More recently, the government has created a number of new states in an attempt to reduce regional tensions and encourage more integration of the population (Fig. 3.4).

Population control

In May 1989, the Nigerian government introduced a population control policy. The government recommends that couples should limit themselves to having a maximum of four children instead of the current average of six. The dependency ratio (the proportion of the non-working population to the working population) has risen steadily since the 1960s and this has created an extra burden on the economy as well as on the health and education services. Over half of the total population are under 15 years of age and such a high **child dependency ratio** (see Appendix A3) gives the government little choice other than to try controlling Nigeria's population growth rate.

4 The text suggests there is over-reporting of local populations in Nigeria. Suggest ways in which the Nigerian population census could be made more reliable.

5 Bearing in mind the population doubling time for Nigeria of 23.34 years (Fig. 3.4), what resource implications does this have for the country? (See also Figures 1.9–1.11)

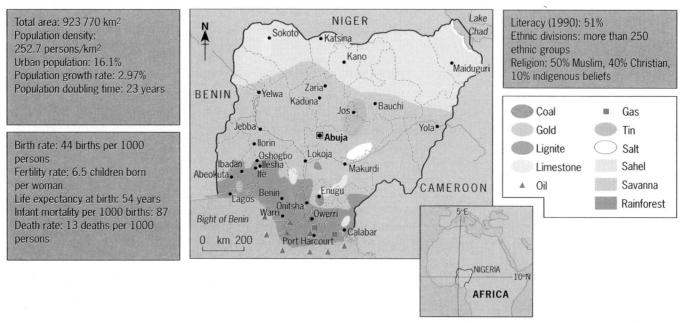

Total area: 923 770 km²
Population density:
252.7 persons/km²
Urban population: 16.1%
Population growth rate: 2.97%
Population doubling time: 23 years

Birth rate: 44 births per 1000
persons
Fertility rate: 6.5 children born
per woman
Life expectancy at birth: 54 years
Infant mortality per 1000 births: 87
Death rate: 13 deaths per 1000
persons

Literacy (1990): 51%
Ethnic divisions: more than 250
ethnic groups
Religion: 50% Muslim, 40% Christian,
10% indigenous beliefs

Coal   Gas
Gold   Tin
Lignite   Salt
Limestone   Sahel
Oil   Savanna
    Rainforest

Figure 3.3 Nigeria: location and basic statistics (1998)

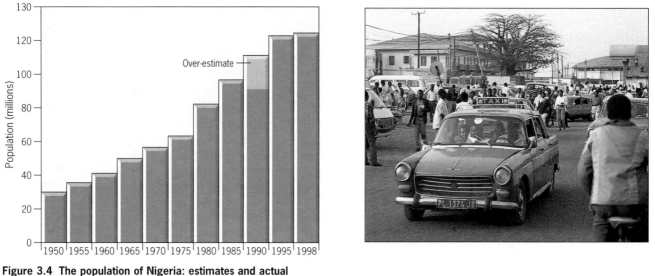

Figure 3.4 The population of Nigeria: estimates and actual

?

6 Divide the graph in Figure 3.5 into three stages. Describe each stage and comment on it.

7a With reference to Table 3.2, use an appropriate mapping technique to show the 1994 population growth rates for five developing countries and five developed countries on a blank base map of the world.
b Suggest reasons for the differences shown.

8 Look at Table 3.3.
a Discuss the factors which may lead to relatively static or declining population growth rates.
b What might be the • social, • economic and • demographic implications of such declining population growth rates?

3.4 World population growth rates

After domestic agriculture became established and settled communities developed, the world population grew to about 300 million by AD 1 (Fig. 3.5). The rate of growth from then on was very slow (about 0.1 per cent per annum).

Since 1750, the world has witnessed a rapid rise in the number of people, with average annual growth rates of 0.5 per cent between 1750 and 1900. During the first half of the 20th century, the world population grew at an average rate of 0.8 per cent and by the second half of the century this increased to 1.7 per cent. In mid-1994, the average annual growth rate was 1.6 per cent.

By 1994, many countries in Africa, Asia and Latin America were experiencing high population growth with annual rates of 2.0–4.5 per cent (Table 3.2). The industrialised nations, such as the United Kingdom or France were experiencing slower growth with annual growth rates of less than one per cent (Table 3.2). In contrast, some countries were even experiencing population decline (Table 3.3).

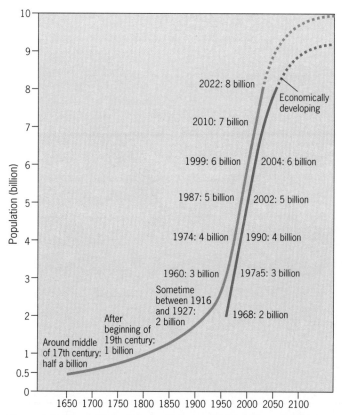

Figure 3.5 The growth of the world's population (*Source:* UNFPA)

Table 3.2 Population growth for selected countries, 1994–2050 (*Source:* UN Population Division, 1994)

Country	Mid-year population 1994 (thousands)	Annual growth rate (%)	Projected population by year 2050 (thousands)
Angola	10 674	3.7	41 182
Australia	17 853	1.4	26 060
Bangladesh	117 787	2.2	238 512
Belgium	10 080	0.3	10 068
Brazil	159 143	1.7	264 349
Canada	29 141	1.2	39 870
China	1 208 841	1.1	1 605 991
Egypt	61 636	2.2	117 398
Ethiopia	53 435	3.0	194 203
France	57 747	0.4	60 475
The Gambia	1 081	3.8	2 762
India	918 570	1.9	1 639 863
Japan	124 815	0.3	110 015
Mexico	91 858	2.1	161 450
New Zealand	3 531	1.2	4 667
Nigeria	108 467	3.0	338 510
Peru	23 331	1.9	43 820
UK	58 091	0.3	61 635
USA	260 631	1.0	348 966

Table 3.3 Annual percentage growth of population for countries with static/declining population (*Source:* The World Bank, 1979; World Development Report, 1994)

Country	1960–70	1970–80	1980–92	1992–2000
Bulgaria	0.8	0.4	−0.3	−0.4
Hungary	0.3	0.4	−0.3	−0.4
Portugal	0.0	0.8	0.1	0.0

Population doubling time

The high population growth rates which we see in many poor nations should be viewed in relation to the population doubling time associated with such rates. With a two per cent growth rate, the population doubling time would be about 35 years, while a growth rate of three per cent means it will take only 24 years for the population to double. Similarly, within a period of 17 years, a country with a population growth rate of four per cent per annum would double itself (Fig. 3.6). Such an understanding of population doubling time is important for assessing demands on both human and physical resources (see section 5.2).

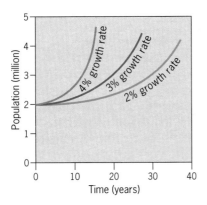

Figure 3.6 Samples of population doubling time

Figure 3.7 World population distribution and density (*Source*: Population Concern)

3.5 Population distribution and density

Population distribution refers to the way in which people are spread out across the earth's surface. In contrast, population density describes the number of people living in a given area. Population density (*PD*) is calculated as follows:

$$PD = \frac{\text{Number of people in an area/country}}{\text{Size of area/country (km}^2)}$$

As such, population density indicates the concentration of people per unit area. It shows the number of people who will be living in each square kilometre if people were distributed evenly over the land.

Both the density and distribution of population vary widely on a global scale (Fig. 3.7). In fact, a majority of the world's population is in developing countries as Table 3.4 and Figure 3.8 illustrate.

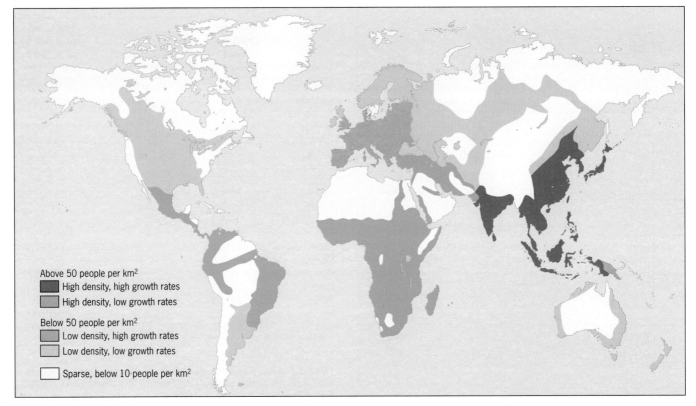

Above 50 people per km²
- High density, high growth rates
- High density, low growth rates

Below 50 people per km²
- Low density, high growth rates
- Low density, low growth rates

- Sparse, below 10 people per km²

?

9a On a blank world map, shade the world's ten most populous nations using Table 3.4.
b Referring to Figure 1.1, draw the North–South dividing line on your map and comment on how many of the largest nations are in the South.

Table 3.4 World's most populous nations (1997). (*Source:* World Development Report 1998/99).

Rank	Country	Population (millions)	World population (%)
1	China	1 227	21.1
2	India	961	16.5
3	United States	268	4.6
4	Indonesia	200	3.4
5	Brazil	164	2.8
6	Russian Federation	147	2.5
7	Pakistan	137	2.4
8	Japan	126	2.1
9	Bangladesh	124	2.1
10	Nigeria	118	2.0

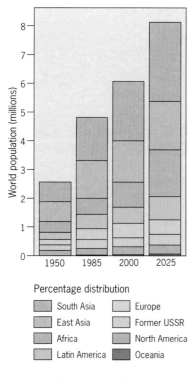

Figure 3.8 World population distribution by major areas, 1950–2025 (*Source*: UN)

Similarly, on an international scale, the population densities of different countries vary (Figs 3.9–3.10). In Western Europe, the UK is one of the most densely populated countries, with 604 people per square kilometre. This national average density figure often hides the fact that population density varies across the country (Fig. 3.11). On a regional scale, population densities also vary, as can be seen in the case of northern England (Fig. 3.12) and on a local scale as in urban areas such as Greater London (Fig. 3.13).

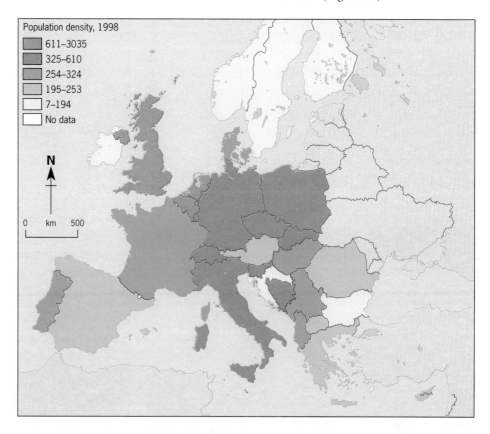

Figure 3.9 International population density: Europe, 1990

Figure 3.10 International population density: Northern Africa, 1990

?

10 Using Figure 3.8 describe the changes and projected changes in the world's population distribution from 1950 to 2025.

11a Describe the variations in population density throughout • Europe and • Northern Africa, as shown in Figures 3.9 and 3.10. **b** Suggest why some countries have high population densities while others have lower densities.

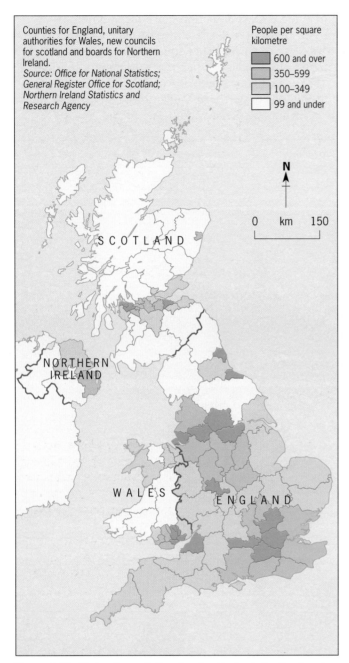

Counties for England, unitary authorities for Wales, new councils for scotland and boards for Northern Ireland.
Source: Office for National Statistics; General Register Office for Scotland; Northern Ireland Statistics and Research Agency

People per square kilometre

- 600 and over
- 350–599
- 100–349
- 99 and under

Figure 3.11 National population density: England, Scotland and Wales, 1996

Persons per km²
- >40
- 20 – 39
- <19

Figure 3.12 Regional population density: Northern England, 1990 (*Source*: Waugh, 1990)

Persons per hectare (1981 census)
- >90
- 60 – 89
- 30 – 59
- <29

Figure 3.13 Local population density: Greater London, 1981 (*Source*: 1981 census)

Lorenz curve and population distribution

The Lorenz curve (Fig. 3.14) is a graph used to show inequalities in distributions. In fact there are many phenomena, such as population, industry and employment, which will show unequal distributions over a given area. On Figure 3.14, the straight diagonal line represents a perfectly even distribution of the population over a selection of continents. The curve shows the level at which population is concentrated within the various regions. The larger the area between the diagonal line and the curve, the greater the concentration of population (or industry, employment, etc.) relative to the total area.

**Table 3.5 Distribution of world population by region, 1998
(Source: Population Reference Bureau, World Population Data Sheet, 1998)**

Region	World population (%)	Cumulative population (%)	World's area (%)	Accumulative area (%)
Africa	12.9	12.9	22.3	20.3
Asia	60.8	73.7	20.3	40.4
Europe	15.2	88.9	20.1	62.7
South America	5.6	94.5	15.2	77.9
North America	5.0	99.5	15.8	93.7
Oceania	0.5	100	6.3	100

?

12a Using the data provided in Table 3.5, draw a Lorenz curve to illustrate the distribution of the world's population (see Appendix A4) .
b Compare and comment on the differences between your own graph and Figure 3.14.

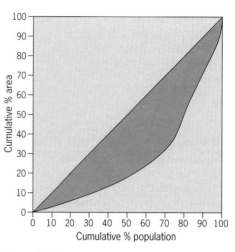

Figure 3.14 Lorenz curve for world population distribution, 1960

Physical factors influencing population density

There are many environmental and human factors which influence population densities. Some of the environmental factors are as follows:

Relief

Mountainous areas are less attractive to settlement than lowland plains. Soils are often thin on steeply sloping land, making it difficult to develop agriculture. Also, at high altitudes air has a low oxygen content and temperatures decrease very rapidly with increased altitude. High mountains, even on the equator, can be as cold as polar areas, with a mean monthly temperature persistently lower than 10°C. Such areas are therefore usually sparsely populated.

Lowland areas, being relatively flat, tend to attract settlement and often support large numbers of people (Fig. 3.15). Communication lines, such as canals, railways, roads and airports, as well as industry, are easily constructed here. This also attracts more people. In addition, lowland areas are usually intensively farmed.

Climate

Where average monthly temperatures rarely exceed 10°C, the range of crops people can grow is limited. Transport is also hampered by frost and snow. In fact, few people live where temperatures are so low, such as in Lapland where there is an average of only one person living per square kilometre. Similarly, people do not tend to live where it is excessively hot and dry. As crop cultivation is impossible in desert regions without expensive irrigation, high population densities are relatively rare in arid areas. For example, in central-west Nigeria, about 50 people live per square kilometre (see Fig. 1.11), while in the Gobi Desert there is an average of only 1.4 people per square kilometre (Fig. 3.16).

In contrast people are attracted to temperate climates, where temperatures are neither too cold nor too hot, and rainfall is distributed evenly throughout the year. Here, intensive crop cultivation is possible. This is clearly seen in the Mid-West USA, known particularly for its corn production. Another example is north-west Europe, which is also one of the most densely populated parts of the world. Similarly, we see high population densities maintained in hot and humid areas near the equator where cultivation takes place all year round, such as the 200–400 people per square kilometre in Bangladesh.

Figure 3.15 Lowland area: the west coastal plain of Taiwan. The main north-south highway crosses the length of the plain, and by 1993 the area had about 80 000 factories.

Figure 3.16 Irrigated vegetable plots in the Gobi Desert, Mongolia, where the average temperatures range from –25 °C in January to 32 °C in July

Figure 3.17 Brunei: tropical rainforest. Brunei is situated on the north-west coast of the island of Borneo and has an annual rainfall of 250 cm along the coast.

13a List all the possible *human* factors which might influence population distribution and densities.
b Assess their impact on world population distribution (Figure 3.8).

14a Study Figure 3.8 and list those regions or countries which are
• sparsely populated and • densely populated.
b For each of the areas you have listed in **14a**, give reasons for the variations in their population densities.

Vegetation

Dense forests, which are difficult to clear, and deserts, where natural vegetation is sparse, are usually regions of very low population density (Fig. 3.17). The most obvious examples of this are the Sahara Desert and the Amazon rainforest.

Conversely, areas of grassland and easily removed broad-leaved woodlands in the temperate regions tend to support dense populations. Examples include the Mid-West conurbations of the east coast of the USA. These areas usually have deep fertile soils which, again, are ideal for agriculture.

Optimum population, over-population and under-population

Optimum population

In economics theory, the **optimum population** of an area is the number of people who, when working with all the available resources and with existing levels of technology, will produce the highest possible per capita income. As such, the optimum population should be able to provide for the highest standard of living possible. We can therefore say that the standard of living is determined by the interaction between physical and human resources as expressed by the following formula:

$$\text{standard of living} = \frac{\text{natural resources} \times \text{technology}}{\text{population}}$$

This concept is a dynamic one, i.e. it changes with time as technology improves, as population totals and structure (age and sex ratios) change, and as people discover new raw materials to replace those which are exhausted or have changed in value.

Over-population

Over-population is a situation where there are too many people, given the existing resources and levels of technology, for them to maintain 'adequate' standards of living. It is also important to stress that over-population is not necessarily associated with high population densities. For example, in countries which are largely deserts, the **carrying capacity** will be small and a few people per square kilometre may represent 'over-population'.

The carrying capacity relates to available resources and the existing levels of technology. It indicates the number of people who can be adequately

15 In relation to the theoretical optimum, what will happen if the size of the population • increases • decreases?

16 Use Table 3.6.
a Work out the population density of both the Netherlands and Bangladesh.
b Describe the standard of living for each country (you could refer to section 1.3).

17a For each country, use the formula to describe the relationship between population and the other factors.
b Suggest additional factors that may affect the link between population and resources.

18 Using specific examples of countries which are • developing and • developed, describe the symptoms of over-population. Figures 3.18 and 3.19 may help you.

supported by the productive capacity of the land (in terms of food output, water availability and the general resource base). If the carrying capacity is exceeded, given existing levels of technology, then a country or region may be described as over-populated. In this case, living standards are lowered and the resource base may be damaged from over-use. Theoretically then, if the numbers of people were reduced, or if new technology resulted in a more productive use of resources, then standards of living should improve.

The Netherlands and Bangladesh: a comparison

The Netherlands and Bangladesh are two countries which we might consider as over-populated. In fact it is clear that there are large, densely populated areas in both countries (Table 3.6). The Netherlands is not well endowed with natural resources but it has been able to use technology to produce high-quality agricultural products for export to generate income (Fig. 3.18). Bangladesh also has insufficient mineral and energy resources, but it has not been able to use technology to generate export income (Fig. 3.19) in the same way.

Under-population

Under-population is the opposite to over-population. It occurs when far more resources are present in an area than can be used by the people living there. In theory, Canada is still under-populated in that it *could* support a population of 50 million and still maintain its standard of living (Fig. 3.20). In 1994 the population of Canada was 29.1 million and the population density was three people per square kilometre. Australia is another country which we can classify as under-populated. Both Canada and Australia could export their surplus food, energy and mineral resources and still have high incomes, good living conditions, high levels of technology and high levels of immigration (Table 3.7). It is also likely that, if the population were to increase, standards of living would rise because of increased production and exploitation of resources.

Table 3.6 Selected indicators of development (*Source:* Human Development Report; 1998; World Development Report, 1998/99)

	Total population, 1997 (millions)	Land area (km²)	Life expectancy at birth, 1996 (years)	GNP per capita, 1997 (US$)	Human Development Index, 1995	Adult literacy, 1997 (%)	Urban population 1997 (%)	Exports, 1996 (US$ million)	Imports, 1996 (US$ million)
Netherlands	16	3 730	77	25 820	0.941	99	89	225 473 Machinery, foodstuffs, chemicals	199 932 Machinery, foodstuffs, chemicals, minerals, fuels
Bangladesh	124	114 000	58	270	0.371	38	19	4 508 Jute, fish	7 614 Machinery, foodstuffs, petroleum

Figure 3.18 Intensive, mechanised farming in the Netherlands

Figure 3.19 Basic farming methods in Bangladesh

Figure 3.20 Under-population: Canada has more resources than can be fully exploited by its population

Table 3.7 Selected indicators of development (*Source:* Human Development Report; 1998; World Development Report, 1998/99)

	Total population, 1997 (millions)	Land area (km²)	Life expectancy at birth, 1996 (years)	GNP per capita, 1997 (US$)	Human Development Index, 1995	Adult literacy, 1997 (%)	Urban population 1997 (%)	Exports, 1996 (US$ million)	Imports, 1996 (US$ million)
Australia	19	7 686 850	78	20 540	0.932	99	85	78 805 Agricultural produce, oil, gas, textiles, machinery	79 568
Canada	30	9 916 140	79	19 290	0.960	99	77	234 311 Cars, machinery, chemicals, foodstuffs, tobacco, metals	211 509 Machinery, clothing, paper, iron, steel

3.6 Factors of population change

There are three major factors of population change: fertility, mortality and migration. These variables account for population change over time and space. While fertility and mortality are discussed below, see Chapter 4 for migration.

Fertility
There are a number of methods for measuring fertility.

Crude birth rate
The crude birth rate (CBR) is the most common measure of fertility. It gives an overall picture of the number of births per 1000 population in a year, i.e.:

$$CBR = \frac{\text{total number of births}}{\text{total population}} \times 1000$$

However, CBR does not take into account the age and sex distribution of the population.

Age-specific fertility rate
The age-specific fertility rate (ASFR) is a measure of the number of children born to each age group, in relation to the number of women in that age group.

19 Use the standard of living formula to describe the relationship between population and resources for Canada and Australia (Table 3.7).

20 Using library resources, find an example of a developing country that you consider to be under-populated. Write a feature for a news magazine assessing its characteristics.

Table 3.8 USA age-specific fertility rates, 1988 (*Source:* US Dept of Health and Human Sciences)

Age	Births	Population	Rate
10–14	10 588	8 144 000	1.3
15–19	478 353	8 924 000	53.6
20–24	1 067 472	9 574 000	111.5
25–29	1 239 256	10 928 000	113.4
30–34	803 547	10 903 000	73.7
35–39	269 518	9 660 000	27.9
40–44	39 349	8 198 000	4.8
45–49	1 427	7 135 000	0.2

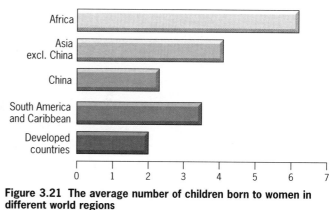

Figure 3.21 The average number of children born to women in different world regions

21 The average family size in developing countries tends to be much larger than in developed countries. Use Figure 3.21 to respond to this comment, suggesting reasons for your observations.

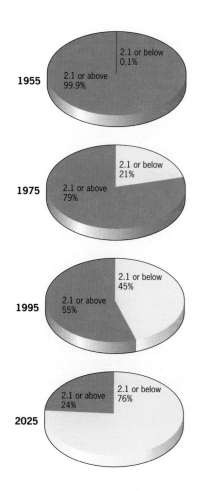

Figure 3.22 Replacement level fertility, 1995–2025 (*Source:* WHO The World Health Report 1998)

Seven age groups are conventionally used across the span 15–49 years. ASFRs are normally expressed per 1000 women in each age group (Table 3.8).

Total fertility rate

The total fertility rate (TFR) is one of the most useful measures of fertility. It is the average number of children born to a woman during her lifetime. This varies noticeably across the world. For example, in Sierra Leone, there was a 1994 TFR of 6.5, while the UK had a TFR of only 1.8. The TFR is obtained from the total of all the age-specific fertility rates and assumes that these remain constant throughout a woman's child-bearing years. Like any other statistical estimates, the TFR value does not necessarily mean that women will, in future, continue to have that number of children.

Replacement level fertility

The replacement level fertility (RLF) is the level at which each generation of women has only enough daughters to replace themselves in the population. The 'replacement' levels vary for different populations, depending on the level of mortality and the sex composition of the population. For example, while in theory we could say that a woman with two daughters has replaced herself twice, in practice these births may only just reach the actual 'replacement level' if child mortality is high. Consequently, a total fertility rate of 2.12 children is usually considered as the replacement level. This is because mortality may prevent a proportion of the female children from reaching their productive years and also, on average, slightly more boys are born than girls. Since 1995 there has been a steady decline in replacement level fertility across the world (Fig. 3.22).

Mortality

Mortality is the ratio of deaths to the population of a given area. Mortality is often measured using such indices as crude death rates, infant mortality rates or life expectancy.

Crude death rate

The crude death rate (CDR) gives an overall picture of mortality and is expressed as the number of deaths per 1000 population in one year, i.e:

$$CDR = \frac{\text{total number of deaths}}{\text{total population}} \times 1000$$

According to the 1994 population data, Sierra Leone had a CDR of 25 per 1000 while the CDR for the United Kingdom was 11 per 1000. This means that for every 1000 people in the United Kingdom, 11 deaths were recorded in 1994.

The CDR can be very misleading, though, because the index is generally influenced by the age structure of the population. For example, although

Table 3.9 Infant mortality rates and life expectancy for selected countries, 1996 (*Source:* World development Report, 1998/99)

Country	Infant mortality (per 1000)	Life expectancy at birth (years)
Malawi	133	41
Burundi	97	47
Sierra Leone	174	38
Nepal	85	57
Switzerland	5	79
United Kingdom	6	77
Germany	5	77
Sweden	4	79
Mexico	32	72
Colombia	25	71
Peru	42	68
Bangladesh	77	58
India	65	62
Australia	6	78

Table 3.10 Life expectancy at birth (years) in world regions (*Source:* UN)

	1950–5	1980–5	2020–5
Africa	37.8	49.4	64.5
S. America	51.1	64.2	72.3
N. America	69.1	74.4	77.5
E. Asia	42.7	68.4	75.9
S. Asia	39.9	54.9	70.1
Europe	65.3	73.1	77.2
Oceania	60.8	67.9	74.9
Former USSR	64.1	70.9	76.7
World	46.0	59.5	70.5

22a Using Spearman's rank correlation (see Appendix A1), analyse the relationship between infant mortality rates and life expectancy for the countries listed in Table 3.9.
b Comment on your result.

23 Using Table 3.10, choose a suitable graphical technique to show changes in life expectancy for all the world regions listed.

France and Togo both had CDR values of 13 per 1000 in 1994, a person can expect to live on average some 22 years longer in France than in Togo. The age structures of the two populations in this case are significantly different. While 15 per cent of France's population is aged 65 years and over, only 3 per cent of the population in Togo are within this age group.

Age-specific death rate

Unlike the CDR, the age-specific death rate (ASDR) is a mortality measure for just one age group in the population. The ASDR is calculated using the formula:

$$\text{ASDR} = \frac{\text{number of deaths in a specified age group}}{\text{population of the age group}} \times 1000$$

It is also expressed as a number per 1000 per year. The age-specific death rate of the population aged 0–5 years is generally referred to as 'child mortality'.

Age- and sex-specific death rate

Usually, age-specific death rates are calculated separately for each sex because of the differences in mortality between the sexes – women tend to live longer than men (Fig. 3.23). An age- and sex-specific death rate (ASSDR) is therefore the number of deaths during a year among persons of a given age and sex per 1000 people of that age and sex category, i.e:

$$\text{ASSDR} = \frac{\text{number of deaths in a specified age and sex category}}{\text{population of age and sex category}} \times 1000$$

Figure 3.23 What a difference! (*Source:* Quillin, 1992)

Infant mortality rate

The infant mortality rate (IMR) is a measure of the number of deaths of infants before their first birthday, per 1000 live births in a year. Since children are much more susceptible to sickness and disease than adults, the number of infant deaths recorded in a country is usually a reliable indication of the state of health of the country. This is especially so, because children respond easily to the state of their mother's health and the state of pre- and ante-natal services. Countries such as Malawi, Burundi, Sierra Leone and Afghanistan have very high infant mortality rates (Table 3.9).

Life expectancy

Life expectancy measures the average number of years a person can expect to live. High mortality in the early age groups often lowers the average life expectancy. Similarly, as general mortality declines, life expectancy will increase (Table 3.9). Just like the age-specific death rate, life expectancy can be calculated for different sexes.

24 Using the annual population growth rates for a range of countries listed in Table 3.2, estimate the time it will take for the population of each country to double (see section 3.4).

Maternal mortality rate

Maternal mortality rate (MMR) is a measure of the number of women who die as a result of complications in pregnancy and childbirth. It is expressed per 1000 live births in a specified year. MMR is higher in many poor countries, especially in Africa where women are 200 times more likely to suffer a pregnancy-related death than Western European women. There are a variety of reasons, but the higher MMR for developing countries generally results from poorer access to health facilities; higher fertility rates (giving women less time to recover from previous pregnancies); and a poorer diet (lowering a woman's resistance to illness).

Calculation of population growth rates

The difference between the crude birth rate and the crude death rate is the rate at which a population is either increasing or decreasing (see Tables 3.2, 3.3). This is referred to as natural population change but it takes no account of the effects of migration. When the net effects of migration are considered, this is known as actual population change.

With a CBR value of 45 per 1000 (4.5 per cent) and a CDR value of 15 per 1000 (1.5 per cent) recorded for Nigeria in 1994, the annual population growth rate is calculated as follows:

$$4.5\% - 1.5\% = \text{annual growth rate of } 3.0\%$$

Demographic transition model

Following a study of changes in birth and death rates in several developed countries in North America and Western Europe, researchers have developed a model which suggests that all countries pass through similar population cycles, or **demographic transition stages** (Fig. 3.24). The model suggests that changes in birth and death rates are linked to the development process.

25a From Figure 3.24, describe how the population total changes through each stage of the demographic transition model.
b Use Tables 3.2 and 3.3 to decide whether you could add a fifth stage to the model. If so, describe its characteristics.

26a With reference to Figure 3.25, make a list of the factors which brought about changes in the birth and death rates in the United Kingdom between 1700 and 1940.
b Describe how both the birth and death rates reacted to each of the factors you have listed.

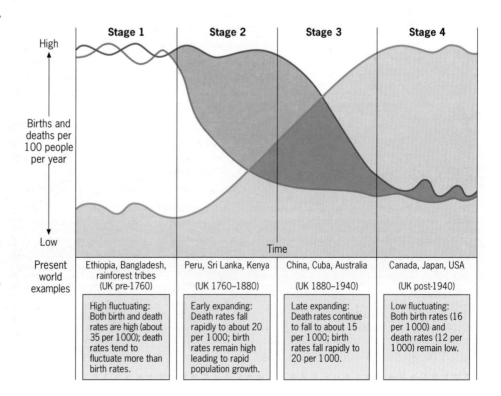

Figure 3.24 The demographic transition model

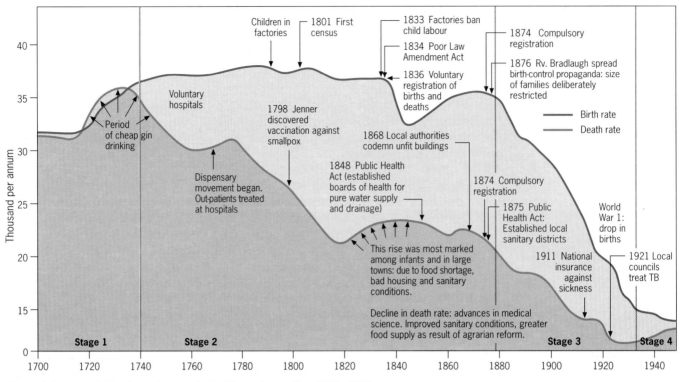

Figure 3.25 United Kingdom: changes in fertility and mortality, 1700–1940

?

27a Study Figures 3.26 and 3.27 and decide which stage of the demographic transition model each country in north Africa has reached in relation to birth and death rates.
b Suggest what you think will happen to the total population of each country over the next few years. Give your reasons.

Although the dynamics of population change in developed countries has been generalised here, the model helps us understand the reasons for population growth in the developing countries.

Many factors contribute to variations in both birth and death rates. All countries therefore have differing demographic transitions, depending on the social and economic circumstances which influence their birth and death rates. For example, changes in fertility and mortality may be affected by a variety of factors such as legislation, medical advances and even fashion (Fig. 3.25).

Although the developed countries have passed through the four stages of the demographic transition, most developing countries experience persistently high birth rates. Stages 2 and 3 of the demographic transition model are more typical, therefore, of most developing countries in the late 20th century.

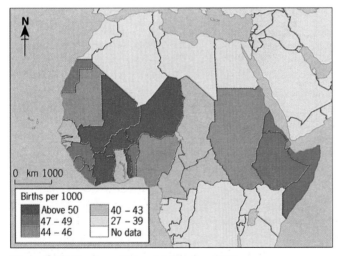

Figure 3.26 Northern Africa: birth rates, 1992

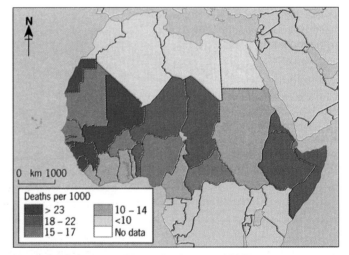

Figure 3.27 Northern Africa: death rates, 1992

3.7 Factors affecting fertility

There are various factors which particularly affect fertility in the developing countries. Some of these are outlined below:

Demographic factors

Families often try to compensate for high infant and child mortality by having a large number of children (Fig. 3.28). This is in the hope that some of the children will survive. In fact, social scientists have calculated that, in sub-Saharan Africa, where the average IMR is over 100 deaths, a woman must have an average of 10 children to be 95 per cent certain of a surviving adult son.

Where a population has a high child dependency ratio (see section 3.3 and Appendix A3), the result of a declining IMR will be more children surviving into adulthood. This can have long-term implications for future population growth rates. For example, more female children will survive to reach child-bearing age. Thus the birth rate remains high – even if fertility rates have since declined. This is a case of past fertility and mortality rates affecting future population growth and is known as **population momentum**.

Evidence of population momentum can be seen in the high rates of adolescent pregnancies that are currently characteristic of many developing countries. Babies born to young women aged 15–19 is an emerging concern throughout the developed and the developing world. In 1995, 17 million (13 per cent) of babies worldwide were born to teenagers. Nine in every ten of these babies (13 million) are born in the developing world and they constitute about 13 per cent of all children born in these countries.

Economic factors

In many developing countries, children are regarded as an economic asset. This means that they are viewed as producers rather than consumers and so parents (or other adults) will encourage them to contribute to the family income (compare with section 5.6).

Whereas children in developing countries are used as income generators, in the developed countries they are often viewed as a financial burden. For example, in the United States it is estimated that the cost of supporting a child to the age of 18 is in excess of US$100 000. The economic motivation for having many children in developed countries is therefore reversed.

Social and cultural factors

There is a strong correlation between increasing female literacy and decreasing fertility rates (see section 6.5). In fact, low literacy rates and high drop-out rates from school, especially among girls, mean that many young women enter into marriage and so have children early (see Table 6.9). Similarly, women's reduced access to formal employment and other income-earning opportunities means that they are forced to devote most of their time and energy to child-bearing and **informal** home and agricultural work (see Table 6.4). In contrast, developed countries show that with 'emancipation', women are more likely to have fewer children, and at a later age, than in developing countries.

There is no doubt that family size will reduce if the socio-economic conditions of many poorer nations improve. However, opinions differ as to how to reduce fertility rates in the developing countries (Fig. 3.29).

We also need to view high fertility rates in the cultural context. This is because in many developing countries, cultural factors play a significant role in the number and frequency of child birth and, hence, in the size of families. For example, in some African countries religious traditions emphasising ancestry and descent require babies to be named after dead relatives. People therefore view a lack of children as evil and childless couples as cursed. Demographic

Figure 3.28 Fai Mankoh (left) has six wives and 36 children. Some traditional African societies seek to increase the numbers of surviving children through family structures: polygamy is practised in Nigeria, Ghana, Mali and Cameroon.

28 Read Figure 3.29.
a Identify the two opinions on how best to reduce fertility rates in developing countries.
b Which view do you agree with? Give your reasons.
c Devise a plan to promote the successful adoption of your view for reducing fertility rates in a developing country.

Birth of a new world order

THE truth about population has become dangerously obscured. A proper concern for women's rights, and for the alleviation of chronic poverty, have ossified into ritual condemnations of anyone making a priority of population. Old shibboleths have persisted decades after their demolition by the empirical evidence of demographers.

None have persisted more obdurately than the idea that 'development is the best contraceptive'. From this perspective, doing anything about reducing human numbers becomes dependent on first reducing poverty – on the grounds that this was how things had happened in the world's richer nations when they went through their demographic transition. Only as per capita income rises will people be persuaded to have fewer children.

Unwelcome though this may be for the development lobby, this is basically cobblers. In country after country, average fertility rates have been falling dramatically over the last 20 years – with or without the necessary increases in per capita income.

Bangladesh is one of the most interesting examples of this so-called 'reproductive revolution'. It is one of the world's poorest nations, with high infant mortality and a largely agrarian society, in which most families still depend on children for labour and security in old age. But between 1970 and 1991, fertility rates declined from 7 to 5.5 children per woman (a 20 per cent reduction). And the key to that was the increase in the number of married women using contraception: up from 3 per cent to 40 per cent.

In short, contraception is the best contraceptive, not 'development'. Some researchers have gone as far as to say that differences in contraceptive prevalence (the percentage of women using contraception) explain about 90 per cent of the variation in fertility rates, and that for every 15 per cent increase in contraceptive prevalence, each woman will bear on average one child less.

What's more, though women's education is indeed one of the key factors in increasing contraceptive prevalence, it is not a precondition of it. In Egypt itself, where illiteracy still exceeds 50 per cent in many rural areas, contraceptive use has doubled in 10 years (making it the first Muslim country with more than 50 per cent of couples using contraception) and fertility rates are down from an average seven children per woman in the early 1960s to four today. That drop has been achieved largely through an unprecedented media blitz, including the screening of up to 600 hours of material relating to population and family planning every year.

To argue that the availability of contraception is the key determinant in reducing average fertility does not mean that one abhors any the less strongly either the poverty or the illiteracy of women taking advantage of that contraceptive availability. But it does rather change one's perception of what we can realistically do to address these problems.

For one thing, availability on its own is not enough. Fertility surveys around the world have shown that what really counts is quality of care, real freedom of choice (between different contraceptives) and the degree to which family services are integrated into overall reproductive healthcare strategy.

That's what makes the Cairo conference programme for action such an astonishing document. It's at least as much about women's reproductive rights and healthcare services as it is about family planning per se. It's a triumph for women's organisations which have gone on pointing out the obvious in the teeth of male-dominated health departments concerned only about the increasing number of 'contraceptive acceptors'; that coercion is not only heinous but counterproductive; that 'empowering' of women to take control of their own fertility will fail and keep on failing.

At long last the penny seems to have dropped. Family planning is an important health measure in its own right. Where women have six or more children, the lifetime risk of dying from maternal causes is five times higher than where they have two or less. The welcome convergence between the family planning establishment and mainstream women's organisations has been highly significant in the drafting and promoting of the Cairo programme for action.

Figure 3.29 Cairo Population Summit, September 1994 (*Source*: Jonathon Porritt, *The Guardian*, 2 September 1994)

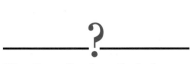

29a Draw four hypothetical population pyramids to reflect the characteristics of the four stages of the demographic transition model (Figure 3.24).

b Comment on the development of the population structure shown by your graphs.

and cultural factors come together when, as part of their 'bride price', women in some African cultures, e.g. Nigeria, are obliged to produce as many children for their husbands as possible. When these women become widowed, any claim on their deceased husband's property is denied. As a result, the only security women have is their children, which suggests why many women would like/need to have as many children as possible.

Modernisation and the changing fertility trend

As people adopt Western culture in many developing countries, some traditional customs become less important. As a result, there is less emphasis on high fertility, particularly with a declining child mortality and increasing familiarity with family planning programmes. Recent demographic household surveys show that birth rates have fallen by 15–25 per cent in Botswana, Zimbabwe and Kenya. Similarly, social scientists report a fertility decline of over 10 per cent in southern Nigeria.

3.8 Age-sex structure of population

The age-sex structure of a population is best illustrated as a population pyramid, which is another form of bar graph (Fig. 3.30, see Appendix A5). The population is normally divided into five-year age groups, e.g. 0–4; 5–9; 10–14 on the vertical axis. The horizontal axis represents the percentage of the total male or female population in each age group and is divided according to gender.

Figure 3.30 Population by age and sex, 1950, 1990 and 2025 (*Source:*** US Bureau of the Census, Center of International Research, UNDIESA, 1991)**

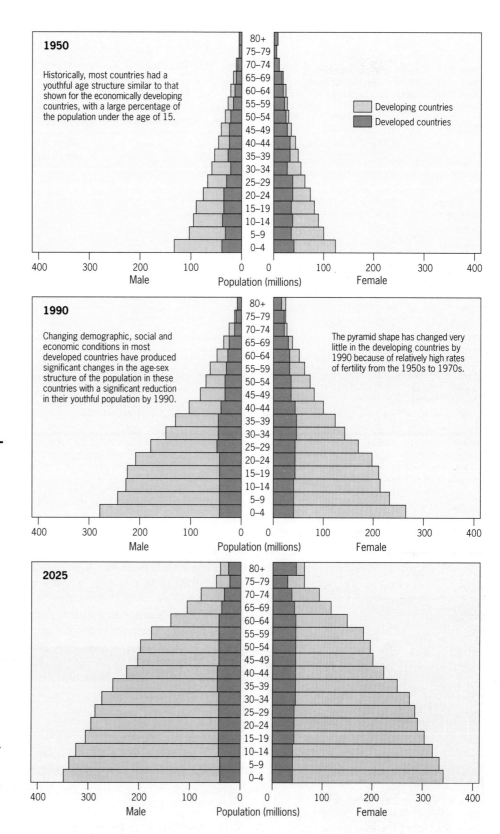

30 Use Table 3.11. On a blank world map, draw pie graphs for each region showing the percentage in each age sector for 1990 and 2025. Compare the differences in the proportion of elderly people between developed and developing regions.

31a Discuss the social, economic and demographic factors responsible for the varying proportion of elderly people in different regions of the world.
b What implications does the growing proportion of elderly people have for service provisions such as health care and transport?
c Research government policies arrived at improving the living conditions of elderly people in your country.

32 Essay: With reference to specific countries, describe and explain the social and economic implications of • top-heavy and • broad-based population structures.

As well as illustrating the effect of past changes, population pyramids can also indicate both short- and long-term future changes in population.

We can use population pyramids to show the results of migration, the age and sex of migrants and the effects of wars and major epidemics. Certain population pyramid shapes are also characteristic of each stage of the demographic transition model.

Elderly people and population structure

An essential feature of the world population structure is the growing proportion of elderly people. We consider the elderly population to be 65 years old and above and this is usually the retirement age for many countries, including the UK (Fig. 3.31).

Table 3.11 The world's oldest nations, 1997–2015 (*Source:* The World Bank, World Development Indicators 1999.)

Country	Percentage population 65+ 1997	2015
Japan	15.5	25.4
Sweden	17.3	21.1
Italy	16.6	21.1
Switzerland	14.7	20.7
Germany	15.5	20.5
Greece	16.6	20.3
Finland	14.4	19.9
Belgium	16.0	19.0
Austria	14.8	18.9
United Kingdom	15.8	18.7
Czech Republic	13.3	18.7
Spain	15.9	18.6
Bulgaria	15.0	18.6
Netherlands	13.4	18.2
Slovenia	12.8	18.1
Denmark	14.7	18.0
France	15.4	18.0
Croatia	13.6	18.0
Estonia	13.3	17.9
Latvia	13.7	17.7
Norway	15.7	17.6
Hungary	14.2	17.1
Portugal	16.1	16.6
Canada	12.2	16.5
Lithuania	12.6	15.7
Australia	11.8	15.2
Ukraine	13.9	14.9

Table 3.12 Percentage of elderly people by regions, 1990–2025 (*Source:* US Bureau of the Census, Center for International Research, International Database on ageing)

Region	Year	65 years and over	75 years and over	80 years and over
Europe*	1990	13.7	6.1	3.2
	2010	17.5	8.4	4.9
	2025	22.4	10.8	6.4
North America	1990	12.6	5.3	2.8
	2010	14.0	6.5	4.0
	2025	20.1	8.5	4.6
Oceania	1990	9.3	3.6	1.8
	2010	11.0	4.8	2.8
	2025	15.0	6.6	3.6
Asia*	1990	4.8	1.5	0.6
	2010	6.8	2.5	1.2
	2025	10.0	3.6	1.8
South America/Caribbean	1990	4.6	1.6	0.8
	2010	6.4	2.4	1.2
	2025	9.4	3.6	1.8
Near East/North Africa	1990	3.8	1.2	0.5
	2010	4.6	1.6	0.8
	2025	6.4	2.2	1.1
Sub-Saharan Africa	1990	2.7	0.7	0.3
	2010	2.9	0.8	0.3
	2025	3.4	1.0	0.4

* Data excludes the former Soviet Union

Of all the world regions, Europe has the highest proportion of population aged 65 and over (Table 3.12), although Japan, too, is dealing with the problems of an ageing population (see section 4.7).

The 'oldest old'

The term 'oldest old' refers to the population 80 years and over. Persons in this category constituted 16 per cent of the world's elderly population in 1992, i.e. 22 per cent in the developed countries and 12 per cent in the developing countries. In many European countries, the population aged 80 and over represented about 25 per cent of the elderly population (Table 3.11).

Figure 3.31 Increasingly growing old: by the year 2025 it is estimated that more than 1 in 10 Europeans are likely to be 75 years old or older

Summary

- Reliable population statistics are essential for effective government policies and planning.
- Unreliable data in the developing countries can act as an obstacle to development.
- The concepts of optimum, over- and under-population relate to the size of population, the available resources and the existing levels of technology.
- The world's population is unevenly distributed. Some areas are over-populated, while others are under-populated.
- Fertility, mortality and migration are the three components of population change.
- All countries pass through demographic transition stages which are linked to the development process.
- The population structure typical of developing countries consists of a high percentage of people under 15 years, resulting in a high child dependency ratio.
- Many developed countries are characterised by an ageing population.

4 Population movements and urbanisation

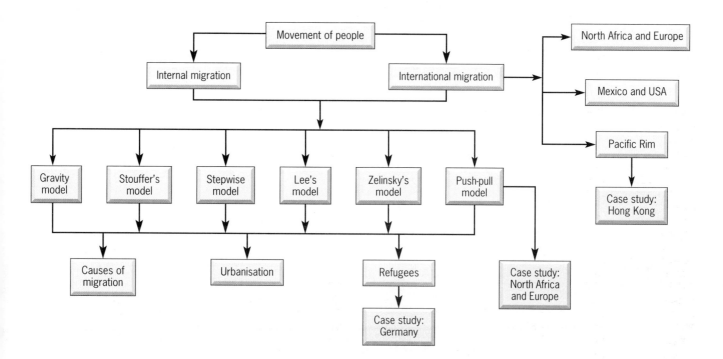

4.1 Introduction

In both the **developed** and **developing countries** patterns of human migration are a result of changing social, economic, political and environmental circumstances. In this chapter we will discuss some of these causes of migration. Over recent years, attention has increasingly centred on the issue of internal population movement, particularly in the developing countries. International migration is another area of growing concern which has implications for both developing and developed countries – not least in its effects on the allocation and utilisation of resources.

4.2 Historic population movements

Early migration

Historical evidence suggests that early human groups spread outwards from north-east Africa. The earliest human remains found in Europe are approximately half a million years old. This indicates that people had already migrated from East Africa to Europe (often now referred to as the **old world**) by that time. These migrations took place during periods of glacial advance in the last ice age when water taken up in ice sheets lowered the sea's surface to create land bridges. These made it easier to migrate (Fig. 4.1). It took humans an estimated 3 million years to spread over much of the earth's surface.

Ethnic (racial) diversity

As people inhabited different parts of the world, they grouped together and developed their own distinctive identities. The term 'race' refers to descent from one of these distinctive groups. Long periods of interbreeding and inter-regional migrations have since resulted in a great mixing of races and racial diversity.

Figure 4.1 Major migrations: early peoples and during the nineteenth and first half of the twentieth centuries

Table 4.1 Population total increase in Western Europe, 1750–1980 (*Source*: J N Biraben (1979) *Essay sur l'evolution du Nombre des hommes*, 1979; UN World Population trends 1981, UN Population Bulletin 14, 1982)

Year	Population (millions)	Increase since previous year; average per year, per 1000 population
1750	111	—
1800	146	5.5
1850	209	7.2
1900	295	6.9
1950	392	5.7
1960	425	8.1
1970	462	8.4
1975	474	5.1
1980	484	4.2
projected		
2000	512	2.8
2100	504	—

For example, the Caucasoids met Mongoloids (American Indians) in North and South America and through intermarriage produced the Mestizos. The world became a 'multi-racial' (pluralistic) place at a very early stage primarily because of early migrations and intermarriages.

We can see differences between the ethnic groups in both their physical and cultural characteristics, e.g. language, dress and even diet. It is therefore possible for us to identify the major races:

• Negroid: includes the indigenous peoples of Africa south of the Sahara, their descendants and the people from Melanesia (Pacific Islands).
• Mongoloid: includes most of the peoples of Asia, the Inuit (eskimo) and the North American Indians.
• Caucasoid: refers to peoples originating from Europe and North Africa.

Migration during the industrial revolution

Apart from the early migrations, the world's major mass movement of people occurred during the industrial revolution in Europe. This was a time when Europe experienced a population 'explosion' (Table 4.1). In fact, one of the major characteristics of the industrial revolution in Europe was high population growth due to rapidly declining death rates while birth rates remained persistently high (see section 3.6 and Fig. 3.24). This led to population pressure which, alongside social changes, encouraged many people to migrate, especially to North America (known as the **new world**) (Fig. 4.1). An estimated 40 million Europeans emigrated to North America and other relatively uninhabited regions, such as Australia and South Africa, between 1820 and 1900.

1 Use Figure 4.1 to write an historical account of the early movement of people across the world.

2 Read Figure 4.2.
a How did Europe cope with its labour problems after World War 2?
b In what ways were the **immigrants** to Britain different from those migrating to other European countries?
c In your group, discuss what you consider to be the results of such migration.

3 In 1963 President Pompidou stated that 'immigration is a means of creating a certain easing in the labour market, and of resisting social pressure'. Comment on this statement saying whether or not you agree with it.

Post-World War 2 and the migratory balance

The direction of population movements from Europe was reversed after World War 2. This was a time when the devastated European economies needed rebuilding and Europe was suffering from serious labour shortages because of men lost in fighting. The European governments encouraged migrants, usually from the European colonies, to work in industries such as transport, care and construction (Fig. 4.2).

During 1956, 30000 West Indians arrived in the UK: most came by boat to Southampton and then train to London.

THE SECOND WORLD WAR led to unforeseen new demands. By 1944 Germany had seven million foreign workers. Every fourth German tank, lorry, and field gun was made by a foreigner. Much of this, of course, was forced labour.

But at the end of the war, in 1945, the consensus of expert opinion was that most European countries would not be able to provide enough employment for their own citizens. The big worry was Western Germany which had received eight million refugees from the East. But in fact the reverse happened. The expanding economies of the West European countries soon took up the slack and before long attention was swivelling outwards to foreign sources of labour. In Britain it began in 1940 with a cargo of West Indian immigrants. They were closely followed by Indians and Pakistanis. The numbers of immigrants increased year by year until, in the late fifties and early sixties, Britain's economy went into the permanent doldrums. Ironically, at this time, racism and xenophobia pushed anxious governments into building high walls of protection to limit the immigrants who no longer wanted to come. All in all, in this time of immigration Britain absorbed 800000 workers and their families – small fry compared with what was going on in some other European countries...

The British have the feeling that the great influx of Commonwealth immigrants in the last two decades is a special British phenomenon – a legacy of Empire. But this is only true inasmuch as the British tend to have black workers rather than white ones. But all European countries have experienced what the British have experienced – a great influx since the war of large numbers of foreign workers. In Germany they are nearly all white – Greeks, Turks, Yugoslavs, Spaniards, and Italians. In France the principal groups are Portuguese, Spanish and North African. In Belgium they are mainly Italians, Turks, and Greeks. In Holland, more similar to Britain, there are large numbers of Indonesians and people from the Dutch West Indies, Although Turks, Greeks and Italians are numerous too.

They are the new proletarians – doing the menial jobs, poorly paid with little job security (unless they are Italians or Greeks, fellow members of the EEC), separated from their families, living in housing that is often appalling.

Willy Brandt succinctly summed up their contribution when he said: 'In every way, foreign workers help us to earn our daily bread... although foreign workers are in Germany because at home they live in indigent circumstances, Germany needs them urgently. They're dependent on us. But we are even more dependent on them for otherwise they would not be here.'

Figure 4.2 Attracting workers to the industrial centres of Europe (*Source: Jonathan Power, 1972, The New Proletarians, Community & Race Relations Unit of the British Council of Churches)*

4.3 Definition of migration

The United Nations defines migration as the movement of a person or persons from one place to another, involving a permanent (one year or more) change of address. There are different types of migration classified according to whether the movement is within a country (internal migration) or from one country to another (international migration).

Internal migration

This involves movement between regions within the same country and over relatively short distances. There are various types of movement in this category depending on their direction (Table 4.2 and Fig. 4.3).

International migration

International migration involves relatively long-distance movements between countries. **Emigration** is the term used to describe the departure of a person from one country to live permanently in another. Conversely, immigration is the entrance of a person into a country with the aim of living there permanently (see Figs. 4.1 and 4.24)

4a Using the media or your library, research recent examples of both migration types.
b Identify some of the difficulties each type of migrant had to face as they moved. Consider how the people in the host area responded to the migrants.

Table 4.2 Types of internal migration

Type of migration	Direction of movement	Reason and example
Rural-to-urban	People moving from countryside to urban areas	People searching for work led to: • growth of cities in Europe during industrial revolution, • rapid urbanisation in developing countries in late twentieth century.
Urban-to-rural	People moving from the city or town to the countryside	Many people see cities as unattractive and in developed countries people try to move away from the urban areas. This process is referred to as **counter-urbanisation**, e.g. England's South-East where families move out of London into the semi-rural home counties.
Inter-urban	People moving from one town or city to another	Changing work opportunities force people to relocate.
Intra-urban	People moving within the same urban area or city	Increased transport results in high levels of residential mobility, e.g. post World War 2, people moved to the edge of cities (suburbanisation).
Rural-to-rural	People moving from one area of the countryside to another	Common in agricultural communities where there is a need to change farming locations, e.g. sheep shearers migrating between ranches in the USA and Australia; nomadic pastoralists, northern Africa.
Transmigration	Forced, or government-organised, mass movement of people	Indonesia, from the 1980s: several million people were moved to the country's less populated outer islands, from Jakarta and other overcrowded cities. In 1999 this resulted in conflict in East Timor. 200 000 people were displaced by the fighting, forced to flee to the countryside surrounding the capital, Dili.

Figure 4.3 Squatters near Curitiba, southern Brazil. Large plantations have taken up much land and left many people homeless and landless, forcing them to move close to the cities in search of work. In 1980 18.45 million people migrated within the South-East region of Brazil. In contrast, 35.14 million people migrated to the relatively inaccessible Central-West region. Brasilia has grown rapidly mainly as a result of rural-urban migration.

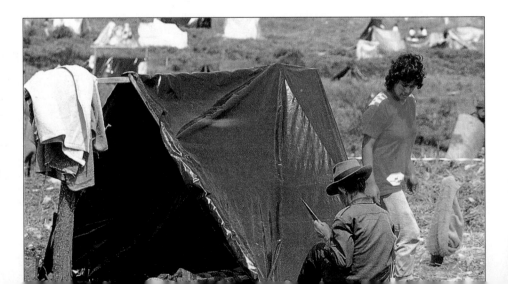

4.4 Migration theories and models

There are two main categories of migration models. First are those which try to predict and explain migration using some mathematical or probability concept. An example of such an approach is the gravity model. Second, there are largely descriptive models which focus on various social factors that may influence patterns of migration. Whether expressed in mathematical or descriptive form, migration models generally provide some specific explanation for population movements.

Gravity model

The gravity model is based on E G Ravenstein's laws of migration (1885). He developed these to explain the migration process in late-nineteenth-century Britain.

An essential feature of the gravity model is its suggestion that migrants tend to move over short distances, with the number of migrants decreasing as the distance over which migration takes place increases. This idea is known as the **distance decay effect** which states that the volume of migration is inversely proportional to the distance travelled, and directly proportional to the relative sizes of the origin and destination places (Fig. 4.4). This is mathematically expressed as follows:

$$M_{ij} = \frac{P_i P_j}{D^2_{ij}}$$

where M_{ij} = the volume of migration from place i to place j
P_i = the population size of place i
P_j = the population size of place j
D^2_{ij} = the distance between places i and j

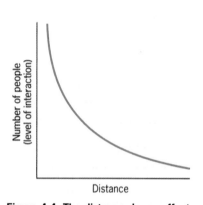

Figure 4.4 **The distance decay effect**

?

5a For the five largest cities in the country where you live, find out: • the population size of each, • the distance between each city and the capital.
b Calculate the *predicted* interaction between each city and the capital using the formula provided.
c List the factors which could lead to more or less interaction between cities than you have predicted using the gravity model.

Stouffer's intervening opportunity model

Stouffer's migration model suggests that the level of movement of people between two places is dependent upon the type and number of **intervening opportunities** between them. Intervening opportunities are the nature and number of possible alternative migration destinations that may exist between place A (migration origin) and place B (migration destination). An essential feature of this model is that the nature of places, rather than their distance, is more important in determining where people move to. People will move from place A to place B based on the real or perceived opportunity at place B (e.g. work). According to

Stouffer's model, therefore, the number of persons moving over a given distance is directly proportional to the number of opportunities at that distance, and inversely proportional to the number of intervening opportunities.

Using Strodbeck's (1949) version of this method, the basic idea of Stouffer's Intervening Opportunity model can be mathematically expressed as follows:

$$y = k \, \frac{\nabla x}{x}$$

where y = the expected number of migrants from a place to a particular concentric zone or distance band around that place

∇x = the number of opportunities within this band

x = the number of opportunities intervening between origin and midway into the distance band

k = a constant of proportionality

Stepwise migration model

The stepwise migration model is a behavioural one developed from E G Ravenstein's laws (1885) that population movements occur in stages and with a 'wave-like' motion. According to this idea, major settlements, such as capital cities, tend to attract migrants from the smaller cities, which in turn attract migrants from smaller towns and villages. Migration therefore occurs in 'steps' and in the form of a 'ripple' that stretches across an entire region (Fig. 4.5).

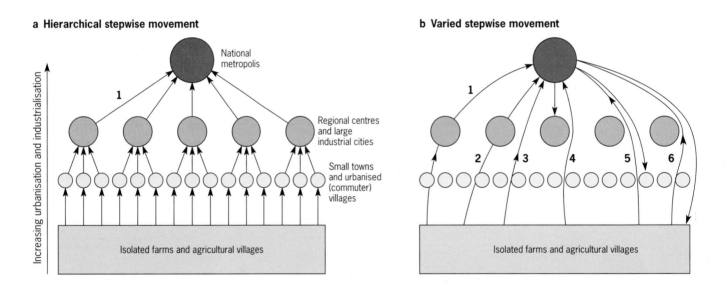

6 Referring to Figure 4.5, draw your own version of the stepwise model identifying the stages of Chinese migration.

Types of stepped migratory movement originating from rural areas:

1 Progressive movement from rural area to small town, to regional centre to national metropolis
2 Progressive movement from rural area to regional centre and then national metropolis
3 Direct movement from rural area to national metropolis
4 Intention to move from rural area to national metropolis but eventually residing in regional centre
5 Intention to move from rural area to national metropolis but eventually residing in small town
6 Intention to move from rural area to national metropolis but eventually returning to rural area without residing elsewhere

Figure 4.5 Stepwise migration model (*After:* Ravenstein)

Table 4.3 Pacific Rim countries: overseas Chinese

Country	Ethnic Chinese population in millions
Thailand	7.0
Hong Kong	5.5
Malaysia	4.88
Indonesia	4.12
Singapore	1.99
USA	0.894
Canada	0.4
Philippines	0.6
Australia	0.17
UK (for comparison)	0.126

Stepwise migration in China

Several events in China have led to increasing numbers of Chinese emigrating to countries of the Pacific Rim. A famine in the early 1960s, resulting from a change in political direction, caused many Chinese to escape to nearby countries such as Thailand and Malaysia. The adoption of the 'Open Door' policy, in 1978, also resulted in a steady stream of Chinese migrants moving to the urban centres around the Pacific. In the early 1990s, there were about 30 million Chinese living in Pacific Rim countries (Table 4.3).

We can see the influence of such Chinese migration by looking at Malaysia. Here, one-third of the population are indigenous Chinese and most of these, as in many other Pacific Rim countries, are successful business people who maintain their cultural and economic links with China. They are often reluctant to break with Chinese traditions and religions, and usually regard Chinese as their first language. In fact, many have now left Malaysia, 'stepping on' to greater cultural tolerance and better business opportunities in Singapore.

There are also 400 000 Chinese in Canada, with two-thirds of these living in Vancouver and Toronto. Most Chinese here come from Hong Kong, though, showing the 'stepwise' progression, as a typical feature of international migration.

Lee's migration model

Lee's model tries to explain the factors of migration in terms of positive and negative characteristics of both the origin and destination places. Migrants must expect to receive some added advantage in moving from one place to another. Also, potential movements from an origin, such as a rural area, to a final destination, such as a capital city, are often influenced by the existence of possible alternative destinations. These present themselves as intervening opportunities for migrants whose movements to the final destination may be slowed down or even stopped by these intervening places (Fig. 4.6).

Intervening obstacles may prevent migration from taking place, or may reduce the numbers moving. Distance may be such an obstacle (see gravity model), while social or economic factors may also act as obstacles.

Key
- – Negative factors
- + Positive factors
- 0 Neutral factors

Figure 4.6 Lee's general migration model

Zelinsky's model of mobility transition

Zelinsky's model of mobility transition is a parallel theory to the **demographic transition model** (see section 3.6). Zelinsky's model attempts to describe definite regularities in migration types through space and time. In doing so, it seeks to explain the pattern of migration from what Zelinsky considered to be the pre-modern traditional society through the different stages of modernisation to the advanced industrial society. The essential feature of the model is based on Rostow's stages of economic growth (see section 6.6).

Zelinsky's model suggests that as modernisation proceeds, different forms of migration patterns emerge. Once a particular pattern of migration is started, it rises steadily until it reaches its peak and then declines. Thus different types of population movement succeed one another as the dominant wave (Fig. 4.7).

?

7a How might long-distance travel be affected by modern developments in transport, such as Concorde?
b Might these developments in transport mean that another stage could be added to Zelinsky's model? If so, describe the main features of this stage.

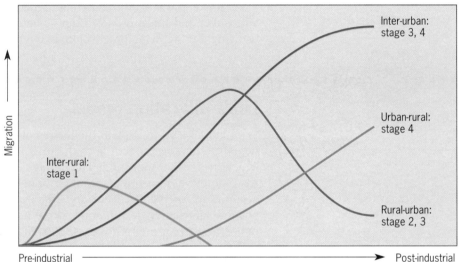

Figure 4.7 Zelinsky's mobility transition model

Stage 1: occurs mostly in a subsistence economy. People move about very little and usually only make daily journeys to work in the fields, or less frequent journeys from village to village to sell farm produce.

Stage 2: migration to other countries and cities becomes important. People begin to move home in search of better opportunities. Farm mechanisation reduces the demand for rural workers while industrialisation provides work in urban areas.

Stage 3: overseas emigration tends to fall. Movement from the country-side to the cities remains important. Migration from one city to another and within particular cities also occurs.

Stage 4: migration from the countryside to the cities declines and urban-rural migration (counter-urbanisation) begins. People tend to move home frequently but within or between cities e.g. $\frac{1}{5}$ of the population of the USA change residence annually. Ease of travel encourages daily long-distance journeys for e.g. work or education. Long-distance travel for holidays is another feature of this stage.

Migration between North Africa and Europe

It has been estimated that about six million people from North African countries now live within the European Union (Fig. 4.8). It is also now evident that increasing numbers of people are arriving in Europe from countries south of the Sahara. While we could consider distance an 'obstacle' to migration, this movement suggests that the environmental and political push factors (see push-pull model, section 4.5) in the semi-arid origin countries, e.g. Chad and Ethiopia, are much stronger than the distance obstacle. Italy and France are the most popular destinations with migrants from North Africa. We can explain this by proximity, but also by historic ties. Algeria, Morocco, Tunisia, Libya, Mali, Chad and Burkina Faso are all former colonies of France and many people in these countries still speak French as their main language, despite subsequent independence.

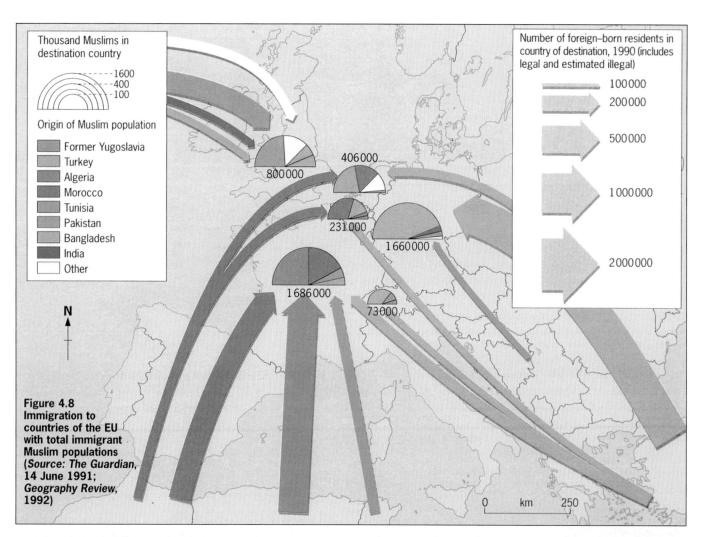

**Figure 4.8
Immigration to
countries of the EU
with total immigrant
Muslim populations
(Source: The Guardian,
14 June 1991;
Geography Review,
1992)**

The impact in Italy and France

Both Italy and France have been under great pressure
to tighten their immigration policies. This is principally
because of the rapid increase in the numbers of
migrants during the 1980s, especially from North
African countries such as Senegal, Ghana and the Cape
Verde islands.

Italy

Italy introduced visa requirements from July 1990 for
'visitors' from the Mahgreb (or North African countries).
Italy's 2000 km coastline makes it particularly
vulnerable to landings of illegal immigrants and the
authorities fear that such migrants will find it easy to
travel into other countries of the European Union since
internal border controls were abolished (1994).

France

France has prohibited 'new' immigration since 1974.
None the less, the composition of immigrant groups
seen in 1975 is a pattern which has continued
throughout the 1980s and early 1990s (Fig. 4.9). In
fact, there is a clear relationship with the location of
the origin of each group. Distance travelled obviously
determines the type of migrant most likely to move.

People joining family members already resident in
France are still allowed entry, and this leads to an
inflow of 120 000 immigrants a year. In 1990, 440 000
Algerians, 50 000 Tunisians and 16 000 Moroccans
entered Marseilles on tourist visas which entitle them
to stay for up to three months. Many immigrants in
France are Muslims (Fig. 4.8), but unlike the French,
they often have large families and take cheaply-paid
work. Because most migrants enter France now as
refugees, the processing of their applications can take
months. During that time, refugees have rights to both
reside and work in France.

?

8 Study Figure 4.8.
a Describe the geographical pattern of the origin and
destination of Muslim migrants in West Europe.
b Using this information, find evidence for some of the likely
issues that such immigration could cause.

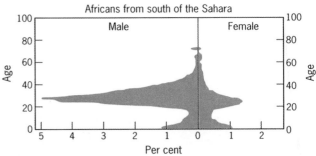

Figure 4.9 France: population pyramids for selected immigrant groups

?

9a Describe the composition of each of the immigrant groups in France as shown in Figure 4.9.
b Comment on the numbers of • dependants, • those who are economically active, and • the implications for France.
c With reference to an atlas, suggest reasons why the composition of migrants from south of the Sahara is different from the other groups of immigrants in France.

10 How far is the scale of migration *from* countries in North Africa consistent with Zelinsky's model? Have these countries reached the same stage of development as European countries at the turn of the century (when large-scale international migration also occurred)?

4.5 Causes of migration

The traditional models of migration suggest that population movements largely reflect inequality in the distribution of resources and opportunities. These differences force people either towards or away from an area.

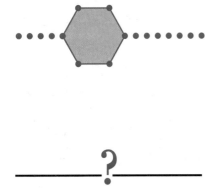

Push-pull model

Imbalance in both economic activities and opportunities creates the potential 'push' and 'pull' forces which drive and sustain population movements (Table 4.4). According to the migration models, the operation of these two forces (push and pull) generally determines the level, type and nature of migration.

On the one hand, the 'push' factors are features of the home area which create pressures and so cause people to move away. For example, unemployment, natural disasters and political/religious crises. On the other hand, the 'pull' factors operate at places outside the migrant's home area to attract individuals to a new location. In fact, the major reason why people move from one place to another is economic. The main pull factor is therefore the promise of work, and the person in search of work is thus known as an **economic migrant** (Figure 4.10, see Fig. 4.2).

?

11 Read Figure 4.10 and identify some of the major problems which result from large-scale internal migration.

12a Study Figure 4.11 and make a list of all the different reasons indicated for migration.
b Using Table 4.4 and all the reasons you identified in **a**, sort all the 'push' and 'pull' factors into the following:
• physical factors
• economic factors
• social factors
• political factors.

Table 4.4 Factors affecting migration (*Source:* Selmes (ed), 1985)

Push		Pull	
Natural disaster	Bereavement	Political asylum	Marriage
Heavy taxes	Inaccessibility	Higher education	Promotion
Harsh climate	Poverty	Resource exploitation	Scenic quality
High rents	Discrimination	Fertile soils	High living standards
Growth of family	Unemployment	Lack of natural hazards	Good welfare services
Persecution	Lack of housing	Propaganda	Freedom of speech
Planning decisions	Civil unrest	Relatives and friends	Good wages

China's 'gold coast' pulls millions in search of work

Every few minutes a public address system outside Shanghai railway station broadcasts warnings to a forecourt packed with people. They are told that it is illegal for employers to recruit workers at the station and it urges those who have arrived in the city in the hope of finding work to go home.

Despite the regulations, a man in a suit and camel-hair coat negotiates with potential employees. There are shouts of 'Wenzhou!' or 'Ningbo!', as private bus operators tout for custom to fill seats to other boom towns along the coast. Elderly men and women in tattered clothes beg for pennies.

One young beggar, her 10 months old baby swaddled to her chest, asked for a contribution to her train fare home. She and her husband had spent all their savings to get here, she said, but now had nothing to eat.

The scene is repeated in stations throughout southern and eastern China.

About 140 million people in the countryside do not have enough work, according to official estimates. Frenzied construction and industrialisation near the coast acts as a magnet. In Guangzhou, the capital of Guangdong province next to Hong Kong, 100 000 people arrive each day.

The railways cannot cope. Last month up to 50 people died in a stampede at the station in Hengyang, in the central province of Hunan. More than half were young women under the age of 20. Local officials said 160 000 people were leaving the town each day.

But there is work for many. Much of coastal China is a building site, staffed by migrants who are a source of cheap labour for local and foreign investors. After a spate of murderous factory fires late last year, the official media has railed against conditions. The labour ministry said it would set up a telephone hotline for abused workers.

In Shanghai, most of those still job hunting at the station are from the neighbouring, but poor province, of Anhui. One young man is with a group of about 30 from one village. 'What can we do?' he asked. 'There's no work there.' Two men came from the village last year. They live in a dormitory on a construction site in Pudong, the new town over the river from old Shanghai, where office blocks and factories have shot up.

City officials said 2.5 million of Shanghai's population of 13 million are migrants. The local media blame them for an increase in crime. It is claimed that 80 per cent of bicycle thieves are migrants. Murder, rape and armed robbery increased by 80 per cent in 1993.

Taxi-drivers, who are protected by metal grilles and reinforced plastic, said they will not pick up migrants. 'It's not safe. Shanghai is lawless these days,' one said.

Despite recent efforts to slow down the Chinese economy, industrial output in January was still up more than 30 per cent on last year. Shanghai's economy grew by 15 per cent last year and hopes to achieve 12 per cent this year, three per cent above the national target.

But the boom is unevenly spread. So each year, one of the world's great annual migrations gathers momentum, as poor farmers take off to claim their share of the benefits.

Figure 4.10 The uneven spread of wealth results in one of the world's great annual migrations (*Source:* Simon Long, *The Guardian*, 2 March 1994)

At the walls of Citadel Europe

The Guardian, 14 June 1991

Most of today's emigrants wish to change their identities and, in so doing, reject what they leave behind in their homeland. They are not fleeing to any particular country, but from the Soviet Union.

Today's wave of emigration from the USSR is also very different from the migration of peoples in demo-cratic states. A form of 'security' still reigns here; while people will have been exposed to all manner of persecutions, they have also been subject to the will of the state. These people long to free themselves from this imposition; to flee constraints and pressures of totalitarianism.

They also want, quite simply, to see those things which for so many long years remained forbidden fruit. Yet ask someone today why they want to emigrate and one will probably hear this: 'I'm just sick and tired of this dirt, the fear of hunger, the endless time spent standing in queues.'

Fear of Fortress Europe

The Guardian, 14 June 1991

Economic deprivation and political repression have driven large numbers of people to leave developing and southern European countries and move to the richer north. The break-up of the former Eastern bloc has opened the door to the West for hundreds of thousands of immigrants. Meanwhile, the abolition of internal borders within the EC after 1992, accompanied by new restrictions to keep out non-EC migrants, is acting to encourage refugees to enter the EC while they can.

Calls to shut out immigrants

The Guardian, 19 Nov. 1991

Poles, Ukrainians and other second-world-war refugees were initially recruited followed, increasingly, by Commonwealth immigrants from the Caribbean. London Transport, the National Health Service and other employers actively recruited in the West Indies for workers.

Across the river and into the States

The Guardian, 19 Nov. 1991

'There isn't any work in Mexico,' says Hernandez. 'That's why the frontier is the way it is.' He is not exaggerating. Unemployment in Mexico runs at 40 per cent. Another 20 per cent of adults are estimated to be underemployed. Mexico's population stands at about 85 million, of which 40 million are under 18 years of age. In El Paso, 69 per cent of the inhabitants are of Mexican origin.

Figure 4.11 Some causes of migration

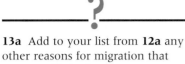

13a Add to your list from **12a** any other reasons for migration that you can think of.
b For each reason, decide whether it is an example of 'selective' or 'non-selective' migration.
c Discuss some of the problems resulting from each example for the • receiver and • loser states.

Selective migration

Depending on the reason for migration, some types are more '**selective**' than others. For example, if famine is the cause of migration, everybody will want to move in search of food. In this case, migration may be described as 'non-selective'. On the other hand, if the cause of migration is to find work then it is usually the young adults (often without families) who will move (see Fig. 4.9). This type of migration is clearly more selective in that it involves only certain people.

Religious migration

Religion is a powerful factor causing people to move across the world (Fig. 4.13). Traditional, usually temporary, pilgrimages include Hindus, Jains, Sikhs and Buddhists journeying to Varanasi in north-east India, while many thousands of Roman Catholics tend to head either to Rome (residence of the Pope) or to Lourdes (where in 1858 a girl saw visions of the Virgin Mary).

4.6 Rural-to-urban migration and urbanisation

Rural-to-urban migration has been an important feature of population movement, especially in the developing countries from about the 1970s (see Fig. 4.3). This urban-oriented movement of people has given rise to the swiftly growing number of cities – a process known as **urbanisation**. On a global scale, nearly half of the world's population live in urban areas and this trend is expected to continue (Fig. 4.12).

The global pattern of urbanisation

Generally, there are higher levels of urban population in the developed than in the developing countries (Fig. 4.14). In fact, 75 per cent of the population in developed countries live in big cities and towns compared with 25 per cent in developing countries. However, there is a wide variation in the level of urbanisation between countries both in the developed and developing worlds.

The growth of cities in developing countries

According to the United Nations' standard definition of urbanisation, settlements of over 20 000 people are generally classified as urban. Similarly, we consider settlements of more than 100 000 people to be cities, while we refer to settlements of more than 10 million people as megacities.

When we look at the global urban population we can see that the rate at which cities are growing in the developing areas is phenomenal. In terms of

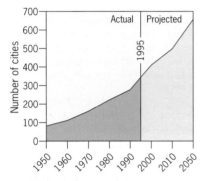

Figure 4.12 Projected growth in the number of cities with more than 1 million inhabitants, 1950–2025

Figure 4.13 Pilgrimage to Mecca, Saudi Arabia: it is the ambition of most Muslims to travel to the birthplace of Mohammed at least once in their lives

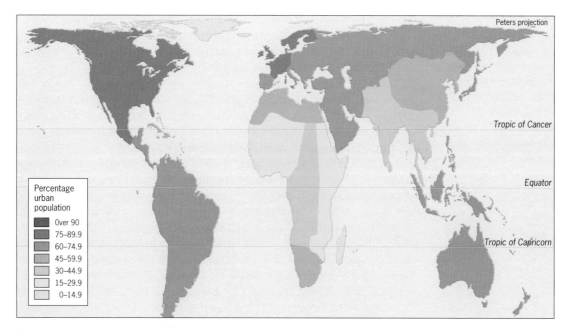

Figure 4.14 World pattern of urbanisation

?

14a Using a suitable graphical technique, illustrate the variations in the levels of urbanisation in the regions shown in Figure 4.14.
b Comment on the pattern shown.

absolute totals, 25 per cent of the people resident in cities in the developing countries far exceeds the total urban population of the developed countries. It is estimated that by the year 2015 the urban population in the developing countries will rise to 49 per cent of the world's total population.

The rates of urbanisation are particularly high in South America and Sub-Saharan Africa (Table 4.5). In 1960, only 14.9 per cent of African people lived in cities. This rose to 24.2 per cent in 1980 and by the year 2015, it is estimated the proportion of the urban population in Africa will be as high as 44 per cent.

Table 4.5 Levels of urbanisation as a percentage of total population (*Sources:* World Development Report 1994; Human Development Report 1998, and World population Data Sheet 1998)

	Urban population as percentage of total population			Average annual growth rate of urban population (%)
	1970	1992	1998	1995–2015
Egypt	42	44	43	2.5
Ghana	29	35	35	4.2
Kenya	10	25	27	4.6
Pakistan	25	33	28	4.1
India	20	26	26	2.8
China	18	27	30	2.9
Thailand	13	23	31	2.6
USA	74	76	75	1.1
Mexico	59	74	74	1.7
Jamaica	42	54	50	1.9
Peru	57	71	71	2.0
Argentina	78	87	89	1.3
UK	89	89	90	0.2
France	71	73	74	0.5
Poland	52	63	62	0.7
Italy	64	70	67	0.1
Australia	85	85	85	1.1

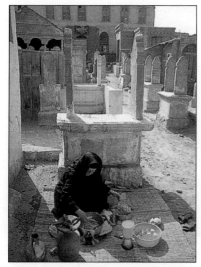

Figure 4.15 Lack of living space in Cairo, Egypt: 1000 people migrate into the city every day and many are forced to live on roof tops. Others, some 3 million, find space in the city's cemetery, 'City of the Dead'.

Consequences of increasing urbanisation in developing countries
One population issue for many countries is that cities grow at the expense of surrounding rural areas (see section 9.3). The consequences of this are felt at both the local and national levels (Fig. 4.16). In developing countries, the most obvious result of large numbers of migrants moving to urban areas is overcrowding (Fig. 4.15). We may describe such places as over-populated when

?

15 Study Figures 4.15 and 4.16.
a Explain how rural-to-urban migration causes poverty in cities.
b Discuss the effects of rural-to-urban migration on resources in
• rural areas, • urban areas,
• in a country as a whole.

the resources available (including land) cannot meet demand. As a result, at a national level, the rapid growth of urban areas demands investment through urban-oriented development programmes. Conversely, rural and peripheral areas tend to lack such investment.

During the last four decades, many cities in the developing world have witnessed a rapid increase in population, with cities such Amman, Curibita, Dar es Salaam, Dhaka, Khartoum, Lagos and Nairobi reaching one million inhabitants. Estimates show that the number of mega-cities in the developing countries is expected to rise over the next 50 years.

Development observers have blamed the poor living conditions experienced by many people in the developing countries, on high rates of urbanisation. It is estimated that 500 million people around the world live in inadequate conditions. The poorest urban inhabitants often live in illegal settlements or shanties in and around major cities. These are characterised by over-crowding, housing deficiencies, inadequate water supply or non-existent waste and sewage services. Recent figures suggest that 30 -60 per cent of the poorest urban inhabitants in the developing countries have no access to water, sewage and health services. Children who live in the shanties are 50 times more likely to die before the age of 5 compared to those in the developed countries. Other problems associated with growing urbanisation include unemployment, poverty and violence.

The concern over the growing rate of urbanisation in the developing countries and the social, economic and political problems associated with this trend, led to the second United Nations Conference on Human Settlements (Habitat II), held in Istanbul in June 1996. Among other issues, the conference addressed the growing deterioration of living conditions among urban settlers. The Habitat Programme agreed upon during the conference was aimed at achieving two objectives:

• housing for all - this emphasised the right to safe and healthy housing.
• sustainable human settlements - this focused on the ecosystem's capacity to sustain urban life styles.

For housing projects to be feasible, the need for the decentralisation of resources and political power was emphasised in the Habitat Programme. The document also states that citizen participation, government transparency, and

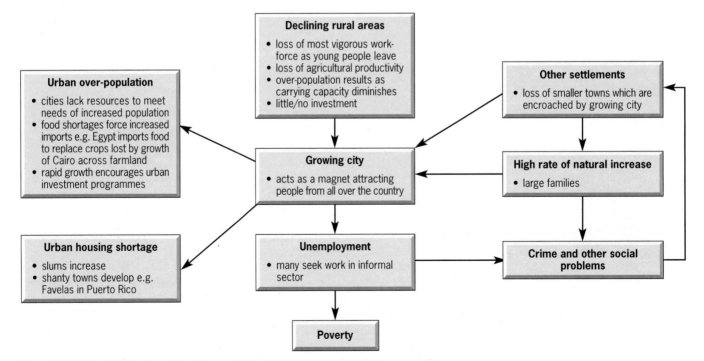

Figure 4.16 The effects of rural-to-urban migration in developing countries

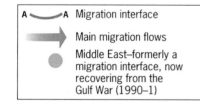

A ⌒ A Migration interface

→ Main migration flows

● Middle East–formerly a migration interface, now recovering from the Gulf War (1990–1)

Figure 4.17 North-South migration pressure-points (*Source: Geofile*, Jan. 1992)

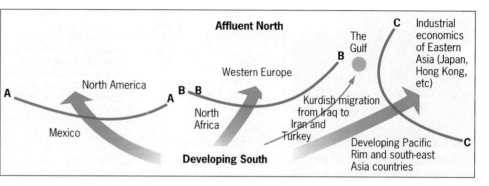

international co-operation are all directly linked to the creation of new and sustainable housing facilities.

4.7 International migration

The pressure from people wanting to migrate from developing countries to developed countries in search of economic security, has increased since the **economic gap** between the rich North and the poor South has widened. Migration occurs across the traditional **North-South divide** (see section 1.1), and there are three 'pressure points' where migration flows are strongest (Fig. 4.17). The first of these, migration between North Africa and Europe, we have already considered in the case study in section 4.4.

Mexico and the United States
The United States government is keen to attract the immigration of highly qualified professionals. In fact, in November 1990, the government passed a new immigration law specifically to make it easier for professional people to enter the USA. At the same time, though, the government is concerned about the continuing immigration from Mexico.

During the 1980s a total of 8 million migrants entered the USA. This was the largest number for a single decade since the beginning of the l900s. Of these 8 million, 3.5 million were Mexicans who took up US residence between 1980 and 1989. In 1990, more than one million people were caught trying to enter the USA and were sent back to Mexico (Fig. 4.18). Although most migrants are Mexicans, a considerable number also reach the Mexican border from countries in South and Central America. It has always been relatively easy to enter Mexico from the south and many people, especially from Central America, have taken advantage of this with the intention of 'stepping' on to the USA.

Pacific Rim countries
In this part of the world, large-scale migration between, and to, Pacific Rim countries has occurred only since World War 2. Historically, this is because neither the Chinese nor the Japanese have wanted to emigrate, while migrants originating in Europe went to other areas such as Australia, Canada, the USA and South America. However, numerous factors have, over the last few decades, encouraged greater numbers of migrants throughout the region:

- Increasing population pressure; e.g. with a population size (l24 million) double that of the UK, pressure increases because the mountainous areas of Japan mean much of the land is unsuitable for human settlement.
- Difficult political situations; e.g. China's Cultural Revolution of the 1960s resulted in widespread famine. Those peasants who could, then emigrated to either Malaysia or Singapore (see section 6.7).
- Different levels of development; e.g. civil wars have prohibited development in some countries, such as Vietnam and Cambodia, while successful industrialisation exists in such countries as Hong Kong and Singapore. War refugees and economic migrants are therefore common between such countries.

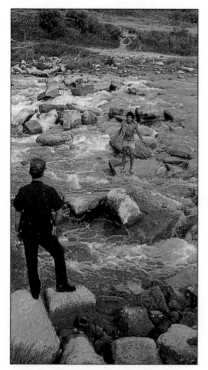

Figure 4.18 'Wetback' tries to enter the USA from Mexico illegally by crossing the Rio Grande River. It is estimated that for every person caught, at least one other succeeds.

16a Using an atlas, identify the Pacific Rim countries and their gross domestic products (GDP).
b Classify the Pacific Rim countries into those which have experienced:
• net immigration, • net emigration over the last two decades.
c Describe the relationship between the net migration and GDP for each country.

The migration problem in Hong Kong

From the late 1980s the number of Chinese emigrating from Hong Kong increased considerably (Table 4.6). This was partly in response to the expiry of Britain's 99-year lease of the island from China, with Hong Kong's subsequent return to Chinese rule in 1997. Additionally, other residents were 'frightened' into leaving China because of the Tiananmen Square massacre in Beijing on 4 June 1989. Facing serious challenges to its authority, the Chinese communist government massacred over 2000 students demonstrating for democracy and against party corruption. Subsequent emigration occurs as a 'brain drain' sees the departure of professionals and intellectuals seeking more secure working environments in other western countries (Table 4.7). To combat this, China has actually urged Hong Kong to persuade its professional and well educated would-be migrants *not* to leave. The Chinese authorities fear that the economy of Hong Kong will be damaged if this type of selective migration (see section 4.8) continues. In fact, by the end of 1989 about 30 per cent of companies in Hong Kong had themselves organised jobs abroad for their emigrating and professional staff. The intention is to attract the employees *back* to Hong Kong after they have received their foreign passports.

Table 4.6 Hong Kong: emigration (*Source:* Hong Kong government, quoted in *Financial Times*, 6 March 1991)

Year	Number of emigrants
1980	22 400
1981	18 300
1982	20 300
1983	19 800
1984	22 400
1985	22 300
1986	19 000
1987	30 000
1988	45 800
1989	42 000
1990	62 000

Figure 4.19 Hong Kong: Vietnamese migration routes

Table 4.7 Destination of emigrants from Hong Kong (thousands) (*Source: Financial Times*, 22 June 1989)

Country	1986	1987	1988	1989 (est)
Canada	5.6	16.3	24.6	16.4
USA	7.7	7.4	11.8	12.6
Australia	4.4	5.2	7.8	10.9
Others	1.2	1.1	1.6	1.9
Total	**19.0**	**30.0**	**45.8**	**42.0**

Immigration to Hong Kong

Since the 1970s, large numbers of Vietnamese 'boat people' have been arriving in Hong Kong (Fig. 4.19). These migrants are hoping to improve their economic well-being, as well as to avoid a Communist regime which they see as threatening and hostile. However, once in Hong Kong they are forced to live in overcrowded camps. The problem of where to settle the boat people has never really been solved by the international community. Many are encouraged to return to Vietnam but most wish to settle in Canada, which accepted 75 000 during the first wave of emigration.

Other countries, apart from Canada, have also accepted many boat people. However, by 1995 it had become harder for the Vietnamese to prove genuine political refugee status and so avoid being forced to return to Vietnam.

?

17 You are the personnel manager for a Hong Kong based company. Write some publicity material aimed at your well-qualified and well-trained employees to persuade them to stay with you in Hong Kong.

18 Use Tables 4.6 and 4.7.
a Draw a graph with a logarithmic scale on the vertical axis to show the increasing scale of emigration from Hong Kong.
b Draw divided bars to represent the destinations of emigrants from Hong Kong for each year.
c In light of the selective nature and scale of migration, discuss the likely social and economic problems Hong Kong might face in the future.

Table 4.8 Foreigners living in Japan, 1988 (*Source: Financial Times Survey*, 10 July 1989)

Country of origin	Number
North and South Korea	677 140
China	129 269
USA	32 766
Philippines	32 185
UK	8 523
Thailand	5 277
Vietnam	4 763
Brazil	4 159
Malaysia	3 542
Canada	3 510
West Germany	3 222
France	2 744
India	2 730
Australia	2 585
Indonesia	2 379
Bangladesh	2 130
Pakistan	2 063
'no nationality'	1 658
Singapore	1 084
Cambodia	1 021
Total	**941 005**

?

19 Read Figure 4.20 and answer the following:

a How has Japan attempted to solve the problems of an ageing population?

b Why might the Japanese authorities have to change their attitude towards immigration in the future?

20a Using Table 4.8 draw proportional symbols on a base map of the world to show the countries of origin of foreign workers in Japan.

b Describe the pattern of migration shown by your map and decide which migration models it relates to (sections 4.4 and 4.5).

21a Using Table 4.9 and a base map, draw a flow diagram to illustrate the various destinations of asylum seekers as shown for 1998.

b Suggest reasons for the patterns of migration shown on your map.

22a Using the data provided in Table 4.10 draw a graph to show the changes in numbers of refugees arriving in each of the regions between 1989 and 1998.

b Comment on the changes that have occurred during this period.

Japanese migration

Japan has had a long history of opposition to immigration, due partly to its strong sense of cultural identity. However, by the end of 1988 there were almost one million foreigners living in Japan (Table 4.8). Legal immigration in Japan is restricted to skilled workers and so most of the immigrants from Europe, North America and Australia are professional people employed by international companies. In contrast, there are at least 200 000 illegal immigrants in Japan and many of these are from the northern Chinese province of Fujian.

The Japanese are undecided on their future immigration policies. The acute shortage of unskilled labour in Japan partly explains why there is so much Japanese production overseas (it has been estimated that by the year 2000 one fifth of Japanese manufacturing output will be produced by Japanese companies located abroad). Japan's labour shortage, coupled with its ageing population, presents the authorities with serious problems (Fig. 4.20).

LIFE expectancy in Japan is the highest in the world. By the year 2025, 25% of the Japanese will be aged over 65. The high welfare costs associated with old age began to concern the Japanese government in 1986, when the 'Silver Columbia' project was adopted. This aimed to settle aged Japanese in purpose-built villages abroad, where medical and other expenses were expected to be cheaper. So far the programme has not met with much success – the elderly Japanese were apparently not interested in villages near Melbourne in Australia – but the attempts continue. In 1989 it was planned to set up a colony of retired academics and other professionals on the coast of Spain between Barcelona and Lloret de Mar, near the village of Canet de Mar (*Financial Times*, 24 July 1989). In 1991 a new scheme, 'Extended Leisure Stays Abroad', was begun on the Atlantic coast of Senegal, 80 kilometres north of Dakar. A retirement city is to be built on an area of 400 sq km; it will have its own airport and twenty-six golf courses. The Japanese government is still encouraging voluntary expatriate settlement in Australia (a village is to be built in Wollongong), Uruguay and Hawaii, an earlier venture in the Philippines came to an unfortunate end when it was overrun in a military coup (*Financial Times*, 24 February 1991). If these schemes do not succeed, Japan may in the end have to relax its immigration regulations so that young immigrants from South East Asia can enter the country to look after its elderly people.

Figure 4.20 A different migration problem in Japan (*Source: Geofile*, no. 184, 1992)

4.8 Refugees and international response

In the early 1990s there were an estimated 20 million people on the move throughout the world (Fig. 4.21). By the late 1990s this figure was estimated by the United Nations High Commisioner for Refugees (UNHCR), to have increased to over 100 million people, i.e. one in every 60 human beings. At the beginning of the new millennium, refugee populations of over 10 000 are to be found in 70 countries around the world. Never in recent history have such large numbers of people, in so many parts of the globe, been forced to leave their own countries and communities to seek sanctuary elsewhere.

The original UN definition of 'refugee' was based on the concept of individual persecution. According to this definition, a refugee is a person who is 'unable or unwilling to return to her or his homeland for fear of persecution based on reasons of race, religion, ethnicity, membership of a particular social group or political opinion'. This original definition was not designed to deal with the large-scale flows of people which are now common phenomena. Apart from persecution, other circumstances often compel people to migrate, such as the consequences of development models and economic systems that have failed to provide for people's most basic survival needs. The denial of access to agricultural land is another reason for the large-scale flows of people characteristic of some developing nations. It is these unconventional 'environmental' refugees that have shown most increase in recent years, with

1 Mexico: up to 100 000 Guatemalans in exile	diaspora to Jordan, Syria, Lebanon and Gaza	20 Pakistan: more than one million Afghanis in exile
2 Colombia: 900 000 displaced by political violence	12 Iraq: more than one million displaced	21 Sudan: more than 400 000 refugees, mostly from Eritrea and more than four million internally displaced
3 Bosnia and Herzegovina: almost 2 million uprooted	13 Iran: about two million Afghani refugees	
4 Sierra Leone: 1.6 million internally displaced	14 Afghanistan: up to 1.2 million internally displaced	22 Ethiopia: up to 400 000 refugees from Kenya, Somalia, Sudan
5 Liberia: more than 800 000 displaced	15 Nepal: 115 000 refugees from Bhutan, Tibet	
6 Ivory Coast: up to 700 000 people have fled the Libarian civil war	16 Myanmar (Burma): up to one million displaced or forcibly relocated	23 Uganda: 265 000 refugees, mostly from southern Sudan
7 Algeria: 165 000 refugees from Western Sahara	17 Thailand: more than 100 000 from Cambodia, Laos and Vietnam	24 Burundi: one million displaced in camps
8 Cyprus: 265 000 internally displaced		25 Democratic Republic of Congo: more than 320 000 displaced from surrounding countries
9 Turkey: up to 2 million inetrnally displaced Kurds	18 Sri Lanka: more than one million displaced by war	
10 Azerbaijan: 500 000 internally displaced	19 India: more than 300 000 Sri Lankans, Tibetans, Bangladeshi Chakmas and Afghanistans	26 Angola: up to 1.2 million displaced
11 Palestinians: over 3 million have fled since the		27 East Timor: 600 000 displaced

Figure 4.21 Major migrations: estimated number of refugees and displaced persons fleeing to neighbouring countries (*Source: The Guardian*, 2 April 1999)

an estimated 25 million people moving as a result of environmental catastrophe at the end of the twentieth century.

Migrant or refugee

The large numbers of people moving between nations during the late 1990s was a result of a number of dramatic political events. With perestroika and the collapse of communism in the Soviet Union, over half a million Jews emigrated to Israel between 1986 and 1995. Until the unification of Germany in 1990, vast numbers of economic migrants left East Germany for the Federal Republic (see case study). The Gulf War (1991) led to temporary migrations with Iraqi Kurds crossing the borders to Turkey and Iran (Fig. 4.17). In addition, immigrant workers from developing countries, resident in Kuwait at the time of the Iraqi invasion, were forced to return home. By March 1991, 35 000 Sudanese, 100 000 Bangladeshis, 100 000 Sri Lankans and 200 000 Indians had left the Gulf. Their countries of origin thus lost much-needed earnings (remittances from the Gulf had amounted to one third of Bangladesh's foreign exchange earnings).

As a proportion, there are more people who migrate from one developing country to another, rather than from a developing to a developed country. Consequently, the developing countries suffer as a result of population movements caused by push factors such as civil war and environmental degradation. The people who are affected by such problems are, respectively, often referred to as war refugees or environmental refugees who may, or may not, consider themselves to be persecuted.

Overall, people who migrated in the 1990s arrived at their destinations in groups rather than individually and this caused confusion over the definitions 'migrant' and 'refugee'. The term refugee has therefore become increasingly confused with the term migrant.

The world's refugee burden

The huge increase in refugee numbers is far outpacing the ability of the world community to respond. The annual budget of the UNHCR is unable to meet the demand for food and shelter, much less to invest in repatriation or rehabilitation of refugees. The annual budget of the UNHCR was increased to $1 billion in 1994, yet the total annual cost of supporting asylum seekers (a small part of the overall problem) has for a long time surpassed $5 billion. By the late 1990s, the UNHCR was providing protection and assistance to 27.4 million people around the world, of whom 14.5 million were refugees (Fig. 4.23).

Refugees often bring alien customs, dietary preferences and religious practices to the country where they are seeking sanctuary. In the developing countries, they tend to congregate in the poorer areas of such megacities as Dhaka, Calcutta, Karachi, Lagos, Sao Paulo and Mexico City, where the city services are already stretched to capacity (see section 4.6). In other cases refugees are forced to crowd into refugee camps with inadequate facilities. Wherever they find temporary sanctuary, resettlement is never easy and assimilation is rare. In many cases, refugees face hostility from the locals who see their presence as a threat.

The refugee problem is now more widespread than ever before; it is an international problem with implications for both the developed and developing nations. The result of political instability and civil war in some developing countries is often a huge wave of migration away from the crisis area. At the beginning of 1996, 1.7 million Rwandans and more than 200 000 Burundians were confined in refugee camps in Zaire and Tanzania. Another 230 000 Rwandans remained in Burundi. Since the 1994 genocide in Rwanda, when approximately 1 million people died, another 2 million Rwandans sought refuge in Zaire, Tanzania, Uganda and Burundi (Fig. 4.23).

In the same way, war in the former Yugoslavia caused the movement of 3 700 000 people. In Serbia, hundreds of thousands of Yugoslavs from Bosnia and Croatia (largely of Serb descent, but some Croats and Muslims) have remained for a long time in refugee camps since the end of the war. The absence of security and justice as well as scarce job opportunities and the devastation of many rural and urban areas, have generated friction and continue to make the resettlement of refugees in this region difficult.

Table 4.9 Number of refugees received in each region 1989–1998

Region of asylum	1989	1990	1991	1992	1993	1994	1995	1996	1997	1998
Eastern Africa	3 142 490	3 264 830	2 818 530	2 985 580	3 098 500	2 344 920	2 001 940	1 564 480	1 563 370	1 503 450
Middle Africa	408 100	485 620	555 020	473 070	600 000	1 843 110	1 433 000	789 800	414 360	377 900
Northern Africa	938 800	951 440	900 950	950 830	972 540	955 860	776 420	5 898 130	560 570	574 460
Southern Africa	40 600	43 510	50 900	56 390	296 690	94 200	93 980	25 590	9 860	14 590
Western Africa	77 600	834 330	948 610	926 490	1 476 100	1 514 100	1 386 600	1 363 500	933 410	800 460
Africa	**4 608 590**	**5 579 730**	**5 274 010**	**5 393 360**	**6 443 830**	**6 752 190**	**5 691 940**	**4 341 500**	**3 481 570**	**3 270 860**
Eastern Asia	339 050	348 040	358 280	341 770	290 240	297 910	289 820	297 050	294 800	295 200
South-central Asia	6 135 340	7 372 530	7 765 460	6 421 820	4 588 410	3 824 010	3 379 230	3 694 810	3 611 340	3 509 930
South-eastern Asia	167 080	168 950	161 070	112 620	115 320	111 890	101 700	144 990	189 850	204 290
Western Asia	118 010	36 760	580 440	894 770	818 280	784 430	708 900	672 080	634 470	735 310
Asia	**6 759 480**	**7 926 280**	**8 865 250**	**7 770 980**	**5 812 250**	**5 018 240**	**4 479 650**	**4 808 930**	**4 730 460**	**4 744 730**
Eastern Europe	27 000	45 100	75 310	62 340	51 540	64 150	64 370	253 070	252 500	144 530
Northern Europe	293 300	339 790	419 640	531 150	414 620	105 760	135 400	408 900	416 100	423 420
Southern Europe	29 220	30 290	31 920	1 278 900	857 010	453 430	963 210	832 320	752 770	679 680
Western Europe	439 200	457 290	646 290	1 150 700	1 356 030	1 253 200	938 000	1 671 600	1 519 400	1 420 200
Europe	**788 720**	**872 470**	**1 173 160**	**3 023 090**	**2 679 200**	**1 876 540**	**2 100 980**	**3 165 890**	**2 940 770**	**2 667 830**
Caribbean	7 400	6 000	1 600	6 030	5 020	3 340	4 780	2 420	2 030	1 830
Central America	1 163 000	1 160 600	852 510	854 200	97 190	87 040	75 660	68 720	66 110	57 230
South America	29 470	27 250	26 510	22 750	22 650	18 690	47 120	16 490	15 090	15 120
Latin America & Caribbean	**1 199 870**	**1 193 850**	**880 620**	**882 980**	**124 860**	**109 070**	**127 560**	**87 630**	**83 230**	**74 180**

The world's refugee burden is carried mainly by the poorest sectors of the global community (Table 4.9). The 20 countries with the highest ratio of refugees have an annual per capita income average of $700. For example, Mozambique's neighbours have little means to support people fleeing from drought and agricultural failure, both problems exacerbated by civil war. In Malawi, where 800 000 Mozambicans found sanctuary, one person in nine is a refugee. The refugee burden is particularly great in Malawi since the country is among the dozen poorest nations in the world, with a GNP per capita of $170.

It is now widely held that the likely increase in numbers of environmental refugees could become one of the most critical of human crises in modern times. The phenomenon is evidence of rapid environmental and political change, often marked by extreme deprivation, fear and despair. Countries such as Jordan, Egypt and Pakistan have found themselves recently with acute shortages of water. Countries which have experienced rapid population growth, such as Kenya, the Philippines and Costa Rica, can rapidly switch from a state of land abundance to one of land shortage. Whole regions have found that their protective ozone layers have been critically depleted within a single generation. The entire earth seems set to experience the changes brought by global warming in a relatively short period. Any of these environmental catastrophes, together with their associated social, political and economic dimensions, can create refugees in exceptionally large numbers. This is one of the greatest challenges facing human society in this millennium.

Assistance is provided to those who cannot meet their own basic needs, and in the absence of other resources, UNHCR distinguishes five types of assistance:
- emergency assistance, which includes measures to meet basic needs, usually in case of a new refugee influx. The assistance does not normally exceed a period of twelve months.
- care and maintenance, which covers assistance once survival is no longer threatened. It involves meeting basic needs on a more routine basis, pending the identification of durable solutions (i.e. voluntary repatriation, local settlement and resettlement). Assistance usually takes the form of providing food, water, household utensils, medical care, shelter, transportation, basic education, vocational training, etc.
- voluntary repatriation, which cover preparations to the country of origin, transportation, etc. In most cases, it also involves activities in the country of origin, including organising reception facilities and assistance during the initial phase of reintegration.
- local settlement assistance, which may be provided to refugees who cannot return home. It aims to promote their self-sufficiency and local integration.
- resettlement, which may be offered to refugees who are admitted temporarily to a country of asylum, who cannot return to their home country and who face particular protection problems. UNHCR facilitates permanent settlement in third-world countries through securing resettlement places, medical screening, arranging for travel and measures to facilitate the integration of the refugee in the country of resettlement.

Figure 4.22 Types of assistance provided for refugees

Table 4.10 Top ten asylum applications (totals) by country of origin: Europe, 1989–1998 (*Source:* United Nations High Commission for Refugees UNHCR statistics 1998)

Origin	Austria	Belgium	Denmark	Finland	France	Germany	Greece	Italy	Netherlands	Norway	Spain	Sweden	Switzerland	UK	Total
Yugoslavia, Federal Republic[1]	24 880	16 520	6 890	3 620	11 100	460 860	300	2 950	25 680	13 700	540	104 600	75 600	21 460	7 687 000
Romania	30 950	18 110	1 270	740	31 770	275 220	420	5 720	9 760	620	9 820	5 330	6 350	4 740	400 820
Turkey	10 870	8 210	620	630	48 360	235 700	4 610	1 510	7 920	560	190	4 520	30 530	18 210	372 440
Iraq	9 390	1 230	8 100	750	2 190	46 740	13 140	3 120	33 090	2 490	2 030	23 550	3 900	8 130	157 850
Bosnia and Herzegovina	4 620	2 880	14 740	60	1 560	46 080	—	—	25 330	8 140	1 520	31 150	19 120	160	155 360
Sri Lanka	990	960	2 440	240	23 460	50 570	450	310	15 810	3 280	90	1 480	29 990	23 950	154 020
Bulgaria	4 220	4 940	620	300	3 130	83 550	170	1 100	2 300	330	1 850	5 930	1 340	2 550	112 330
Iran (Islamic Republic)	8 190	1 330	2 860	420	2 110	48 650	1 620	460	21 300	2 420	1 940	13 390	1 710	5 150	111 550
Somalia	660	1 340	9 010	2 870	1 910	16 430	90	2 440	29 240	4 220	320	10 810	8 100	23 640	111 080
Dem. Republic of the Congo	550	18 340	120	330	29 710	27 960	60	370	7 340	130	1 050	770	6 070	15 350	108 150

[1] Including former Yugoslavia

The endless diaspora

The history of the past 50 years, and the 1990s in particular, has been forced exodus of populations from their homes and great waves of people fleeing state-inspired terrorism, ethnic cleansing and human rights abuses. The Office of the UN High Commissioner for Refugees (UNHCR) believes there are now more than 25 million people who have been forced to leave their countries and another 25 million who are now internally displaced within their own countries but unable to return to their lands or villages.

They are, says the writer William Shawcross, the "fourth world", living without rights, home or, most often, hope of return.

But the official figures are are just the tip of the iceberg. Many millions have been displaced by the partitions of countries, massive development programmes and the tactics of rural depopulation to facilitate land grabs. Mostly, like the Palestinians, these people never register on the official statistics.

And in an increasingly insecure, globalised world, where populations are burgeoning in the poorest countries, abject poverty has caused millions of economic and environmental refugees to flee the land. It is possible that more than 75 million have been forced to uproot in the last 60 years. Internal displacement of populations is now as significant in humanitarian terms as the more conventional flights across state boundaries. History suggests that most of these population flows were made to happen – aggressors usually win – and that the first law of diasporas is that return is painfully slow.

The reality of the refugee crisis, which is now a worldwide phenomenon as countries implode, is that few refugees return for good. Only 250 000 people, a fraction of the millions displaced in the Balkans in the past decade, have returned and very few of them to their previous homes.

Even before the exodus of the past few weeks, Croatia had 90 000 refugees from Bosnia Herzegovina along with 62 000 displaced Croats and Serbs; in Bosnia Herzegovina itself there were more than 383 000 Muslims and ethnic Croats expelled by the Serbs who now mix with 107 000 internally displaced people. Meanwhile in the republic of Sraska there are more than 300 000 "ethnically cleansed" Serbs. Thousands of others are now living precariously in Albania, Montenegro, and Macedonia. Few are expected ever to return.

But the figures are dwarfed by what has happened outside Europe in the past few decades. The great diasporas this century include the Jews and Armenians fleeing genocide, massive forced relocations under Stalin, millions of people fleeing communism, and more than 20 countries – including Mozambique, Cambodia, Bulgaria, Turkey, Western Sahara, Cyprus, Angola, Sri Lanka, Sudan, Iraqi and Georgia, Sierra Leone, Ethiopian and Eritrea – have been torn apart by populations fleeing repression.

History also shows that despite clear warnings and increased concern by the international community, it is next to impossible to stem the tide of refugees.

But there have been some notable successes: in the 1990s, conflicts in Central America, Southern Africa and South-East Asia and Afganistan have been largely resolved or have stabilised, and almost 10 million people have been repatriated.

But 15 million from these and other wars have still not returned to their own country, let alone to their homes or lands, which have often been destroyed or occupied by others. Many millions of people remained displaced from the cold war years, the collapse of old ideologies and formation of new states, even the second world war. Some are only now returning.

The modern state knows that it is easier than ever to make people flee. New forms of warfare, the spread of light weapons and cheap land mines can easily panic populations. The use of mass evictions and expulsions as a weapon of war has now become common as a way for states to establish culturally or ethnically homogeneous societies, such as in the Caucasus or in the former Yugoslavia.

The UNHCR suggests that the speed at which these flights and expulsions are taking place is quickening. In recent years, the exodus of more than a million Iraqi Kurds, up to 4 million people in the former Yugoslavia, over a million Rwandan citizens and two million people within and from Liberia have been notable.

The people most usually affected, say the humanitarian agencies who were left to pick up the pieces, are the most marginalised. Minority groups, the already stateless, indigenous populations and others in poor or medium poor countries who have little or no representation.

"The forced displacement of minorities, including depopulation and re-population tactics in support of territorial claims and self-determination, has become an abominable characteristic of the contemporary world," says Sadako Ogata, the UN High Commissioner for Refugees.

The lot of the refugee or the displaced person is increasingly hard. Globally, there is mounting rejection of refugees, and states have been quick to erect physical and administrative barriers. On top of the physical and emotional pain, asylum seekers may spend years in fear of expulsion, be denied the right to settle permanently, to work, be disqualified from welfare benefits or be kept in detention or, most often in the poorest countries, in camps.

The geography of exodus is more complex than ever. Several regions are locked into a pattern of strife and displacements that are intensely difficult, perhaps impossible to resolve. In the Caucasus six countries, Abkhazia, Armenia, Azerbaijan, Chechenia, and North and South Ossetia, are all importing and exporting refugees between them in a linked regional conflict. Similarly in central Africa, Angola, Burundi, the Central African Republic, Rwanda and Zambia and four other countries are now producing ever more uprooted people.

Increasingly, too, says the UNHCR, the actual movements of people is becoming more complex, with millions being constantly relocated, expelled and received for short periods. In many cases people have effectively been held as hostages and moved, according to political expediency or whim, between three or even four countries. Many a tiny minority have the means or the will to flee to the richer countries. Of these, only Australia, New Zealand, Canada, the US, Ireland and Chile have any permanent resettlement programmes. In most other countries the walls are going up.

Paradoxically, says the UNHCR, many people have found it impossible to flee. In Bosnia and Sri Lanka, government and opposition forces desperate to maintain control over civilian populations have forcibly prevented people leaving the country. The international community's proposal for safe havens has seldom worked and indeed, has often denied the human right of people to go elsewhere.

If the people now fleeing the cost over ever returned, they may find life harder than ever. The traumas of flight and exile can be matched by the return which, although often portrayed as joyful, can be harrowing as exile itself.

Humanitarian agencies report but people returned forcibly can feel as insecure as when they left. Voluntary returnees may have over optimistic ideas of what they will find and are often thrown into conflict for increasingly sparse land resources. Mostly, the social and physical infastructure has been destroyed, there is no work and no help.

Figure 4.23 Major refugee and internally displaced peoples (Source: *The Guardian*, 2 April 1999)

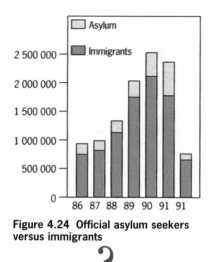

Figure 4.24 Official asylum seekers versus immigrants

?

23a If one of the main intentions of developed countries is to encourage potential migrants from developing countries to stay at home, assess the value of the following solutions:
• increase the amount of aid to developing areas
• encourage investment in developing areas
• reinstate border controls and legal barriers to immigrants entering developed countries
• allow some immigration to compensate for the declining workforce (resulting from lower fertility rates in developed countries, see sections 3.4, 3.6–3.8).

Asylum seekers or economic migrants?

As shown by the example of Italy (see section 4.4), many of the developed countries are tightening up their immigration laws. Since it is now harder for a migrant looking for better economic opportunities to gain permanent residential status in a developed country, many are now using the 'refugee route' to gain permission to stay (Fig. 4.24). Perhaps it is more appropriate to use the term **asylum seeker** to describe those economic migrants who call themselves refugees (Table 4.9).

The European Union and immigration laws

To gain entry to the EU, increasing proportions of migrants sought asylum in the early 1990s (Fig. 4.25). However, a person is only allowed to appeal for asylum once within the country of her/his choice and if this application is turned down, s/he has no choice other than to return to their country of origin.

Although individual European countries still have their own immigration laws, the EU intends to align all the separate immigration procedures. The aims of such a single policy are to slow down the rate of immigration, to allow for legal immigration and to assist the social integration of future immigrants.

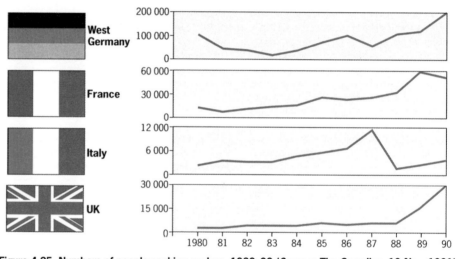

Figure 4.25 Numbers of people seeking asylum, 1980–90 (*Source: The Guardian*, 19 Nov. 1991)

Refugees in Germany

With the dramatic political events of 1989, and the collapse of communism (Fig. 4.26), there was a huge upsurge in the numbers of people moving from Eastern Europe, including the former Soviet Union, into Western Europe. As frontiers across Europe were lifted, the first large-scale movement of people was of former East Germans migrating into the old West Germany, followed by migrants from other countries (Fig. 4.28, see Fig. 4.8).

Results of refugees

The long-term consequences of migration into former West Germany, as well as immigrants arriving since unification, have concerned the German authorities. Some economists view the migrant 'guestworkers' as a boost to the economy. The migrants will provide much needed labour to replace Germany's own, ageing workers (see section 3.8). Conversely, other observers highlight the problems of rising unemployment – for both nationals and migrant workers. During times of

recession and social hardship, people often look for a scapegoat (Fig. 4.28).

Figure 4.26 The fall of the Berlin Wall 9 November 1989. In 1988, 50 000 people had emigrated from East to West Germany; in 1989 there were 300 000 emigrants.

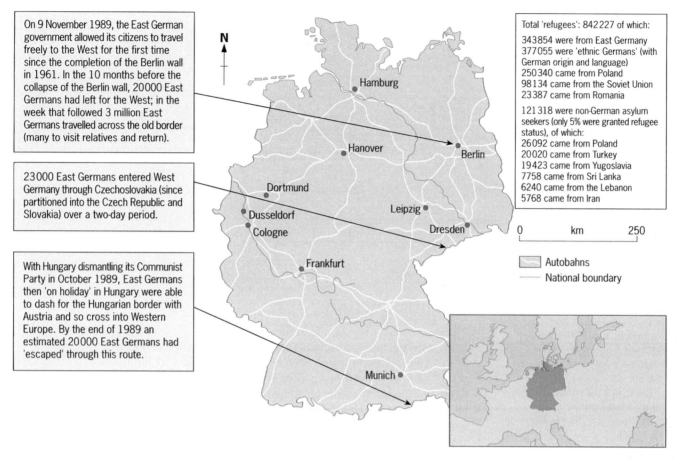

On 9 November 1989, the East German government allowed its citizens to travel freely to the West for the first time since the completion of the Berlin wall in 1961. In the 10 months before the collapse of the Berlin wall, 20000 East Germans had left for the West; in the week that followed 3 million East Germans travelled across the old border (many to visit relatives and return).

23000 East Germans entered West Germany through Czechoslovakia (since partitioned into the Czech Republic and Slovakia) over a two-day period.

With Hungary dismantling its Communist Party in October 1989, East Germans then 'on holiday' in Hungary were able to dash for the Hungarian border with Austria and so cross into Western Europe. By the end of 1989 an estimated 20000 East Germans had 'escaped' through this route.

Total 'refugees': 842227 of which:

343854 were from East Germany
377055 were 'ethnic Germans' (with German origin and language)
250340 came from Poland
98134 came from the Soviet Union
23387 came from Romania

121318 were non-German asylum seekers (only 5% were granted refugee status), of which:
26092 came from Poland
20020 came from Turkey
19423 came from Yugoslavia
7758 came from Sri Lanka
6240 came from the Lebanon
5768 came from Iran

0   km   250

⬜ Autobahns
— National boundary

Figure 4.27 Migration into Germany

Figure 4.28 Social tension and racial violence sweep Germany: Turkish immigrants, originally temporary 'guestworkers' but staying in Germany permanently, become 'scapegoats' with residents blaming them for unemployment, scarce housing resources and poor social services.

Summary

- Population movement is an essential feature of human society.

- Migration has occurred in 'waves' throughout history giving rise to multi-racial societies.

- Migration can be categorised into two major types: internal and international. Each type has implications for available resources and development.

- Rapid urbanisation in the developing countries mostly results from the mass exodus of people from rural to urban areas.

- Environmental disasters, political unrest and the spread of disease have led to large scale migration from one developing country to another.

- Increasing poverty in many developing countries has resulted in the growing numbers of people migrating to the developed countries as economic migrants.

- Many developed countries are tightening their immigration policies in response to the increasing refugees, economic migrants and asylum seekers from the developing countries.

- The breakdown of communism in Eastern Europe increased the immigration problem in Western Europe and other developed areas.

- Racial tension has increased in many areas as more people are on the move. This accounts for the rise of nationalism in many West European countries.

5 Population policies and food supply

```
Population growth          Food supply  ──────▶  Case study: The Green Revolution

Limits to growth model     Malthusian theory     Boserup's theory

        Case study: Mauritius    Case study: China    Case study: Europe
```

5.1 Introduction

While some countries are experiencing rapid population growth, others are faced with declining numbers (see Tables 3.2 and 3.3). Population policies therefore vary according to each country's **demographic** situation. On a global scale, while governments recognise that population is rising fast, there seems to be no consensus as to the best way to control this growth. Opinions are divided along cultural, religious and ideological lines as to the need for population control.

Growing populations, which characterise many **developing countries** (see sections 3.4–3.8), have serious implications on the availability and use of resources (Fig. 5.1). Debt, dependency on cash crops and lack of investment all place the production of essential commodities, such as food, under great stress. In this chapter, we will examine reasons for the unequal distribution of food supply and then discuss specific policies which are geared towards controlling population growth and decline.

?

1a Design a questionnaire (see appendix A2) to investigate people's attitudes to population control.
b Carry out the questionnaire survey and find out how your interviewees would combat over-population.
c Do responses vary with age, gender, social, and ethnic groups?
d Summarise your findings, stating whether, and how, opinions are divided over population control.

• The average American consumes 300 times as much energy as the average Bangladeshi. The 16 million babies born each year in the rich North will have four times as great an impact on the world's resources as the 109 million born in the poor South.

• UNICEF estimates that preventing 7 million babies dying each year will lead to the prevention of between 12 and 20 million births by the end of the century. There will undoubtedly be a time-lag while parents gain confidence in the improved survival chances. However, no country has ever managed to achieve a low birth rate while infant deaths remain high.

• The United Nations states that 'food supplies might be adequate if they were evenly distributed in relation to needs'.

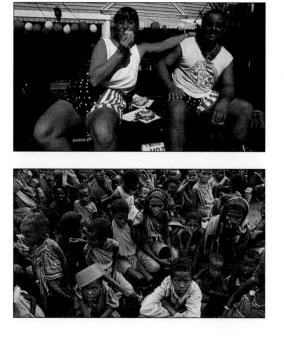

Figure 5.1 Population and resource issues (*After: New Internationalist,* Oct. 1987)

• Population growth rates are slowing down everywhere in the world. According to the United Nations Fund for Population Activities (UNFPA), the world's population will stabilise at around ten billion by approximately the year 2050 (double what it was in the early 1990s). In some countries numbers are already declining.

• People who do not have access to contraception still plan their families. In Greece, where contraception was not legalised until 1980, women bore an average of only 2.3 children in 1978. In theory these women could have had many more children.

• In the poorer countries, scarcity among the poor is partly due to an uneven distribution of land ownership and lack of person power in rural areas, for example, in South America, 47 per cent of the land is owned by just 2 per cent of the people.

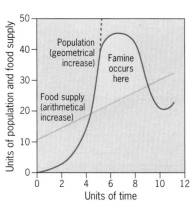

5.2 Population growth and food shortages

There are two main theories relating to population growth and food supply.

Malthusian theory

Thomas Malthus was an English clergyman and economist who lived from 1766 to 1834. In his text *An essay on the principle of population*, 1798, Malthus expressed a pessimistic view over the dangers of **over-population** (see section 3.5) and claimed that food supply was the main limit to population growth.

Principles of Malthus

Malthus believed that the human population increases geometrically (i.e. 2, 4, 8, 16, 32, etc.) whereas food supplies can grow only arithmetically (i.e. 2, 4, 6, 8, 10, 12, etc.) being limited by available new land. Malthus added that the 'laws of nature' dictate that a population can never increase beyond the food supplies necessary to support it (Fig. 5.2).

Checks

According to Malthus, population increase is limited by certain 'checks'. These prevent numbers of people increasing beyond the **optimum population**, which the available resources cannot support (see section 3.5). Malthus identified two types of check which limit further population growth. Preventive, or 'negative', checks are methods which people can choose to reduce human fertility e.g. abstinence or delaying marriage. Conversely, 'positive' checks are anything which increases mortality e.g. low living standards and unhealthy living conditions resulting in disease, war and famine.

At the time Malthus was proposing his ideas, inadequate food and clothing were common features of daily life in the then rapidly growing urban areas of England. Towns were heavily polluted by new factories during these early stages of the industrial revolution and malnutrition and disease were frequent.

Malthus saw the checks as nature's way of controlling excessive growth in the population, and they fall into three categories:
1 Misery: This includes the effects of disease, famine or war, i.e. 'all the causes which shorten the duration of human life'.
2 Vice: Malthus warned against the dangers of practising any kind of 'family planning', believing that it could only lead to promiscuity.
3 Moral restraint: Delayed marriage and abstinence from sexual relations were considered highly advisable by Malthus in order to avoid the consequences of over-population.

Malthusian theory and food supply

As long as fertile land is available, Malthus believed that there would be more than enough food to feed a growing population. However, as population increases so do the demands for food. There is therefore greater pressure to farm more intensively and cultivate poorer, more **marginal land**. According to Malthus, though, food production can only increase to a certain level determined by the productive capacity of the land and existing levels of technology. Beyond the ceiling where land is used to its fullest extent, over cultivation and, ultimately, soil erosion occur, contributing to a general decline in food production. This is known as the **law of diminishing returns** where, even with higher levels of technology, only a small increase in yield will eventually occur. These marginal returns ultimately serve as a check to population growth. Malthus did acknowledge that increases in food output would be possible with new methods in food production, but he still maintained that limited food supply would eventually take place and so limit population.

Figure 5.2 Representation of Malthus' view on population growth and food supply

2a Draw a continuous flow diagram putting the following labels in sequence according to Malthusian theory:
• Increased demand for food
• Economic distress
• Early marriage
• Population growth
• Suffering and delayed marriage
• Food prices drop
• Increase in wealth
• Food prices rise
• Less demand for food
• Population decrease
• Increased demand for food
b Explain why your diagram illustrates the pessimistic view of Malthusian theory.

The carrying capacity of the land

The **carrying capacity** refers to the number of plants, animals or humans which can be adequately supported (carried) by the land (see section 3.5). The maximum carrying capacity of the environment is referred to as the saturation level, while for populations it is the **population ceiling**. Malthus was the first to suggest the idea of a population ceiling and assess different scenarios when a population approaches carrying capacity (Figs 5.3–5.4).

Figure 5.4 Population change and resource limits

S–curve: population growth adjusts gradually to the carrying capacity; population growth rates slow down and the population total stabilises around the maximum number of people who can be supported by the existing carrying capacity.

J–curve: population growth may overshoot the carrying capacity causing fluctuations in growth rates; such fluctuations gradually diminish until the population total stabilises around the level of the carrying capacity.

Figure 5.3 Population growth adjustments to carrying capacity

3 Study Figure 5.3.
a Describe how the population rates change as the carrying capacity is reached.
b Which of these possible scenarios is the most realistic? Explain why (see section 3.5).

4 Study the relationship between population growth and carrying capacity in Figure 5.4. Suggest what events or government policies could produce:
a the curve x.
b the curve y.
c the curve z. Describe how the population rates change as the carrying capacity is reached.

5a Decide whether each statement in Figure 5.1 supports or contradicts Malthusian theory.
b Essay: Rapid population growth is the only explanation for poverty. Discuss.

Figure 5.5 Opposing views on the reasons and outcomes of population growth

Limitations of Malthusian theory

Anti-Malthusians criticise the theory as being too simplistic. A shortage of food is just one possible explanation for starvation, disease and war (Fig. 5.5). In fact, Marxists argue that the theory's reasoning (geometric population growth which outruns an arithmetic increase in food supply) ignores the reality that it is actually only the poor who go hungry. Marx claimed that poverty results from the poor distribution of resources, not physical limits on production. Except on a global scale, the world's community is not 'closed' and so does not enjoy a fair and even distribution of food supplies. Even so, Malthus could not possibly have foreseen the spectacular changes in farming technology which mean we can produce enough food from an area the size of a football pitch to supply 1000 people for a year, i.e. there is enough land to feed the whole world.

Thus evidence of the last two centuries contradicts the Malthusian notion of food supply increasing only arithmetically. Rather than starvation, food surpluses exist and agricultural production increases. In 1992 European surpluses reached 26 million tonnes and there are indications that this trend will continue, contrary to Malthusian theory.

Figure 5.6 Boserup's view on the relationship between population growth and food supply

?

6 Using Figure 5.6, draw a graph similar to Figure 5.2 to illustrate Boserup's theory. (Note that the carrying capacity will increase in stages, as the intensity of cultivation increases.)

?

7 Write a summary of Malthus' and Boserup's ideas and compare their views on the relationship between population growth and food supply.

8 Why do you think some commentators refer to the Malthusian viewpoint as 'pessimistic'?

9a With reference to Table 5.1 and evidence from other chapters, find specific examples to justify the viewpoints of the economists and environmentalists on population and resources.
b Organise a class debate to determine which of the viewpoints is more convincing.

Boserup's theory

In 1965, Esther Boserup, a Danish economist, asserted that an increase in population would stimulate technologists to increase food production (the optimistic view). Boserup suggested that any rise in population will increase the demand for food and so act as an incentive to change agrarian technology and produce more food (Fig. 5.6). We can sum up Boserup's theory by the sentence 'necessity is the mother of invention'.

Boserup's ideas were based on her research into various land use systems, ranging from extensive **shifting cultivation** in the tropical rainforests to more intensive multiple cropping, as in South-East Asia. Her theory suggests that, as population increases, agriculture moves into higher stages of intensity through innovation and the introduction of new farming methods. The conclusion arising from Boserup's theory is that population growth naturally leads to development.

Limitations of Boserup's theory

Like Malthus, Boserup's idea is based on the assumption of a 'closed' community. In reality, except at a global scale, communities are not 'closed' because constant in- and out-migration are common features. It has therefore been very difficult to test Boserup's ideas. This is because migration usually occurs in areas of over-population to relieve the population pressure which, according to Boserup's theory, then leads to technological innovation.

In addition, Boserup herself admits that over-population can lead to unsuitable farming practices which may degrade the land. Consequently, some geographers have partly blamed population pressure for **desertification** in the Sahel. From this it is clear that certain types of fragile environment cannot support excessive numbers of people. In such cases, population pressure does not always lead to technological innovation and development.

Economists versus environmentalists
The conflict between the views of Malthus and Boserup continues today. We can see this controversy in the debate between optimistic economists and pessimistic environmentalists (Table 5.1).

Table 5.1 Economists versus environmentalists

Proponent	View of people and resources	View of population growth	Example of belief
Economist's view Professor Julian Simon, University of Maryland, USA	People are the 'ultimate resource' – not the problem; every newly-born human is a fresh source of ingenuity who can provide many more solutions to problems than they can ever cause.	Population growth is responsible for technical improvements in social infrastructure, e.g. transport and communication, which sustain further high population growth.	Energy provision is one of the global problems of the late 20th century: Simon sees future generations as the discoverers of new forms of much-needed energy.
Environmentalist's view Paul Ehrlich; neo-Malthusians	People are condemned to live in poverty and hunger because of food shortages, lack of development and limited resources; natural environments can only support a limited population.	People always reproduce faster than food supplies will increase.	Deforestation, global warming, desertification, depletion of the ozone layer, wars and AIDS are all signs of an impending Malthusian crisis.

5.3 Application of Malthus and Boserup

There is evidence to suggest that the ideas of both Boserup and Malthus may be appropriate at different scales. On a global level, the growing suffering and famine in some developing countries today may reinforce Malthusian ideas. On the other hand, at a national scale, some governments have been motivated by increasing population to develop their resources and so meet growing demands.

Population and resource crisis in Mauritius

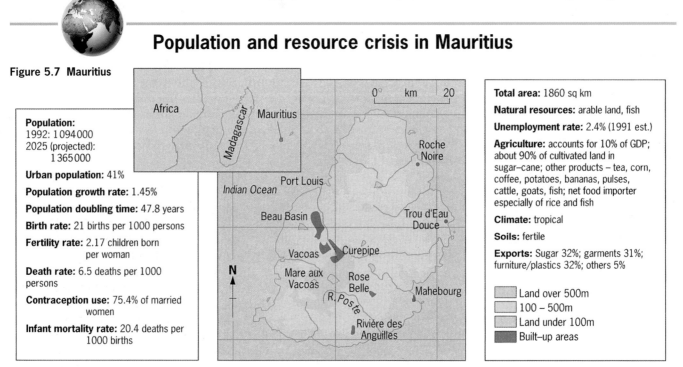

Figure 5.7 Mauritius

Population:
1992: 1 094 000
2025 (projected):
1 365 000

Urban population: 41%

Population growth rate: 1.45%

Population doubling time: 47.8 years

Birth rate: 21 births per 1000 persons

Fertility rate: 2.17 children born per woman

Death rate: 6.5 deaths per 1000 persons

Contraception use: 75.4% of married women

Infant mortality rate: 20.4 deaths per 1000 births

Total area: 1860 sq km

Natural resources: arable land, fish

Unemployment rate: 2.4% (1991 est.)

Agriculture: accounts for 10% of GDP; about 90% of cultivated land in sugar–cane; other products – tea, corn, coffee, potatoes, bananas, pulses, cattle, goats, fish; net food importer especially of rice and fish

Climate: tropical

Soils: fertile

Exports: Sugar 32%; garments 31%; furniture/plastics 32%; others 5%

Land over 500m
100 – 500m
Land under 100m
Built–up areas

One example where there is a rapidly growing population is the island of Mauritius (Fig. 5.7). Here however, the government has co-ordinated efforts to improve standards of living in spite of this population pressure.

Human expansion

In the 1950s Mauritius was facing a 'Malthusian crisis' when the relationship between its population and resources became unbalanced (Fig. 5.8). A sharp decline in the death rate followed by a rise in birth rate meant increased pressure on the economy, which was almost totally reliant on sugar production.

Figure 5.8 Mauritius: demographic transition, 1890–1992
(*Source: Geography Review*, May 1995)

Falling birth rates

In response to the population increase, by 1953 the Mauritian government had developed an organised family planning programme. This aimed to:

*   improve the social position of the people
*   improve the status of women
*   restrict early marriage
*   provide better health care
*   encourage emigration
*   set up an integrated family planning service.

Gradually, a hierarchical network of government health and family planning clinics developed and by 1985 only 14 per cent of the urban population and 11 per cent of the rural population were more than 30 minutes' travelling time from a clinic.

10 You are researching Mauritius as a possible location for a transnational company. Write a brief description of the history and population geography of the island as background information for your research.

Other factors which contributed towards reducing birth rates in Mauritius included a change in attitude towards family size, postponement of marriage (mainly as a result of harsh economic conditions in the 1960s) and a shift in the status of women as female education improved. As women looked for work opportunities outside the home, their roles changed. Only 22.3 per cent of women were in paid employment in 1975, whereas by 1990 this had risen to 35.75 per cent.

Improved living standards
Although population numbers have always been high in Mauritius (Fig. 5.9), the country has still been able to turn its economy around (Fig. 5.10). This is contrary to Malthus' pessimistic view.

The main routes to increased living standards include diversification of agriculture and investment in industry (see Fig. 5.7). As the workforce became relatively better educated than in other developing countries, economic transformations were considerable. In 1993, the GDP per capita was nearly US$3 000, a 159 per cent increase since 1986.

Figure 5.9 Mauritius: population growth (*Source: Geography Review*, May 1995)

International trade
As an ex-colony of the UK, Mauritius built links with Europe and maintains a stable and democratic government. This encourages a pro-Western stance which, during the Cold War, helped the country's trade relations with the USA.

Many **transnational corporations** (**TNCs**) have since been attracted to Mauritius. This is due in part to the large numbers of well-educated residents. More obviously, though, the TNCs are drawn to the country by its status as an Export Processing Zone (EPZ). This provides numerous financial incentives such as reduced

Figure 5.10 Port Louis, Mauritius: with economic growth and social change, the capital now has the appearance of an international centre

corporation tax, free repatriation of capital, guarantees against nationalisation of companies and investment in transport. In addition Mauritius has a good supply of cheap labour ready to work in the transnationals.

The EPZ status, together with the more recent creation of a Free Port at Port Louis, have helped to improve the resources side of the population-resources imbalance. This works as the TNCs import raw materials into Mauritius for manufacture and then export as finished goods. One aspect of this is that Mauritius is now a textile exporter of world rank although it grows no cotton. Most raw materials are imported and the main resource provided domestically is the labour force.

?

11 Comment on the trend of natural population increase since the family planning programme was introduced (Figures 5.8 and 5.9).

12 Work in small groups.
a Using the Mauritius scheme, design a programme to reduce birth rates in another developing country which has a high population increase.
b Describe what prior research you would do, and how you would implement your programme.
c Get another group to evaluate your work and make modifications to improve the programme.

13a Compare the experiences of Mauritius with the theories of Malthus and Boserup.
b To which theory is Mauritius closer?

14 A poor country's fragile economy cannot keep up with population growth, so people will just get poorer and poorer. Use evidence from Mauritius to comment on this view of development, stating whether or not you agree with it.

15a Identify a finite resource in your country and find out the rate at which it is being exploited.
b What adjustments may be needed in order to conserve this resource?

5.4 The geography of food

Inequalities in world food distribution
In 1995 we globally produce enough food to give the whole world's population an adequate and balanced diet (see Fig. 5.1). We need, therefore, to question why so many people often go without food (Fig. 5.12). It is also important that we understand the reasons for these inequalities in world food distribution.

Farming systems and food output
The main source of food for all people is agriculture. Throughout the world it employs more than one billion people and they work in a great variety of farming systems. A farming system relies on a series of inputs which produce a series of outputs (Fig. 5.11). Each system is affected by a number of different social, economic, political and environmental factors.

Subsistence agriculture
In most developing countries much agricultural production relies on labour intensive methods. Traditionally, these consisted of ecologically sustainable practices such as shifting cultivation and **bush fallow** (Fig. 5.13).

However, such farming customs have not been able to provide enough income for the rapidly growing populations of developing countries. In response to this, large-scale rural-to-urban migration occurs (see section 4.6) and there is a decline in the level of **subsistence agriculture** as farmers switch to more commercial methods.

Commercial agriculture
Commercial agriculture is characterised by high capital investment in machinery and inputs such as chemical fertilisers (Fig. 5.14). While these increase agricultural output, they tend to reduce the need for farm labour. Commercial farming systems were originally introduced into developing countries by colonialists producing goods for their home market. With the decline of colonialism, the production of export crops in these old colonial areas, e.g. Brazil (see section 9.5), has increased. In some cases, such crops provide countries with their main source of revenue. Over three quarters of the exports from tropical countries are in the form of primary produce and there are many examples of countries which rely heavily on the production of just one crop (Table 5.2). This means that certain developing countries depend heavily on particular agricultural products, such as tobacco, cotton and coffee, placing both the national economy and farmers at the mercy of fluctuating world markets (see Chapter 8).

16 Use Figure 5.12.
a Which countries have
• the lowest levels and
• the highest levels of calorie intake
b Comment on the global pattern of food supply (see Figure 1.1).

17 Read Figure 5.1 and give your personal response to the spatial inequalities in world food distribution.

18a Using Figure 5.12, trace the outlines of countries with a low low calorie intake.
b Use your tracing to overlay a map of different farming systems
c Describe the relationship between levels of calorie intake and farming types.

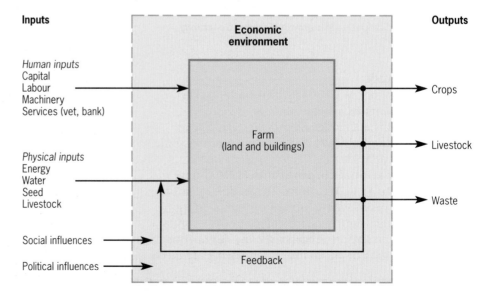

Figure 5.11 Agriculture as a system

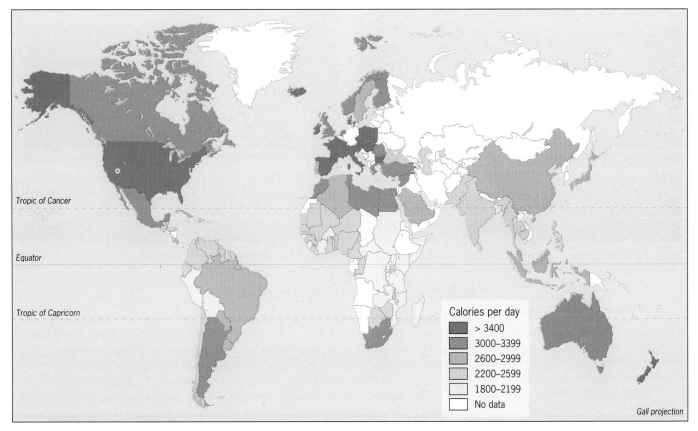

Figure 5.12 Average daily calorie intake by country, 1991 (*Source:* FAO). Malnutrition frequently leads to disease and often death; high rates of infant mortality are characteristic of countries with high levels of undernutrition. An estimated 14 million children in Asia and Africa die every year from diseases caused by malnutrition.

Table 5.2 Examples of countries reliant on a limited range of agricultural produce in their exports, 1990

Country	Type of produce	Named produce as % of agricultural exports	All agricultural produce as % of merchandise exported
Réunion	Sugar	93.3	79.2
Cuba	Sugar	92.3	88.2
Uganda	Coffee	92.2	86.4
Ghana	Cocoa	85.8	41.2
Jamaica	Coffee	81.2	19.9
Swaziland	Sugar	78.3	38.1
Martinique	Bananas	66.4	60.8
Sri Lanka	Tea	66.2	39.0
Bangladesh	Jute	64.8	12.7
Ecuador	Bananas	60.0	28.7

Internal political crisis and food availability

Internal political crisis and inter-tribal conflicts often disrupt daily life and sometimes produce thousands of refugees (see Figs. 4.24–4.25). During the latter part of the twentieth century, many countries in Africa have experienced such political upheavals. For example, Rwanda, Somalia, Chad and Ethiopia are countries which have recently witnessed large-scale population movements as people have been forced to flee from danger zones or from areas with little or no food supplies.

Food aid

One way the international community has responded to the increasing need for food in conflict areas is through the provision of food aid (Fig. 5.15).

Despite such aid efforts, many people still suffer from hunger and starvation (see Fig. 5.1). Both short-term and long-term food aid programmes have been vital during immediate crises, but such aid cannot remove the more long-lasting food problems. Countries receiving aid may also find themselves tied financially to the donor country (see section 2.5).

Figure 5.13 Subsistence agriculture

Figure 5.14 Commercial agriculture

19 Study Figures 5.13 and 5.14.
a Compare the differences between the two farming systems.
b Suggest how each system may affect people in terms of: • use of resources, • employment, • food supplies.

5.5 Increasing food production

Only about 10 per cent of the world's land surface is regularly farmed. In most parts of the developing world, ownership of land is crucial to one's economic status. This is because many developing countries are agrarian in nature, engaging 60–65% of the population. In contrast, less than 3% of the population in the developed world is engaged in the agricultural sector.

However, modern farming methods mean more can be produced per unit of land area than is usually produced in the developing world. The harsh weather conditions in many developing countries are known to have some adverse effects on agricultural production. These include factors such as insufficient rainfall, which can contribute to desertification, and too much rainfall, which can lead to erosion of soil nutrients.

In light of this global shortage of farming land and the increasing world population, people have tried firstly, to bring more land into cultivation and secondly, to increase production from current farming land. Land reclamation has been tried in a number of countries with varying degrees of success. More recently, some have suggested that widespread application of genetically modified crops (cross-reference GM food) offers the only global solution to the growing shortage of agricultural farmlands, but the issues regarding the safety, the ethics and environmental concerns about this method of farming have made it very controversial.

Figure 5.15 Care International delivering corn to Angola, December 1991: between 1980 and 1990 the USA supplied over 60 million tonnes of food aid

The Green Revolution

Technology is one of the key factors for increasing food production on available agricultural land. Since the end of World War 2, technological advances were made through a 'package' of ideas known as the Green Revolution. This saw the development of new high-yielding varieties (HYVs) or modern varieties (MVs) of staple crops such as wheat, maize and rice.

In 1943 investors from the USA established a research project with the Mexican government to improve local wheat and maize varieties. Yields of both wheat and maize increased threefold and researchers took the new seeds to the Indian sub-continent.

By 1960, the International Rice Research Institute had established a similar project at Los Banos, in the Philippines, to research the world's rice varieties. The first genetically engineered strain of rice was IR8, or 'miracle rice', which increased yields sixfold at its first harvest (Fig. 5.16). Technologists saw this miracle rice as a cure for the world's food problems.

Both the new strains of wheat and rice produced dwarf plants capable of withstanding strong winds and heavy rain. They tolerated dry conditions, while their higher yields allowed farmers to reduce the land area devoted to cereals and so grow other crops.

Problems with HYVs

Rice is the traditional staple crop in most parts of Asia and this is where the new HYV strains of rice were originally introduced. The response of Asians to the HYVs was mixed. Some people complained that the taste was different and so reverted back to their traditional strains. For example, Thailand, the largest rice exporter in the world, was reluctant to adopt the new varieties for fear of losing customers who preferred the 'old' flavours. This explains why only 13 per cent of rice paddies in Thailand is planted with MVs.

Overall, HYVs are expensive. They require a higher level of fertiliser and irrigation, so farmers have to buy a range of chemical fertilisers, pesticides and herbicides. Problems arise, then, with the typical peasant farmer who has little money for such inputs, and often poor access to irrigation. In addition, during the 1970s, farmers discovered that the new types of rice had little immunity to disease (unlike traditional varieties). The farmers therefore had to use more pesticides, often damaging the environment. These and other problems associated with the Green Revolution are outlined in Figure 5.17. Similar consequences may result from an increased application of genetic engineering throughout the world.

Figure 5.16 Transplanting high-yielding rice varieties, Java, Indonesia

Genetic engineering

The Green Revolution has progressed since the early 1990s into genetic engineering where the use of artificial insemination, embryo transfer and tissue culture increases agricultural production.

Some of the arguments for and against genetic engineering are listed in Figure 5.18. In the light of some of the problems associated with the application of science in agricultural production, growing numbers of people are becoming more concerned about the possible harmful effects of genetically modified crops. In the UK, this has led to public demonstration against farmers who are participating in GM trial crops (Fig. 5.19).

Figure 5.17 An appraisal of the Green Revolution

Figure 5.18 (*Source: The Guardian, September 1999*)

?

20 Using Figures 5.17–5.19, evaluate the Green Revolution according to its:
a social benefits and disbenefits
b environmental benefits and disbenefits.

21 Conduct a class debate to discuss the motion: 'The development of GM foods will solve the current world food crisis'. The debate should involve speakers with different perspectives including an environmentalist, an economist, a farmer, a Managing Director of a trans-national corporation, a scientist, a politician and a development aid worker.

22 Essay: With reference to both the developed and developing world, assess the relative successes and failures of the Green Revolution with regard to tackling world food inequalities.

Failed GM firm pays price of bad publicity

James Meikle

The first significant biotech company to run out of money yesterday blamed on its demise on bad publicity surrounding genetic engineering.

Axis Genetics, which is using genetically modified plants for drug research, has begun insolvency proceedings having failed to raise sufficient funds to keep going.

Its difficulties became public, just weeks after Deutsche bank advised big investors to sell shares in multinationals developing GM crops because of "growing negative sentiment".

Scimac, the GM crop industrial body, also warned last month that companies might begin to lose interest in crop trials in Britain if the campaign against them continued.

But its secretary, Daniel Pearsall, said yesterday:

"The industry is committed to the programme. That is there to take technology forward on the basis of good science.

Iain Cubitt, of Axis Genetics, based in Cambridge, said his firm's problems might have been caused by bad publicity surrounding the performance of businesses such as British Biotech, whose shares plunged amid doubts over the efficacy of a new anti-cancer drug.

"We are dealing with GM plants for pharmaceuticals, not food. The performance of publicly-quoted companies has affected the private biotechnology companies [such as the Axis Genetics]," said Mr Cubitt.

One of the four farmers due to plant large-scale trials of GM Mark oil seed rape this month has pulled out, it emerged yesterday, writes Paul Brown

David Rose, who farms near Bingham, Nottinghamshire, made his decision after meeting local residents who voted by 80 to three against the trial.

Plantings in different parts of the country are considered essential by the government to assess the impact of the crops on the countryside.

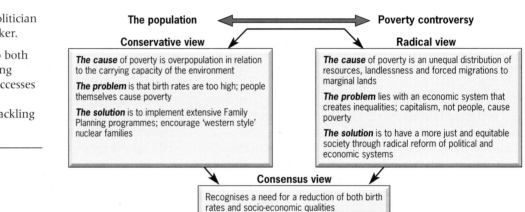

Figure 5.19 Population versus poverty

Arguments for
• Genetic engineering will lead to a growth in world food production. With an increasing global population and improved purchasing power, the demand for food will rise significantly during the next 50 years. Genetically modified (GM) foods could help meet this increase in demand.
• Genetically modified crops can lead to a reduction of pollution. For example, GM Soya beans developed by Monsanto (a transnational company which controls more than three-quarters of the world's trade in cereals), can withstand the effects of chemicals. As a result, farmers can use chemical herbicides to kill weeds in the fields of Soya beans. Because of this, there is no need to plough the fields. This means a reduction in soil erosion, fewer tractor fuel emissions plus the added bonus of saving time and labour.
• Monsanto is developing an oil seed crop, which produces betacarotene. Betacarotene is a good source of vitamin A. A growing number of people around the world are Vitamin A deficient and suffer night blindness as a result. One teaspoon of enhanced oil from this new crop, can provide the recommended daily amount of Vitamin A for an adult.
• The use of biotechnology will mean farmers using fewer insecticides and other chemical products, which in turn will help protect the environment.

Arguments against
• Corporate giants like Monsanto are patenting genetically engineered seeds. The result is that farmers have to pay royalties for the seeds, which they are forbidden by law to save and re-sow. At present eighty per cent of crops in developing countries are grown from seeds saved from the previous harvest. This shift of power from farmers to transnational companies could result in the poor getting poorer and hungrier.
• The so-called 'terminator' seed technologies will almost certainly lead to the big corporations profiteering from hunger. These seeds are engineered to germinate only when a specific chemical, supplied by the company at relatively high prices, is applied.
• The transnationals operate a monopoly on food production and distribution and are now threatening to do so on seeds. They are in a position to buy where and when it is cheapest and sell at a high price.
• The British Medical Association has stressed the need for more research into the links between genetic engineering and new allergies which are becoming more widespread.
• It is not always possible to predict how new varieties of crops will interact with the natural environment and because of this there remains the risk that crops could be destroyed and agricultural land seriously degraded.

Figure 5.20 Arguments for and against genetic engineering (*Source: Grains of Truth, Geographical, October 1999*)

The programme of Action on Development states that countries, as a matter of policy, should 'seek ... reductions in maternal mortality through measures to reduce high-risk births, including birth to adolescents, eliminate all unwanted births and all unsafe abortion, [and] expand cost-effective obstetrical and gynaecological care'.

Figure 5.21 Recommending contraception (Source: UN Draft Final Document of the International Conference on Population and Development, Cairo, 1994)

5.6 Population policies

The first ever world population conference was held in Bucharest in 1974. Since then, a number of international institutions and **non-governmental organisations** (**NGOs**, see section 2.5) have focused on population control. These include the United Nations Fund for Population Activities (UNFPA) and the International Planned Parenthood Federation (IPPF).

Each of the institutions has different ideas and policies for population control and the appropriate strategy to adopt, whether anti- or pro-natalist. These fall into three ideological camps: • the neo-Malthusians; • those who consider the general lack of development to be the real problem, *not* high population growth; • those who believe that high rates of population growth in developing countries will naturally slow down with development. The main thrust of this argument is summarised in Figure 5.20.

Limiting fertility

Providing efficient and hygienic family planning is a major objective of governments and organisations (Fig. 5.21). Each year, about 500 000 women die of complications due to pregnancy, child bearing or unsafe abortions (Fig. 5.23). Over 90 per cent of such deaths occur in developing countries where poor health, frequent child bearing, and poor access to medical care are prevalent (Fig. 5.22). The techniques used vary from coercive sterilisation to health care and education (Table 5.3).

Table 5.3 Methods to reduce population growth

Method of birth control	Examples of use
Contraception	Sub-Saharan Africa (>10%); Iran (22%); Philippines (25%); Haiti (10%); North America (69%)
Family planning programmes and child spacing (controlling of the number of, and intervals between, children)	Reduction of average fertility rate from 6.5 to 3.5 children per woman (years taken): USA (58); Indonesia (27); Colombia (15); Thailand (8)
Abortion	see text
Education	Poorly educated women in Brazil have an average of 6.5 children, those with secondary education 2.5.

Figure 5.22 Number of maternal deaths for every 100 000 live births (*Source:* Of woman born: Reproductive rights and wrong, The N.I. No. 303, July 1998)

Abortion

Abortion includes any means used to terminate a pregnancy. There are an estimated 20 million unsafe abortions each year and more than 70 000 abortion related deaths, most of them in developing countries (Fig. 5.22).

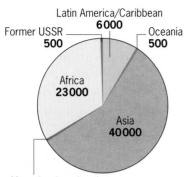

Latin America/Caribbean
6000
Former USSR
500
Oceania
500
Africa
23000
Asia
40000
More developed regions
less than 100

Figure 5.23 Estimated number of deaths from unsafe abortions, 1995

Where abortion is illegal, the number of women resorting to unsafe abortion increases – and so does the danger of them dying or being injured. The moral and ethical issues surrounding abortion are highly emotive, and the practice generates a lot of controversy. In the Russian Federation, abortion is one of the major forms of birth control and each woman has an average of four or five abortions in her life. Similarly, in the USA abortion is considered a constitutional right of women but there is also a growing anti-abortion campaign (Fig. 5.25).

An unplanned pregnancy can be a disaster for a woman. It may affect her physical and mental health. It may cause her to lose her employment, thus ending her financial independence. It may also cause an intolerable strain on the economic circumstances of her existing family. The option of abortion is essential.

Harry Cohen, Labour MP for Leyton

The House Magazine, 12 June 1995

Abortion is violent and primitive. And it thrives on ignorance. People just don't know that the baby is a formed human being, with arms and legs and heart and eyes not a lump of jelly or tissue. The baby gets pulled out bit by bit, or sucked out in shreds by a machine.

LIFE

Abortion is wrong. God wants human beings to continue, this is a sacred order.

Turkey's Chief Cleric, Mehmet Ali Yilmaz

The Guardian, 11 August 1992

Do I acknowledge the pain of abortion? Yes. Do I think the state should control woman's choices? No. Do I think that birth control is a better choice? Yes.
Abortion is indeed a cruel alternative to birth control.

Erica Jong, American novelist and feminist

The Observer, 29 Nov. 1995

Figure 5.24 Attitudes to abortion

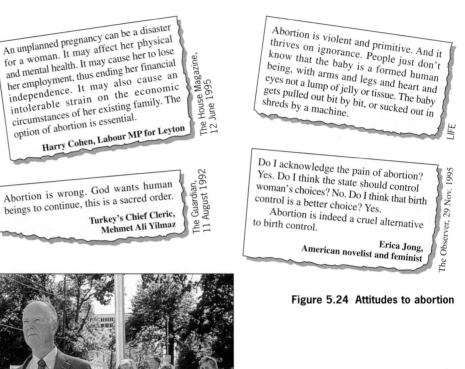

Figure 5.25 Pro-life protesters in the USA, 1993

?

23 In which ways can improvements in the economic status of women influence the number of children they have?

24a Compare Table 5.3 with Figure 5.12.
b Comment on the links between food availability with maternal mortality and fertility.

25 'While ideological positions are divided, the possible effects of abortion on the growing world's population are widely recognised.' Read Figure 5.24 and state your own response to this statement.

26a Research newspaper articles on abortion.
b List arguments for and against abortion.
c Write a speech justifying your own view towards abortion.

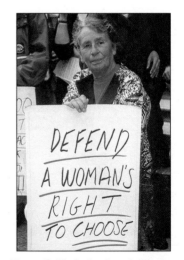

Figure 5.26 Defender of abortion

Population and development in China

China is the third largest country in the world in terms of area. In terms of population, though, China is the biggest nation with 1.23 billion people (1997), who make up 21.5 per cent of the world's total population.

Population changes

In 1949, General Mao Tse-tung took over the country's leadership, proclaiming the People's Republic of China a one-party, centrally planned, state. At that time, there were about 550 million Chinese. However, within ten years, the population had grown to 655 million (Fig. 5.30).

The 'Great Leap Forward' was initiated in 1958 to extend the socialist system of production. Mao hoped to give control to the peasants through industrialisation in rural areas and higher targets for agriculture. These plans, though, ended in disorganised production and famine, with the population declining by about 14 million between 1959 and 1962 (Fig. 5.30). Malnutrition and general distress meant that the average 25 million babies who would normally have been born were either not conceived or did not survive. Infant mortality was thus high, reaching about 284 per 1000. In the late 1990s, the IMR for China was about 38 per 1000, whereas it was 6 per 1000 in the UK.

Population pressure

Between 1955 and 1995, the population of China more than doubled. When increasing most rapidly, China's population grew by almost 24 million per annum, this is equivalent to the population of England and Wales being generated every two years.

The sheer size of the Chinese population puts increased demands on services such as food, housing, education and employment. In fact during the late 1970s, the government feared that further population increases would result in mass starvation by the end of the century (Fig. 5.30). By 1979, therefore, the government introduced a family planning programme. This is a national policy of one child to urban couples, while couples in the countryside are 'allowed' two children and 'may not have three'. The policy met with some success (Fig. 5.33). There were 10 million fewer births in 1979 than in 1970 and during this time the birth rate was halved (see Fig. 3.24). However, the government still found it necessary to extend the single child policy to rural areas by 1981.

The Chinese have defined their optimum population as being around 700–750 million. This would mean a reduction of about one-third of the current population.

?

27 Use Figures 5.28 and 5.29.
a Describe China's population trend.
b Suggest the impact of the Great Leap Forward and famine on the following generations.

28a Make a comparison of China's population • projections and • policies with Malthus' and Boserup's theories.
b To which views are China's policies closest?
c What would be the response of • environmentalists, • economists, to China's strategy?

29 Some Chinese name their child 'the only one' in recognition of the fact that they are unlikely to have any more children. Read Figures 5.31 and 5.32 and identify Chinese attitudes towards government population control.

Population
1992: 1 165 771 000
2025 (projected): 1 590 783 000

Population density: 314.6 persons per km^2

Population growth rate: 1.3%

Population doubling time: 53.4 years

Birth rate: 19.68 births per 1000 persons

Fertility rate: 2.18 children per woman

Death rate: 6.7 deaths per 1000 persons

Literacy: 73% (male 84%, female 62%) age 15 and over can read and write

Contraception use: 71.2% of married women

Infant mortality rate: 34 deaths per 1000 births

Total area: 9 596 960 km^2

Natural resources: coal, iron ore, crude oil, mercury, tin, tungsten, antimony, manganese, molybdenum, vanadium, magnetite, aluminium, lead, zinc, uranium, world's largest hydropower potential

Figure 5.27 China

China's criminal mothers

CHINA first got serious about population control in 1979. The policy of limiting every couple to one child, announced by Deng Xiaoping in 1979, was in place by 1981.

The policy, still in force today, requires women of childbearing age with one child to use IUDs, couples with two children to be sterilised and imposes abortion upon women who get pregnant without authorisation. By the mid-eighties, such birth control operations were averaging more than 30 million a year. Many, if not most, were performed on women against their will.

In 1981, when the Chinese government formally adopted a one-child policy, Chi An, a nurse in the Manchurian city of Shenyang, was recruited to help manage the programme in her factory. Despite her past experiences – she had been forced to end her second pregnancy – she obediently became part of the machine. She was responsible for sterilising women and inserting IUDs; she performed early abortions and assisted in late-term ones.

'The government said there would be a famine without the one-child policy,' she says now. 'We thought we were preventing a catastrophe.'

China draws a cold distinction: killing a newborn is murder; killing an infant even as its head crowns is a 'remedial measure' and a contribution to the public good. There were times when Chi An supervised the 'termination'

of a pregnancy when the woman was in labour. But her conscience was silenced by fear of punishment if she failed to carry out her duty.

Chi An, now director of her factory's family planning clinic, had to sign a 'baby contract' with the Shenyang family planning office. If she kept the number of births in her factory below the target, she would receive a cash bonus and a commendation. If she allowed even one baby to be born over the quota, she would be fined and criticised.

January began with the pleasant task of announcing the names of the lucky women whose applications to bear a child had been approved by the factory family planning committee. The rest of Chi An's time was taken up performing pelvic examinations and pressuring into having an abortion those found to be pregnant. Those who refused 'remedial measures' were locked up in a warehouse until they relented. Factory officials would first threaten them, then Chi An would gently tell them they should go quietly to the hospital, for their own good. She always met her target. But then, in 1984, the factory's quota was slashed from 322 infants to 65. When Chi An complained, her superior told her 'the use of force is a necessary measure. Vice Premier Deng Xiaoping has instructed us: 'To reduce the population, use whatever means you must, but do it'.'

Figure 5.28 The other side of family planning (*Source:* Steven Mosher, *The Guardian*, 28 March 1994)

China admits one-child policy a failure

CHINA's national leaders have been forced to admit that the population is growing at a rate beyond the Government's control. Delegates to an emergency meeting in Peking to deal with the crisis heard that, by the year 2000, there will be 120 million more Chinese than planned.

The growth will deepen the economic crisis in a country where one-fifth of the world's population lives on only five per cent of its arable land and where the Agriculture Ministry recently warned that 20 million people were short of food.

It estimated that within 11 years there would be 1.32 billion Chinese, rather than the 1.2 billion forecast.

The one-child family policy, introduced in 1980 to avoid a fight for food in the mid-21st century, was designed to limit the population to 1.2 billion by the year 2000 and to lower it to 700 million within 75 years.

Figure 5.29 Family planning fails (*Source:* Jonathan Mirsky, *The Observer*, 15 Jan. 1989)

Rural women benefit from birth control

ZHENGZHOU (Xinhua) — Rural women are the biggest beneficiaries of implementation of the birth control policy, which has been pushed nationwide since the 1970s.

Most housewives interviewed share the view they have more energy and time for other pursuits and make their own families rich.

The families all observed the birth control policy. Most couples only have one child, or two children at most. Their per capita income is above 2500 yuan ($301) a year, 1000 yuan ($120) more than the average per capita income for all farmers in the province.

Tian Ju, a 36-year-old woman farmer from Sizhuang Village, Nanshuang Township of Mengxian County, has two daughters. Tian, together with her husband, has been running a workshop for producing felt and shoe-pads since 1992. The couple also contracted with the village for four mu (0.266 hectares) of farmland.

Products from the workshop are selling well in the market. From this alone, Tian earns more than 15000 yuan ($1807) a year. Local villagers all admire the family.

'If this were the past, I would have to try to have a boy,' said the housewife. The survey shows rural women now have a decisive voice on birth. Their opinions are respected by their husbands and relatives, thanks to the improved economic status of rural women and adoption of the birth control policy nationwide.

A total of 3 million rural female farmers in the province have attended training courses of various kinds to become workers in rural enterprises.

Figure 5.30 Good results from family planning (*Source: China Daily*, 1 June 1995)

Figure 5.31 China: percentage age composition (*Source*: *Statistical year book of China*, 1985)

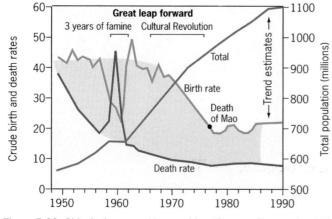

Figure 5.32 China's demographic transition (*Source*: *Geography*, 1989)

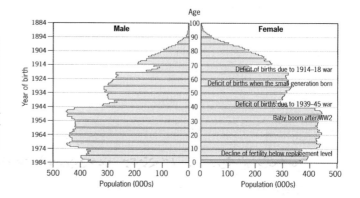

Figure 5.33 China population projections

Eventually, as only one child replaces two parents, China's population will start declining. Such projections are, though, being undermined as couples living in the boom, coastal areas become wealthier (see Fig. 4.10, section 9.6). Because of their economic improvements, they no longer fear the official penalties of increased housing, schooling and medical costs for larger families. Other social factors also limit the effectiveness of the single child policy (Fig. 5.29).

?

30 Read Figures 5.28–5.30.
a What are the moral implications of enforcing the population control policy in China?
b Use all the evidence to assess the short-term and long-term advantages and disadvantages of China's population policy.
c Comment on whether China's one-child policy is a success or failure. Give reasons for your responses.

Europe: declining population

Unlike China, where high population growth rates have been a major obstacle to economic development, some countries are experiencing declining population growth rates. In most cases this trend has occurred without direct government intervention. For many European countries in particular, population projections show that by the year 2050, a decline in population will be a major economic, social and political issue (table 5.4).

?

31a Suggest some social, economic and political reasons why some countries may wish to promote high population growth.
b What are the possible problems that governments' excessive promotion of large families may create for the nation in the future?

32 With regard to population increase and the declining population in Europe (see section 3.4), how can policies encouraging couples to have large families be justified?

Table 5.4 Europe's population decline

Country	1998 (millions)	Projected 2050 (millions)
Austria	8 140	7 094
Belgium	10 141	8 918
Bulgaria	8 336	5 673
Croatia	4 481	3 673
Czech Republic	10 282	7 829
Denmark	5 270	4 793
Finland	5 154	4 898
Germany	82 133	73 303
Greece	10 600	8 233
Hungary	10 116	7 488
Italy	57 369	41 197
Lithuania	3 694	2 297
Netherlands	15 678	14 156
Poland	38 718	36 256
Portugal	9 869	8 137
Romania	22 474	16 419
Russian Fed	147 434	121 256
Slovakia	5 377	4 836
Spain	39 628	30 226
Sweden	8 875	8 661
Switzerland	7 299	6 745
Ukraine	50 861	39 302
UK	58 649	56 667
Yugoslavia	10 635	10 548

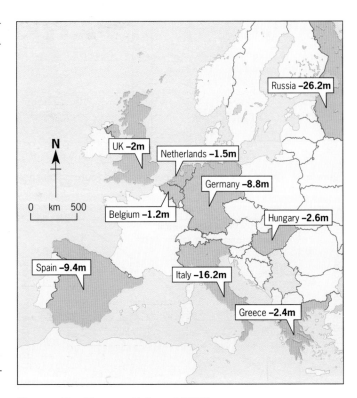

(*Source: The Observer*, 8 August 1999)

Summary

- The international community recognises the need for population control.
- Malthus linked population growth with food shortages, poverty and disease.
- Boserup contradicted Malthus stating that population growth stimulates innovation and increased food production.
- Responses to population growth divide into economic and environmentalist views.
- Food availability is unequal across the world.
- Where there is famine, food aid is supplied for both humanitarian and political reasons.
- Technology and modern farming techniques help to increase food output. This benefits mainly the developed world, while some developing countries still suffer from food shortages.
- The success of the Green Revolution, based on high-yielding varieties of cereals, has been uneven throughout the developing world.
- Population control is a controversial issue with mixed strategies and ideologies.
- A rise in the social status of women in developing countries has led to increasing access to contraception and family planning.
- In developed countries there is a growing anti-abortion movement.
- Some population policies are aimed at controlling fertility, while others encourage couples to have more children.

6 Human resources and industrialisation

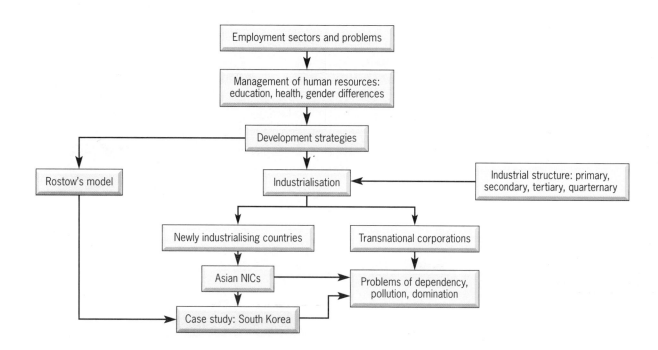

Employment sectors and problems

↓

Management of human resources:
education, health, gender differences

↓

Development strategies

↓

Rostow's model

Industrialisation ← Industrial structure: primary, secondary, tertiary, quarternary

Newly industrialising countries   Transnational corporations

Asian NICs → Problems of dependency, pollution, domination

Case study: South Korea →

6.1 Introduction

The more a country develops its human, as well as its physical and technological resources, the more opportunity it has for transforming itself from economic dependency to self-reliance. In many cases, both **developed** and **developing countries** also view industrialisation as the key to economic change. This path is outlined in Rostow's model of economic development (see section 6.6). We can see that countries which are relatively successful in terms of industrial growth have also made practical use of their human resources. Typically, these countries have managed to bring about economic development and we refer to them as **newly industrialising countries** (**NICs**) (see section 6.7). In this chapter, we will consider how far investment in human resources contributes towards improving people's quality of life and we will examine the role of industry in economic development.

6.2 Employment in the formal and informal sectors

People may work in one of two different sectors of the economy. In the **formal sector**, jobs are officially recognised by the state, they are performed for a wage and they are relatively secure with the hours and working conditions clearly established (Fig. 6.1). Contrastingly, in the **informal sector** people are self-employed and do not receive a permanent wage (Fig. 6.2). While in developed countries an example of informal work is textiles homeworking (e.g. making garments at home for retailers), in developing countries it tends to be characterised by employment in family businesses, as unpaid family work on agricultural small-holdings or as an urban labour force (Fig. 6.3).

The nature of employment in the informal sectors in most developing economies is such that many people are actually **underemployed**. This

Figure 6.1 Employment in the formal sector: metropolitan police give assistance, London, UK

Figure 6.2 Employment in the informal sector: resurfacing mud walls, Kano, Nigeria. Approximately 40–70 per cent of the urban labour force of the developing world work 'informally'.

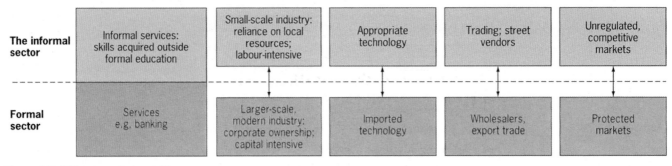

Figure 6.3 Differences between the formal and informal sectors

The informal sector	Informal services: skills acquired outside formal education	Small-scale industry: reliance on local resources; labour-intensive	Appropriate technology	Trading; street vendors	Unregulated, competitive markets
Formal sector	Services e.g. banking	Larger-scale, modern industry; corporate ownership; capital intensive	Imported technology	Wholesalers, export trade	Protected markets

?

1 Use Figures 6.1–6. 3.
a Identify some of the main features of • formal and • informal work.
b With Figure 6.3 to help, make a comparison between the two types of work in both • developed and • developing countries.

2 With reference to Figure 6.4, compare and comment on the relative percentages of people working in the formal and informal sectors in different parts of the world.

3 Use Figure 6.5. In groups, discuss the reasons why large numbers of people employed informally, or who are underemployed, can hinder national economic development.

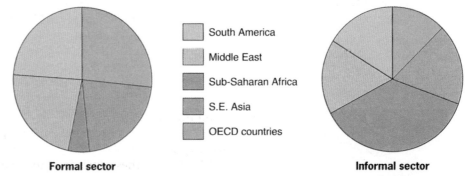

Figure 6.4 Average percentage of world workforce employed in formal and informal sectors (*Source: The Economist: Book of Vital World Statistics*, 1992)

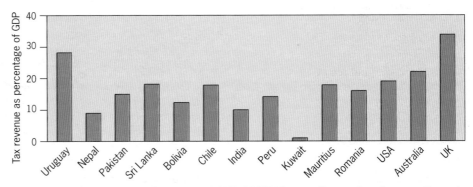

Figure 6.5 Tax revenue (as percentage of GDP, 1995) (*Source*: Human Development Report)

Figure 6.6 The unemployment time bomb (*Source:* International Labour Office)

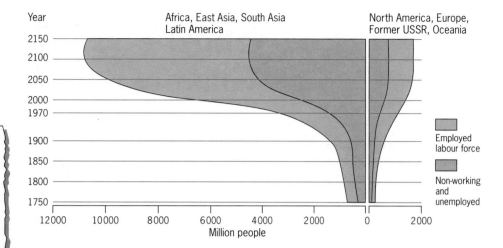

Figure 6.7 Counting the jobless (*Source:* Rosie Waterhouse, *The Independent*, 5 April 1995)

4a From Figure 6.6, estimate how many people in the world will be unemployed by 2150.
b Using information from previous chapters, suggest why unemployment is likely to slow down after 2050.

5 Read Figure 6.7 and refer to section 3.3. Give reasons why it is difficult for both developed and developing countries to obtain accurate statistics on • numbers of people employed/unemployed, • the size of the potential workforce.

usually occurs when work is temporary or seasonal and applies to informal work in both urban and rural areas (see Fig. 6.9). For example, street vendors in many large cities, such as Bombay in India, depend on tourists to boost their income. Their wages will therefore be substantially higher during the 'tourist season' than at other times. In rural areas, landless labourers may only be employed during harvest and so lack that income during the rest of the year.

6.3 Unemployment

Unemployment is a serious world problem with a growing number of people who are out of work or who are facing the threat of being made redundant (Fig. 6.6). In fact, a combination of large numbers of people employed informally, those underemployed and the unemployed make it difficult for authorities to collect accurate labour statistics (see section 3.3). This is true for both developing as well as developed countries (Fig. 6.7).

Impact of unemployment

It is important to understand that unemployment has different consequences for people in both developing and developed countries (Fig. 6.9). In most developed countries, the state often provides for unemployed people through social security schemes (Fig. 6.8). Such schemes are generally non-existent in the developing countries, though, so the unemployed here may have to depend on the support of extended families.

The 'pull', or attraction, of employment opportunities in cities means there is a particularly strong rural-to-urban migration in developing countries (see section 4.5). In fact, these cities tend to have a concentration of both employment and social service provision while the rural areas 'push' people away with their lack of such services. The result is the highest rates of urban growth in the world (Table 6.1, see Fig. 4.17).

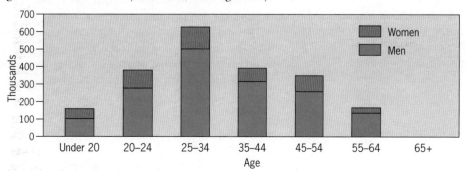

Figure 6.8 UK claimants for unemployment benefits, 1996 (*Source:* Social Security Statistics Stationery Office, 1997)

Figure 6.9 Life in Strathclyde's slums … a world away from India (*Source:* Ian Bell, *The Observer*, 12 Feb. 1995)

Table 6.1 Urbanisation (*Sources:* Selmes et al., 1995, Human Development Report, 1998 and The World Bank Group – World Development Indicators 1999).

Country	Urban population (% of total) 1987	Urban population (% of total) 1997	Urban population annual growth rate (%) 1970–1995
Egypt	48	45	2.5
Ghana	32	37	3.7
Kenya	22	30	7.8
Pakistan	31	35	4.3
India	27	27	3.3
China	38	32	3.8
Thailand	21	21	3.6
USA	74	77	1.1
Mexico	71	74	3.3
Jamaica	51	55	2.2
Peru	69	72	3.2
Argentina	85	89	2.0
UK	92	89	0.2
France	74	75	0.7
Poland	61	64	1.5
Italy	68	67	0.4
Romania	49	57	1.6
Australia	85	85	1.4

?

6 Study the opinions in Figure 6.9.
a Explain why the researchers suggest that unemployment in Glasgow is worse than living in a poor Indian village.
b In your opinion, for long-term unemployment situations, how would life dependent on state benefits compare with life where you are dependent on a large family for support?

Third World label drives Glaswegians to despair

IT IS not a choice most of us will ever face. Which to prefer: a mud hut in southern India's Nilgiri Hills or a home in a Glasgow slum. Two Indian researchers raised the question at the UN World Summit on Social Development, which ends in Copenhagen today.

Stan and Mari Thekaekara said that Glasgow's Easterhouse was 'soulless' and 'demoralised', its abandoned apartments reeking of decay and menace. The penniless tribesmen of the Nilgiri Hills outside Mysore were better off than the unemployed of Easterhouse. 'We had never in India met a man who had been unemployed for 20 years. We have seasonal unemployment, but not for 20 years of purposeless, meaningless existence,' they said.

Easterhouse has a reputation for joblessness, violence, drugs and rotting houses, and its health record is among the worst in Europe.

Yet when newspapers reported that Easterhouse was facing a 'meaningless future' worse than anything confronting India's peasants, locals felt no shock of recognition.

Is life, as one newspaper put it, really 'better in a mud hut than a Glasgow slum'? Have Britain's poor joined the Third – or is it Fourth World?

'My reaction is disbelief,' says Alex Hamilton, project leader with the community-based Easterhouse Project. 'How they could possibly make such a comparison is totally beyond me.'

Lazar Savarimuthli, of the Bangalore-based India Social Institute, is another sceptic. He concedes that India's poor take the initiative, but it is also true that illiteracy rates are high in the sub-continent, that many children do not attend school and there is nothing romantic about 'putting your hand in shit' to survive. 'Don't, ' he advises, 'idolise India's poverty.'

David Black, a worker with the Glasgow Healthy City Project, sponsored by the World health Organisation, argues that you cannot compare radically different cultures: 'The quality of life for the poorest in Glasgow is still better than the quality of life for the poorest in India.'

But what, equally, does 'quality of life' mean to the long-term unemployed or to those for whom drugs offer the only cash economy? The Thekaekaras confessed surprise at the 'surface wealth' of Easterhouse, but claimed that in India lack of jobs was only seasonal, that people in the hills south of Mysore took the initiative, that hope thrived.

You could say more: 13 people have died this year already in Glasgow because of drugs, on council estates suicide rates and early deaths soar above those in middle-class areas, opportunities are few and standards of health are a national disgrace.

What the Indian researchers illustrate, perhaps, is a gulf in perceptions as great as any gulf in wealth. Stan Thekaekara spoke of India's poor 'scavenging in garbage heaps of junk' and found that preferable to the supposed apathy of Easterhouse. Are we insulted or unsurprised? And whoever said Easterhouse was unique in Britain?

6.4 Reasons for unemployment in developing countries

The reasons for large-scale unemployment in the developing countries are varied. Although neo-Malthusians (see section 5.2) blame the high rates of population growth for unemployment and poverty in these locations, rapid population growth is not the only cause of these problems.

One major cause of unemployment in developing countries is **structural adjustment programmes** (**SAPs**) (see section 2.3). Alongside existing unemployment trends, there has been increasing joblessness in the formal sectors since the World Bank and International Monetary Fund (IMF) introduced SAPs. One of the conditions of World Bank and IMF loans to developing countries is that they reduce government (public) spending and adopt privatisation policies (see Fig. 2.12). In practice, such privatisation causes governments to give up control or ownership of companies and corporations and so lose valuable income. The knock-on result of this is that governments then have to remove subsidies on essential services such as health, education and transport, etc. The introduction of SAPs will, according to the World Bank, promote a **free-market economy**.

Since governments in the developing countries have always been the largest employers of labour in the formal sector, the adoption of these SAPs has led to massive job losses in countries such as Ghana, Nigeria, Brazil and Bolivia. In Ghana in particular, 28 000 jobs were lost in one year because of the structural adjustment programme imposed by the IMF.

Overall, unemployment has worsened in both developed and developing countries since the 1970s. World recession has hit manufacturing industry and so primary and secondary workers are particularly affected. This is also due to an increase in mechanisation as well as a growth of the tertiary sector.

6.5 Management of human resources in developing countries

Specific policies aimed at developing human resources include improving health care, education and training in vocational skills. However, before any improvement can be made in these areas, the promotion of better health and education is of paramount importance. This helps to reduce poverty and so bring about economic and social development (Fig.6.10, see sections 3.7, 5.3). However, the financial resources needed to improve education and health care have generally declined in many developing countries over the last 20 years (Table 6.2).

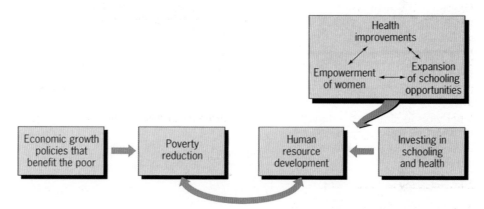

Figure 6.10 Mutually reinforcing cycles: reduction of poverty and development of human resources (*Source: World Development Report*, 1993)

Table 6.2 Government expenditure on health and education (1972–95) (*Sources*: World Development Report, 1992, 1994; Human Development Report, 1998)

Country	% of total government expenditure on education			% of total government expenditure on health		
	1972	1992	1993–95	1972	1992	1993–95
Malawi	15.8	10.4	15.0	5.5	7.8	2.3
India	2.3	2.1	—	1.5	1.6	0.7
Sri Lanka	13.0	10.1	16.9	6.4	4.8	1.4
Chile	14.5	13.3	16.3	10.0	11.1	2.5
Mexico	16.4	13.9	26.0	4.5	1.9	2.8
Brazil	8.3	3.7	—	6.7	6.9	2.7
Kenya	21.9	20.1	16.1	7.9	5.4	1.9
Tunisia	30.5	17.5	17.4	7.4	6.6	3.0
UK	2.6	13.2	11.4	12.2	13.8	5.8
South Korea	15.8	16.2	17.4	1.2	1.2	1.8

?

7a For each country listed in Table 6.2, draw two bars on one graph to show the direction and amount of change in government expenditure on health and education from 1972 to 1992.

b Comment on the trend shown by your graph.

Education

The share of world **GNP** spent on education rose in the mid-1970s and early 1980s. However, by the mid-1990s, spending on education had fallen back to the same level of 5.5 per cent as in 1970 (Fig. 6.11). This reduction in world spending on education hides an even more dramatic fall in education spending in the developing countries, especially in sub-Saharan Africa (Figs. 6.12, 6.14).

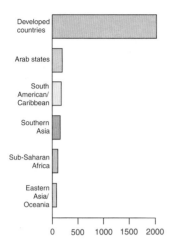

Figure 6.11 The lion's share: World spending on education (per pupil,US$)

8a Describe the regional differences in world spending on education as shown in Figure 6.11.
b Explain why government spending on education is so important to the development process.

9 Refer to Figure 6.12 and 6.15
a Suggest reasons for the gender differences in illiteracy worldwide.
b What are the implications of these gender differences for human development.

10a Referring to Figure 6.14, describe some of the consequences of reduced educational spending on pupils.
b Suggest how such government reductions might influence development in this region.

11a Compare the learning environments experienced by children in the developed and the developing countries as shown in Figures 6.13–6.14.
b What are the positive and negative images being shown in these photographs?
c What quality of life does each image convey?
d Using these images as a basis, make a list of ten factors which are important to you in deciding the quality of life of students.

Figure 6.14 Education in the Ivory Coast: most schools lack any facilities other than a blackboard

Education is also facing limitations in many developed countries because of a reduction in government spending. None the less, the experiences of children in schools here tend to differ greatly, from those in developing countries (Fig. 6.13).

Health

Total annual health spending varies enormously between developed and developing countries (Table 6.3). In 1990, the average amount spent on health per person ranged from less than US$10 in several African and Asian countries to more than US$2700 in the USA. Similarly, there were considerable variations in health spending among countries within Africa. For example, Tanzania spent only US$4 per person on health whereas Zimbabwe spent about US$42 in 1990. In Asia, the amounts spent on health in Bangladesh and South Korea were US$7 and US$377 per person respectively during the same period.

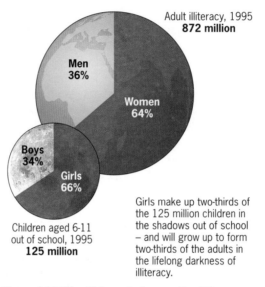

Girls make up two-thirds of the 125 million children in the shadows out of school – and will grow up to form two-thirds of the adults in the lifelong darkness of illiteracy.

Figure 6.12 The lifelong darkness after illiteracy (*Source: The New Internationalist*, No. 315, August 1999)

Figure 6.13 Education in the UK: most schools have access to the latest technology

Table 6.3 Global health expenditure (*Source: World Development Report*, 1993)

Demographic region	Percentage of world population	Total health expenditure (billions $)	Health expenditure as % of world total	Public sector health expenditure as % of regional total	Percentage of GNP spent on health	Per capita health expenditure
Established market economies	15	1483	87	60	9.2	1860
Formerly socialist economies of Europe	7	49	3	71	3.6	142
South America	8	47	3	60	4.0	105
Middle Eastern crescent	10	39	2	58	4.1	77
Other Asian countries and islands	13	42	2	39	4.5	61
India	16	18	1	22	6.0	21
China	22	13	1	59	3.5	11
Sub-Saharan Africa	10	12	1	55	4.5	24
Demographically developing countries	78	170	10	50	4.7	41
World	100	1702	100	60	8.0	329

The extent to which women are free to make decisions affecting their lives may be the key to the future, not only of the poor countries but of the richer ones too. As mothers; producers or suppliers of food, fuel and water; traders and manufacturers; political and community leaders, women are at the centre of the process of change.

Dr Nafis Sadik
(Executive Director of UNPF)

Figure 6.15 The value of women in the development process (*Source: UNPF, The State of World Population*, 1989)

Gender differences

Since the late 1970s, many development experts have recognised that women's active participation in the development process is essential (Fig. 6.15). We now know that women perform approximately two-thirds of the world's work for just 10 per cent of the world's income. In recent studies of 17 developing countries, women's work hours exceeded men's by 30 per cent. Even data from 12 developed countries found that women in formal employment worked about 20 per cent longer hours than men (Fig. 6.16).

Although women participate and are involved in all major economic activities (Table 6.4), some institutional, social, psychological and cultural obstacles still limit or tend to undermine their role in development. This is reflected by the percentage of economically active women shown in Table 6.4 which is a measure of formal jobs. As such, the statistic underplays the many millions of women and men who work in informal jobs (see section 6.2).

Despite the fact that women carry the greater share of work in most subsistence economies (Fig. 6.17), their contribution is lost because of the formal definition of work which looks at economic or monetary value. As a result, non-paid work and services provided by women in many societies remain unacknowledged. Jobs such as cooking, cleaning, caring for the family, harvesting and fetching water are not included in any economic definition of waged work, leaving women unrecognised in most employment statistics (Fig. 6.18).

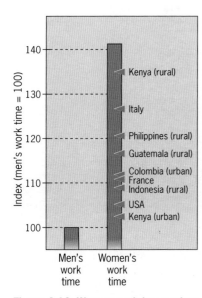

Figure 6.16 Women work longer than men (*Source:* UNDP 1995)

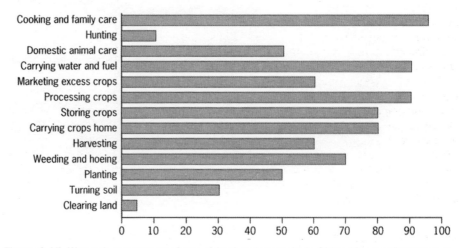

Figure 6.17 Women's percentage share of food system tasks in Africa (*Source:* Barrett and Browne, 1991)

12 Study Table 6.3 and, using a blank base map of the world, choose a suitable cartographic technique to highlight the differences in government health expenditure for all the regions listed.

13 Study Figure 6.17.
a For each of the tasks listed, identify which ones are carried out mostly by women.
b In the light of your findings, discuss how important a woman's role is in supporting a family's existence.

14 Study Table 6.4 and compare the regional variations in: • women as a percentage of the economically active population and • the ratio of females to males in each occupational group.

15a Draw a similar time chart to Figure 6.18 to show the work of a British woman.
b Compare the two charts and assess the differences in the women's lifestyles.

Because of the important role of women for both social and economic functions, particularly in developing countries, governments realise it is necessary to develop the skills and potential of women. This will then bring about further social and economic development (Fig. 6.18). Development experts accept that the physical and economic subjugation of women in the past has held back development in certain countries. In addition, the cultural pressure to have many children (see section 3.7) has serious health consequences for women (Fig. 6.19), so more and more national and international organisations are addressing the issue of women in development. Examples of such organisations are the United Nations Development Fund for Women (UNIFEM), the United Nations International Research and Training Institute for the Advancement of Women (INSTRAW) and Women in Development Expert Group (WID).

Figure 6.18 A day in the life of a typical rural African woman (*Source: Maggie Murray and Buchi Emecheta, Our Own Freedom, Sheba Feminist Publishers*)

Table 6.4 Women's economic activities in selected countries (*Source: The world's women, UN Press, 1991*)

| | | | Occupational groups (females per 100 males) 1980s | | | |
		Women as percentage of economically active population (1990)	Administrative and managerial workers	Clerical/sales service workers	Production and transport	Agriculture
Developed economies	Australia	38	42	138	28	30
	USA	41	61	183	23	19
	France	40	10	164	18	48
	Portugal	37	17	108	34	101
	UK	39	29	225	18	18
Africa	Cameroon	33	6	26	9	82
	Egypt	10	16	23	6	26
	Zambia	28	12	44	6	26
	Gambia	40	17	57	16	98
	Zimbabwe	34	17	57	16	98
South America and Caribbean	Costa Rica	22	29	95	25	5
	Ecuador	19	18	79	13	8
	Mexico	27	18	98	21	5
	Paraguay	21	58	98	21	5
	Venezuela	28	17	86	11	4
Asia	Bangladesh	7	2	29	20	1
	China	43	12	71	55	88
	India	25	2	11	15	31
	Sri Lanka	27	7	35	31	51
	Turkey	34	3	14	9	109

Figure 6.19 The links between female education, human development and economic development (*Source:* Barrett and Browne, 1991)

Break the chain

The World Bank has said the chain of poor maternal health has to be broken by special emphasis being placed on adolescent girls, to stop the cycle of early childbearing, poor health and nutrition, and poverty.

About 500 000 women world-wide die as a result of too many pregnancies, too close together and too young.

The World Bank confirms the situation is worst in developing countries where 'women's disproportionate poverty, low social status and reproductive role expose them to high health risks, resulting in needless and largely preventable suffering and premature death'.

Citing statistics which show that one thousand women die in childbirth each day, Ann Tinker, the organisation's senior health adviser, said the World Bank plans to push for greater investment in 'a holistic approach to women's health', which includes issues such as gender discrimination in nutrition and health care during childhood, early pregnancy and adolescence and violence against women.

Figure 6.20 Maternal health

?

16 Use Figure 6.19 to explain the links between education, health and development.

17 Read Figure 6.20 and assess how frequent pregnancies affect women's health and their contribution to economic development.

Women and education

If access to education and the acquisition of skills are essential for finding secure and waged employment, women are at a distinct disadvantage when compared with men. As seen in Chapter 3, for social and cultural reasons females usually have lower school enrolment and higher drop-out rates in the poor nations of Asia and Africa (Fig.6.21). Social pressures cause women to have children and become principal carer and provider at an early age. An estimated 90 million girls in the world have no education at all and of the 960 million illiterate people in the world, two-thirds are women.

Cultural influences

Apart from unequal access to education, some cultures, religions and traditional customs in the developing world are very repressive to women (see section 3.7). Even in some developed countries, women still do not have equal status with men. In certain Muslim and Hindu societies, such as Pakistan and India, purdah is practised. This is the custom of keeping women in seclusion with clothing that conceals them completely when they go out. This custom often prevents women from taking an active part in social, economic and political activities outside their homes.

Similarly, certain religions, such as Hinduism, actively discriminate against women. Because of their belief, some parents prefer baby boys to girls (see section 5.6). This sometimes results in female infanticide, and widow burning (*suttee*) is still (though very rarely) practised in rural parts of India. Also, as women are generally expected to marry and leave home, their families do not consider the education of female children a priority.

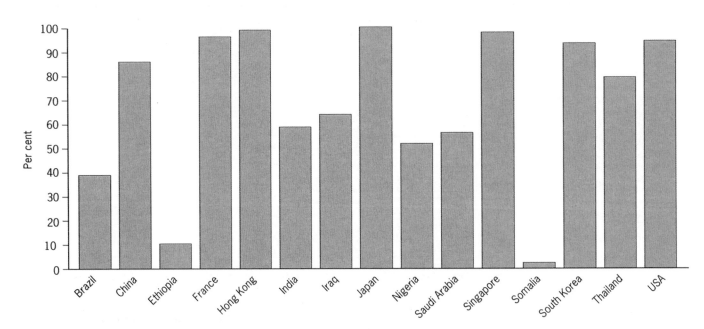

Figure 6.21 Percentage of girls reaching their final year of primary education, 1994 (*Source:* UNICEF, *The Progress of the Nations*, 1994)

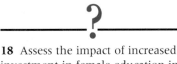

18 Assess the impact of increased investment in female education in the developing countries with relation to:
• population growth rates
• life expectancy
• health care
• family structure
• generation of income.

19 Use all the information in section 6.5. What are the implications of the global variations in health and education spending on human resource development and the potential to industrialise?

6.6 Development strategies and industrialisation

In both developed and developing countries, there are four major categories of industry, or economic activity (Table 6.5).

Table 6.5 Definitions of employment sectors

Economic sector	Definition	Examples from developing countries
Primary	Exploitation of natural resources; includes people working in agriculture, forestry, mining and fishing	Copper mines of Zaire and Zambia; tin mines of Nigeria; growing jute in Bangladesh; oil palm plantations in Nigeria
Secondary	Manufacturing products from raw materials for either domestic consumption or export. Import-substitution industries produce goods protected by tariffs, quotas and favourable taxes. Governments use these to replace imported manufactured goods, boost domestic industry and reduce foreign exchange deficits	Processing cocoa in Ghana and Sierra Leone for export for chocolate production; textiles in India for export for clothing manufacture; producing bread for domestic consumption in Nigeria
Tertiary	Jobs where people provide services to other people and industries	Transport; retailing; financial services
Quarternary	Jobs where people supply information or expertise	Hi-tech; information services; education

The influence of industrialised countries

In the nineteenth century, many countries in Europe and North America experienced rapid industrialisation and urbanisation. Successful industrialisation led to economic growth and prosperity for these now developed countries.

In response to this, many developing countries in the late twentieth century see industry as the basis for their economic development. However, while in many developed countries the industry and service sectors contribute a significant proportion to their GDPs (Table 6.6), the proportions are very different in many developing countries (Table 6.7). The 24 countries that make up the Organisation for Economic Co-operation and Development (OECD), otherwise known as the 'rich man's club', produce three-quarters of the world's industrial output.

20 Use Tables 6.6 and 6.7.
a Choose a suitable statistical technique to measure the relationship between GDP per capita and the percentage contribution from agriculture in both developed and developing countries.
b Comment on your results and suggest reasons for any differences.

21 You are a researcher for the World Bank and have to give a general report on the links between world industrial sectors and economic development.
a Compare the percentage contributions made by:
• agriculture, • manufacturing industry and • services to the GDPs of both developed and developing countries.
b Using triangular graph paper, plot the figures from both tables to show the relative contributions of the different sectors to the total GDPs of both developed and developing countries.
c Write your assessment of world economic development using contrasting countries. Draw conclusions from your comparisons made in a and b.

Table 6.6 Percentage contribution of agriculture, industry and services to gross domestic product in selected (OECD) countries, 1997 (*Sources:* World Development Report, 1998/99, Human Development Report 1998).

Country	GDP (million US$)	GDP per capita (US$)	Percentage contribution of agriculture	Percentage contribution of industry	Percentage contribution of services
Australia	391 045	19 632	4	28	68
Austria	206 239	21 322	2	31	68
Denmark	161 107	21 983	4	29	67
Finland	116 170	18 547	6	37	57
France	1 396 540	21 176	2	26	71
Italy	1 145 370	20 174	3	31	66
Japan	4 201 636	21 930	2	38	60
Netherlands	360 472	19 876	3	27	70
Norway	153 403	22 427	2	30	68
Sweden	227 751	19 297	2	32	66
Turkey	181 464	5 516	17	28	55
UK	1 271 710	19 302	2	32	66

Table 6.7 Percentage contribution of agriculture, industry and services to gross domestic product in selected developing countries, 1997 (*Sources:* World Development Report, 1998/99, Human Development Report 1998).

Country	GDP (million US$)	GDP per capita (US$)	Percentage contribution of agriculture	Percentage contribution of industry	Percentage contribution of services
Algeria	45 997	5 618	12	51	37
Bangladesh	32 838	1 382	30	17	53
Botswana	4 000	5 611	5	46	48
Cameron	9 115	2 355	41	20	39
Ethiopia	6 330	455	56	7	37
Gabon	5 435	3 766	7	52	42
Ghana	6 762	2 032	47	17	36
India	359 812	1 422	27	30	43
Morocco	33 258	3 477	20	31	49
Namibia	3 453	4 054	14	34	52
Panama	8 244	6 258	8	18	73
Sierra Leone	940	625	44	24	32
Tunisia	19 069	5 261	14	28	58
Uganda	6 555	1 483	44	17	39

Rostow's model of economic development

Based on the experiences of the rich industrialised nations, economists during the 1950s and the 1960s developed a number of general theories of economic growth. An American, W W Rostow, published his model in 1960 and this is now called a 'linear-stages' theory of development (Fig. 6.22). We can use it to analyse the experiences of a number of countries at different stages of development (Fig. 6.23).

Rostow's model is particularly concerned with the stages countries go through to achieve economic growth and these are dependent on capital. Rostow proposes that countries can develop if they save 5–10 per cent of their national income and invest these savings in manufacturing industry.

The model gives investment as the key to economic growth. With increasing investment in industry, a country will move from a subsistence-based economy (stage 1) to an economy dominated by the production of consumer goods and tertiary and quarternary industries (stages 4–5).

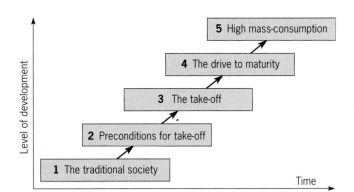

Stage 1: A subsistence economy using limited technology. The society is self-sufficient and relatively isolated.

Stage 2: Outside influences lead to the development of industries based around local resources. Agriculture is more commercialised and becomes mechanised. Improvements in infrastructure encourage trade. Urbanisation begins. Investment in manufacturing industry is 5–10% of GDP.

Stage 3: An important stage lasting 20–30 years during which the country accumulates wealth by trade. Investment in technology for manufacturing to produce goods for exports, thus generating wealth for the next stage.

Stage 4: Economic growth should by now be self-sustaining. This spreads to all parts of the country because of the multiplier effect. More complex transport systems develop and technology continues to improve. Some early infant industries decline. A broad industrial base leads to the creation of wealth which can be invested in social and welfare provision.

Stage 5: Rapid expansion of tertiary activities and high employment in services result in a decline in manufacturing employment. Social and welfare facilities continue to expand. Mature industries thrive using high level technology to produce consumer durables.

Figure 6.22 Rostow's linear-stages model of economic growth

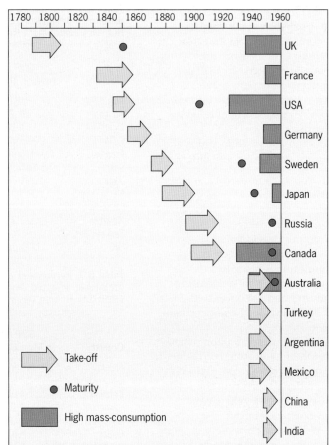

Figure 6.23 Application of Rostow's model in selected countries (*After:* Horsfall, *Manufacturing Industry*, Blackwell, 1977)

22 Use Figure 6.22 to compare and contrast the time lags between the take-off and high mass consumption periods for each country in Figure 6.23.

Rostow's model implies that developing countries need to follow the stages of development experienced by the western industrialised nations (see Fig. 3.24). The model also assumes that developed countries can sell technology to the developing countries to stimulate industrial output in these poorer areas. An increase in wealth, brought about by the use of modern technology, will therefore make it possible for developing countries to invest increasing amounts of their income in manufacturing industry. According to the model, this will enable developing countries to 'take off' economically.

Weaknesses of Rostow's model

Critics of Rostow suggest that the model is too simplistic. They dispute its assumption that the experiences of developed countries are appropriate for all developing countries.

Resources

Countries which were among the first to industrialise, such as the UK, had access to enormous amounts of natural resources both at home and in their colonies. However, developing countries of the twentieth century have access to relatively fewer natural resources. Contrary to Rostow, therefore, it is unlikely that the past experiences of developed countries will, or can, be followed by all the developing countries.

Markets

The UK also had huge world markets to supply during its early stages of industrial development. Although the economies of other European countries and those of North America used tariffs to protect themselves from UK-made

23 Discuss the extent to which Rostow's model applies to the developing countries today. Refer to specific examples in your answer.

24 Could a Stage 6 be added to Rostow's five stages? If so, what would the features of such a stage be? Give reasons for your answer.

goods, and so also prospered, the UK still had the huge market of her colonies. The income from these markets made investments in industry possible, leading to further economic growth. The UK was therefore able to pass through to the take-off stage. The developing countries today do not have such market opportunities either at home or abroad. Their domestic markets tend to be limited in terms of purchasing power, while the conditions of world trade restrict developing countries from competing favourably on world markets (see Chapter 8). This is because of high **tariffs** imposed by developed countries on the import of finished goods. Consequently, developing countries are forced to export materials in only a raw or semi-finished state. Overall, therefore, these problems mean that the capital necessary for investment, as stressed by Rostow, is simply not available.

6.7 The emergence of newly industrialising countries

There were a number of countries during the 1980s and early 90s in Asia and South America that showed a reasonable level of industrialisation. These were known as the newly industrialising countries (NICs) and have experienced rapid growth in their manufacturing output and exports over recent decades. Their economies have expanded much faster than the economies of developed countries in terms of real GDP growth (Fig. 6.24).

We may refer to countries such as Brazil and Mexico as newly industrialising, but the Asian NICs were, in many ways, the most economically successful. This group includes, among others, South Korea, Taiwan, Thailand, Malaysia, Hong Kong and Singapore (Table 6.8).

Some of the reasons for the economic successes of these countries are explained below. However, more recently during the late 1990s, there has been economic downturn especially in East Asia (see case study).

Figure 6.24 Average annual % growth of GDP in selected countries (*Source:* World Development Report, 1998–99)

Table 6.8 General indicators for selected NICs. 1998. (Sources: Population Reference Bureau, World population Data Sheet, Book Edition 1998, The World Bank Group, World Development Indicators 1999, Human Development Report 1998)

Country	Population (millions) 1998	Population growth rate %	% under 15 years	% over 65 years	Average life expectancy at birth	GNP per capita $ 1997	Human Development Index
Brazil	162.1	1.4	32	6	67	4 790	0.809
Hong Kong	6.7	0.4	18	10	79	25 200	0.909
Malaysia	22.2	2.1	35	4	72	4 530	0.834
Mexico	97.5	2.2	36	4	72	3 700	0.855
Singapore	3.9	1.1	23	7	77	32 810	0.896
South Korea	46.4	1.0	22	6	74	10 550	0.894
Taiwan	21.7	1.0	23	8	75	—	—
Thailand	61.1	1.1	27	5	69	2 740	0.838

25 Study Table 6.8.
a Rank the countries listed in order of GNP per capita.
b Using the other indicators of development, comment on the relationship between level of GNP and standard of living.
c Compare the standard of living in these NICs with that of selected African countries in Table 1.6.

The rise of Hong Kong, Singapore, Taiwan and South Korea
The reasons for the success of these Asian NICs (otherwise known as the 'Little Tigers') vary from country to country (Fig. 6.24).

The importance of human resources
Due to a combination of large-scale immigration and high population growth rates, each of the four countries has a large workforce. During the 1950s and 1960s, the NICs specialised in traditional, labour-intensive industries, such as textiles, clothing, footwear and leather products, making the best use of their workforce. During the 1960s and 1970s the NIC governments used this cheap labour as a major resource in their development plans. One obvious result of cheap labour was the relocation of transnational corporations (TNCs),

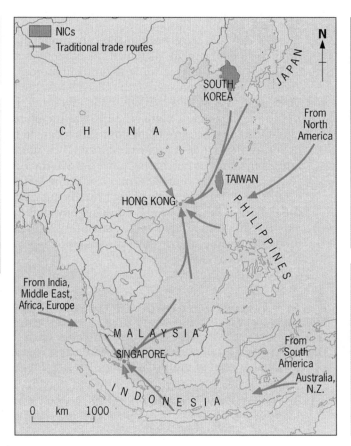

General problems
- Lack a raw material base
- Lack wealthy domestic markets

General advantages
- Relatively well–educated workforce
- Adoption of export–oriented policies
- Beneficial interventionist policies of own governments
- Influence of Japan and the USA in establishing industries and in technology transfer
- Hong Kong used as China's back door

Historical advantages
- Convergence of trade routes
- Influence of British Empire's worldwide trading network on Hong Kong and Singapore
- Hong Kong and Singapore developed as entrepôts, i.e. ports without duties
- Industry, transport links, trade and education of Taiwan and South Korea influenced by Japanese colonial rule and domination until 1945; adoption of Japanese work ethic
- Substantial economic and technical aid and investment given by USA to Taiwan and South Korea, 1951–65

Historical disadvantages
- Immigration since WW2 from China into Hong Kong and Singapore
- Korea devastated and divided after 1950–53 Korean war
- Taiwan received huge numbers of Chinese refugees after 1949 changing the island's demography and politics
- Singapore's withdrawal from the Federation of Malaysia (1965) meant loss of access to raw materials

Figure 6.25 South-East Asia's newly industrialising countries

Figure 6.26 Changing structure of exports from selected NICs 1960–92 (*Source*: World Bank)

particularly those from Japan, to the NICs. The TNCs then gained the economic advantages of low labour costs, while people in the NICs were employed and the countries invested in the industrial process. Since then, the NICs have developed more capital-intensive mature industries, such as electronics, and now export a wider range of products. (Fig. 6.26).

Human influences

With both the colonial and industrial influence of Japan came the adoption of the 'Japanese work ethic'. This is the belief in the virtue of hard work, allegiance to employers and the importance of harmony in the workplace.

We can also see the influence of other countries through political factors. Many capitalist entrepreneurs fled from Communist China and set up businesses in places such as Taiwan and Hong Kong. Similarly, many Chinese from Malaysia migrated to Singapore also seeking greater business opportunities (see section 4.7).

Education

The levels of education in these four NICs are relatively high, certainly higher than in most African countries (see Figs 6.21, 6.12). A common feature of the NICs is that their governments have always shown a commitment to improving the quality of education for their people. In fact, everybody in Taiwan, Singapore, Hong Kong and South Korea has access to primary and secondary school facilities. Even female enrolment in education is high (Table 6.9). Literacy rates are high, and the numbers of people receiving higher education are increasing.

Industrial changes

With such human influences from abroad and a workforce which is being increasingly educated, the NICs have successfully improved both the skills and

26 Study Figure 6.26 and describe the changing structure of exports for each country for the period 1960–92.

27 Explain why the use of human resources has allowed the Asian group of NICs to develop their industries successfully.

28a Assess the influence of Japan in the emergence of the Asian NICs.
b In which ways has Japan benefited from economic ties with these NICs?

29a Draw a diagram to illustrate the linkages which might develop between industries in a typical NIC.
b Describe how these linkages might influence the growth or decline of the economy.

30 Analyse the four Asian NICs and identify common factors in their economic success.

Table 6.9 Female enrolment in education (per cent of total number in educational age group), 1988–90 and female literacy rates, 1989 (*Sources: Human Development Report*, United Nations Development Programme, 1993; Infrastructure for Development, *World Development Report*, World Bank, 1994)

Region	Country	Primary	Secondary	Tertiary	Female literacy rates (age 15–24)
NICs	Philippines	98	75	28	92
	Thailand	88	32	16	96
	Malaysia	93	58	7	83
	South Korea	100	86	28	—
	Singapore	100	71	—	96
Africa	Ethiopia	24	12	1	—
	Malawi	52	3	1	31
	Nigeria	62	17	2	31
	Sudan	43	17	2	14
	Mali	14	4	1	14
	Kenya	93	19	1	49

NB: In most countries primary age group is 6–11 years, secondary age group 12–16 and tertiary age is over 16 years.

productivity of their people. This enables the NICs to use their human resources to the utmost and so develop new areas of **comparative advantage**, that is, provide cost advantages for the production of certain products. For example, the NICs traditionally enjoyed comparative advantages in the textiles and footwear industries because of their cheap labour. However, as living standards have risen in the NICs, labour is no longer as cheap and such products are manufactured more cheaply elsewhere. Countries like India and Bangladesh have developed their own textile industries using even cheaper labour. The NICs have therefore had to diversify their industrial base because of the increased competition and reduction of potential markets.

In response, the NICs shifted to less labour-intensive, more skill-intensive and more technologically advanced industries (Fig. 6.27). These include electronics, machinery, motor vehicles and chemicals.

As the range of skills of the workforce improves, including management techniques, the production process becomes more efficient and technologically more advanced goods will be developed. This trend conforms with the product life theory, which suggests that countries at different stages of development will produce different kinds of products, which will eventually be replaced as technology progresses.

Figure 6.27 Hi-tech industry: working on circuit boards, Taipei, Taiwan

The East Asian Crisis

Although the NICs in Asia and South America have experienced significant growth in levels of economic and social development during the last two decades, a recent down-turn in the economies of these nations has put the sustainability of these economic successes in doubt. The biggest setback to human development in the NICs has been the East Asian economic crisis of the late 1990s, which has mostly affected countries such as Indonesia, the Republic of Korea, Malaysia, the Philippines and Thailand.

A sudden and dramatic crisis in the financial sector of the economies of these countries has resulted in falling GDPs, soaring unemployment, deep cuts in public expenditure, rapid inflation and severe declines in consumption. A dramatic change in the commercial banks' monetary inflows and outflows, and the consequent shortage of funds to invest in the domestic economy, has been blamed for this crisis. The economic growth prospects for these countries have been severely affected by this financial crisis (Table 6.10). During the last five years, government expenditures on healthcare and education in many Asian countries have declined with the growing prospect of a rise in poverty levels, especially in countries such as Indonesia and Malaysia. Many economic observers now believe that this crisis marks the end of the economic miracles that have sustained the NICs during the last few decades as economic growth forecasts for the year 2000 predict a steady decline (Table 6.11).

The international community, through the International Monetary Fund (IMF), has responded to the crisis in East Asia by providing over $100 billion of financial support to the countries affected by sudden economic collapse. However, some observers have criticised this move as too little, too late to ameliorate the effects of the crisis. Given that many emerging nations are particularly vulnerable to financial

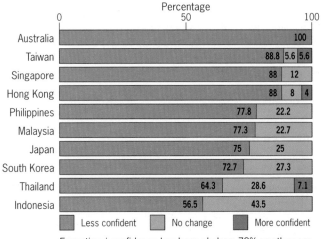

Executives' confidence has been shaken: 79% say they are now less confident of doing business in the country. Only in Thailand (7.1%), Taiwan (5.6%) and Hong Kong (4%) did any respondents say they are now more confident.

Figure 6.28 Doing business in Indonesia (*Source: Far Eastern Economic Review*, Sept. 30 1999)

instability, others have argued that much more needs to be done by both the national governments and the international community to protect people from the consequences of such an economic collapse. Rather than providing financial support, emphasis, according to this viewpoint, should be focused on the human dimension of such crises by protecting people through initiatives that include public employment schemes, food provision for the vulnerable and credit allocations for both small businesses and low-income households.

The economic instability in East Asia has underlined the need for all newly industrialising countries to create systems of insurance for the unemployed, as recently introduced in the Republic of Korea. The Asian crisis also provides an opportunity for national governments in these countries to rethink their economic strategies. If the growth of the last two decades is to be sustained into the next century, there is the need for fundamental social and political changes in relation to national economic strategies in the NICs.

Political instability in East Timor

One recent event that has had an adverse effect on the economic prosperity of the region has been the political crisis in East Timor. Following the 1999 public ballot, 78 per cent of East Timorese voted in favour of independence from Indonesia. As a result, Indonesian forces invaded East Timor during which thousands of civilians were killed and many more were forced to seek refuge in the mountains. This political unrest has

Table 6.10 East Asia: Economic growth forecasts (*Source: Far Eastern Economic Review*, September 30, 1999)

| Country | Economic Growth (%) | | | |
	1997 (actual)	1998 (estimate)	1999 (forecast)	2000 (forecast)
China	8.8	7.8	8.2	8.4
Hong Kong	5.3	−5.1	−1.0	1.5
Taiwan	6.8	4.8	4.5	4.9
Indonesia	4.9	−13.4	−1.7	2.5
Malaysia	7.5	−7.5	3.0	5.0
Philippines	5.2	−0.5	2.4	3.0
Singapore	8.0	1.5	4.0	4.8
Thailand	−1.3	−9.4	1.5	3.0
Japan	−0.7	−2.1	0.9	0.0
South Korea	5.0	−5.8	7.0	5.0

* Forecasts

created unfavourable economic conditions and damaged the confidence of potential investors (Fig. 6.28).

Because of the strategic importance of Indonesia in the East Asian region, western governments have, for a long time, had special interests in this country. For many years, the West has supplied arms to Indonesia and has played a significant role in the economic development of the country. Generous loan facilities from the World Bank have helped maintain investment in all sectors of the Indonesian economy such as health, education and tourism. Many people fear that the

recent political crisis in East Timor will reverse the progress made in development in recent years (Figs 6.29 and 6.30).

Table 6.11 East Asia: Investment and growth prospects (annual average) (*Source: Far Eastern Economic Review*, September 30, 1999)

Country	Gross domestic fixed investment (% of GDP)		Real GDP growth (%)	
	1993–96	2001–10*	1993–96	2001–10*
China	33.2	32	11.6	8.0
Hong Kong	31.1	28	5.1	4.0
India	21.8	24	6.5	6.0
Indonesia	28.5	26	7.5	6.5
South Korea	37.2	30	7.6	5.5
Malaysia	42.6	30	8.8	6.0
Philippines	23.2	24	4.2	6.0
Singapore	36.3	30	9.1	5.0
Taiwan	23.8	22	6.1	5.0
Thailand	41.6	30	8.1	6.0

* Forecasts

How the world bought its stake

International loans
The IMF, the World Bank and Western governments bailed out to the Indonesian government with a £20.60bn ($33 bn) loan, after the rupiah for everybody was hit by the Asian financial crisis in autumn 1997. Not all of the money was dispersed after the government dragged its feet on economic reforms the IMF demanded in return for the bailout. But the World Bank lent an additional £12.5bn ($20bn) for other development projects. Indonesia currently owes the Bank and the IMF £12.75bn and about ($13.5bn) to Western governments.

Commercial bank loans
The rupiah's fall burnt many Western banks, including HSBC, Standard Chartered, Schroders, NatWest and Barclays, which were large lenders to Indonesian companies. At the end of last year Indonesia owed Western banks £30.75bn.

Arms
France and Britain are the biggest exporters of arms to Indonesia. UK exports last year were worth £112m and French exports are roughly double that figure.

Oil and natural gas
Indonesia produced about 1.5m barrels of oil a day last year, just over 2% of world output. Caltex, a joint venture between US companies, Chevron and Texaco, is the biggest oil producer in the country. The state-owned oil company, Pertamina, lost its monopoly over awarding contracts to foreign firms earlier this year after corruption over the deals was exposed.

Tourism
Indonesia attracted 3.9m visitors last year, who spent the equivalent of £3.8bn.

Figure 6.29 The west's economic involvment in Indonesia

Loans to Jakarta test nerve of west

The financial state of Indonesia is so precarious that even the mildest political tremors could send the economy back to the worst days of 1998, when gross domestic product plummeted by 16%, making the country a worse basket case than even Russia.

The strategic importance of Indonesia has long been recognised by the West. In the second world war one of the key allied objectives in the Pacific was to block the Japanese access to what was then the Dutch East Indies, with it's natural resources including oil.

In more modern times the importance has been conferred on the country by its size and scale. It is one of the most populace countries in the world, with 204m people living on hundreds of islands with a surface area of 1905 sq km, two-thirds of the land mass of India. The country's shrinking gross domestic product of $138.5bn makes it the 28th largest economy in the world.

In the period 1989-93, when the Asian model was being lauded throughout the West, Indonesia enjoyed economic expansion on an impres-

sive scale; growth climbed by 7% a year. But as Jeffrey Henderson of the Manchester Business School has observed, despite the veneer of success, it was among the "industrially least advanced of the East Asian economies".

The World Bank is intimately involved too. By March this year the Bank's lending to Indonesia approached $25bn, of which $19.8bn have already been advanced.

Under its current President, James Wolfensohn, the Bank has sort to use Indonesia as a test bed for new standards of good governance and transparency. It has become embroiled in almost every aspect of the Indonesia economy, from the banking system to health care projects and educational schemes. It seeks to hold the Jakarta government to it's promises by publishing agreements on the internet and focusing on parts of the economy such as social security and corruption, which in the Suharto years would considered untouchable.

The Bank's insistence on better governance has meant it has been scrupulous in its dealings. Earlier this year it held up a negotiated $600m

budget support loan to the government because it feared that some of the funds might find their way into the pockets of the pro-government parties before the June 7 elections. Although in the past it has been widely criticised for helping to prop up authoritarian and corrupt the regimes through generous loan programmes, now it is also likely to a halt the programmes in response to the complaints of protesters or non-governmental organisations.

This means, in effect, both the IMF and the World Bank ought to be very sensitive to the present stand-off in East Timor and prepared to freeze, if not halt, lending on the grounds that the money could easily be redeployed to pay the militias and security forces responsible for the bloodshed in East Timor.

The West is plainly concerned about using the financial weapon in Indonesia because of its broader implications. The Jakarta stock market slumped 4% on Monday as the crisis deepened. The risk is that contagion will set in across the region and that the whole of the Asian economic recovery could be jeopardised.

Figure 6.30 (*Source: The Guardian*, 8 September 1999)

With so many commodity producers and so few buyers the price will tend to stay low

Cereals
5 companies
77%

Bananas
3 companies
80%

Cocoa
3 companies
83%

Tea
3 companies
85%

Tobacco
4 companies
87%

Figure 6.31 Percentage market share of transnational companies in world primary commodity trade (*Source:* Christian Aid, *A Raw Deal*, 1992)

6.8 Transnational corporations and economic dependency

Transnational corporations (TNCs) are very large firms with branches, or subsidiary companies, in more than one country. Since World War 2 there has been a considerable increase in the number of TNCs as they have taken over smaller firms. More recently, their numbers are falling as individual TNCs have merged with others. As a result, these bigger organisations hold even more economic power and influence. The main advantage of TNCs is the large scale of their operations which enables them to run efficiently and reduce operational costs. TNCs have the capital to establish large plants which lower unit costs and this allows them to make savings known as economies of scale. Reduced costs from mass production lead to increased profits and so TNCs can invest heavily in research, marketing, advertising and general development. This concentrated investment increases competition in the global markets.

Companies such as Nestlé, Hitachi and Unilever each have turnovers of approximately UK£20 billion per annum. In 1992, this exceeded the total value of the exports of all but five of the world's developing countries. In the mid-1990s, just 500 TNCs controlled 70 per cent of world trade, 80 per cent of world investment and 30 per cent of the global GDP.

Developing countries and TNCs

TNCs have a very powerful influence on developing countries and their economies. In many cases, the corporations control most, if not all, activities involved with a product from producing the raw material, through to processing, packaging, transport, advertising and sales. TNCs now tend to dominate the world's primary production (Fig. 6.31). Unilever, with its subsidiaries Lipton and Brooke Bond, for example, controls at least 30 per cent of world tea production, processing and trade.

Investment

Many TNCs provide developing countries with necessary investment and the provision of skills and technology. None the less, the growing influence and economic power of the TNCs in developing countries can create some long-term economic and political problems for their host nations. For example, a TNC may decide to switch production from one country to another, or it may radically change its production processes and operational strategies by, for instance, either increasing production or closing a branch plant. Such decisions are usually made thousands of miles away at the TNC headquarters.

31 Describe the stages of income generation and regional economic growth which follow the establishment of a TNC in:
• a developed country and
• a developing country.

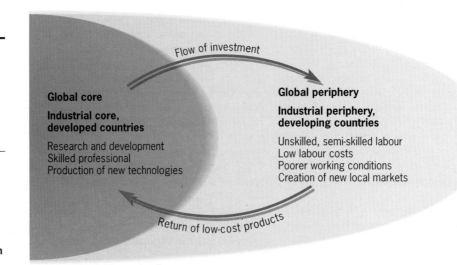

Flow of investment

Global core

Industrial core, developed countries

Research and development
Skilled professional
Production of new technologies

Global periphery

Industrial periphery, developing countries

Unskilled, semi-skilled labour
Low labour costs
Poorer working conditions
Creation of new local markets

Return of low-cost products

Figure 6.32 The international division of labour

Figure 6.33 The structure of a typical TNC: Nike

Decision-making

The headquarters and research and development activities of TNCs are most likely to be based in the developed countries of Western Europe, the USA and Japan, where the companies had their origins. These major decision-making regions constitute the global core, while the developing countries (where the TNCs locate their routine production activities) are the peripheral regions (Fig. 6.32, see section 1.4).

Nike worldwide

An example of a TNC with different operations spread through numerous countries is Nike (Fig. 6.33). Nike operates in more than 80 countries worldwide. The company has three major headquarters in Hong Kong (covering Asia), the Netherlands (covering Europe) and the USA (covering the world). Sections of the operation's functions are divided globally, with design taking place in America, Asia and Europe. Manufacturing of key technical components occurs in America while subcontractors in Asia manufacture whole shoes.

Nike views its Far Eastern subcontractors as partners who are responsible for the quality of goods leaving their own factories. In addition to delegating responsibility to local factories in this way, Nike also involves the local companies in decision-making and some research and development. Company policy also tries to provide some security for factories, workers and their country of location. Nike does this by guaranteeing with the factories that their orders for new products will not vary more than 20 per cent a month.

Overdependency

There are three main ways in which TNCs may affect the future of developing countries:

- TNC economic domination can discourage local investment and damage indigenous enterprise.
- Dependency on the investment and employment provided by a TNC may result in the host country losing control of its own economy, e.g. as the TNC makes decisions for its own profit and not the long-term economic prosperity of the host country.
- The operations of TNCs may affect the welfare of the local community and the protection of the natural environment.

We can see the worst effects of TNCs in the case of the American-owned TNC, Union Carbide in India. The factory, which produced pesticides, was located 5 km from the densely populated Bhopal in Madhya Pradesh. In December 1984, 45 tonnes of methycyanate gas leaked from the factory and drifted over a 7 km area. An estimated 2500 people died and over 200 000

Figure 6.34 TNC damage: Bhopal residents demonstrate against Union Carbide, 1984

were injured from cyanide-related poisoning. The Indian government filed for compensation from Union Carbide but with the closure of the company, victims are still waiting to receive compensation (Fig. 6.34).

Free trade zones

To attract TNCs to locate within developing countries, many of them are establishing free trade zones (Fig. 6.35).

Table 6.12 Advantages and disadvantages of TNCs in the host countries

Advantages to the country	Disadvantages
• Provides secure employment (in the local area) and a guaranteed income.	• Capital intensive nature of modern industry results in relatively small numbers being employed.
• Improves levels of education and skills.	• Wages usually low. Profits usually go overseas.
• Brings investment into the country and boosts exports to help the balance of payments (increased GDP).	• GNP grows at a slower rate than that of the parent company's, widening the gap between developed and developing countries.
• Increased personal income can lead to increased demand for consumer goods and the growth of new industries.	• Decisions are made outside the country and the company could decide to withdraw at any time.
• Widens the economic base of the country.	• Exploitation of the workforce.
• Improvements in roads and other parts of the infrastructure.	• Insufficient attention paid to health and safety factors or protection of the environment.
• Brings new technology to a developing country.	

Figure 6.35 The elements of free trade zones

?

32 Study Table 6.12 and consider whether the advantages of TNCs outweigh their disadvantages for the host countries.

33 Write an article for a current affairs magazine, such as *New Internationalist*, stating your own opinion towards the presence of TNCs in many developing countries. Give reasons and examples to back up your statements.

34 Design your own model of economic development along similar lines to that of Rostow's model (see section 6.6). Include the 'human' side of the industrialisation process, such as health and education, which Rostow's model omits.

Since the early 1970s, the United Nations has been discussing a code of conduct for transnationals to establish rights and duties for both TNCs and the host countries. However, such an international agreement has proved impossible to make, primarily because of the TNCs' economic power and desire to increase their own profits. Even on a national level, when companies are threatened by regulations, they can simply close their operations and shift to another country in search of increasing profits.

Summary

- Development of human resources is essential for successful industrialisation.

- Investment in health and education is an important strategy for developing a country's human resources.

- In the developing countries, most people are employed in the informal sector.

- The weak industrial base of many developing countries means that fewer people are employed in the formal sector.

- Structural adjustment programmes introduced in many developing countries by the World Bank and IMF have led to growing levels of unemployment.

- The important role women play in social and economic activities should not be overlooked in any development strategies.

- Industrialisation has been regarded as essential to economic development since World War 2.

- Newly industrialising countries have managed to industrialise successfully by the efficient management of their human resources.

- Transnational corporations play a vital, but sometimes controversial, role in the industrial development of many countries.

7 Natural resources and development

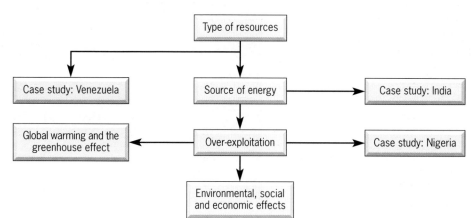

7.1 Introduction

The availability of natural resources is critical for economic development. Equally important are the uses to which resources are put and the need to manage non-renewable resources.

In this chapter, we identify the different types of natural resources and their uneven distribution. We also look at the different rates of consumption between **developed** and **developing countries** and the implications of this for all countries. We can then assess the wide gap between the wealth of the North and the poverty of the South, according to their access to and use of resources. In the light of this, we will consider the issue of **sustainability** and the growing problem of environmental pollution.

7.2 The types, nature and use of resources

A resource is something which people use to survive, to generate wealth or simply enjoy. Clean air, water and food are all basic resources which we sometimes take for granted. In fact, the earth has a vast range of natural resources which are usually divided into two categories: renewable and non-renewable (Fig. 7.1).

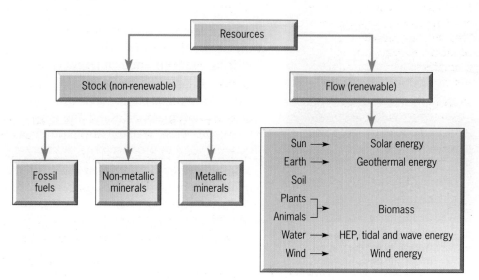

Figure 7.1 Classification of resources

Figure 7.2 Depleting renewable resources: unloading cod at Petty Harbour, the Grand Banks of Newfoundland, Canada, once the world's richest fishery. Scientists 'managing' the Banks set catch limits to allow stocks to recover but the cod catch fell from 810 000 tonnes in 1968 to 150 000 tonnes in 1977 to estimates of existing stock at 120 000 in 1992. In 1993, fishing at Grand Banks was banned altogether because there were barely enough cod to spawn.

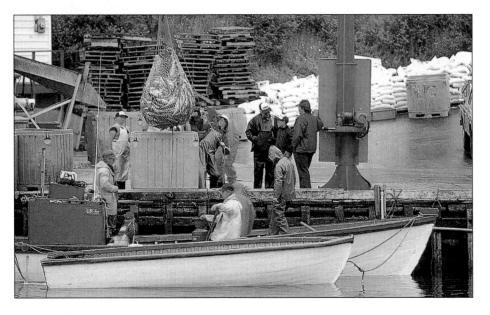

Table 7.1 Estimated reserves of minerals

Mineral	Years
Lead	50
Copper	120
Tin	150
Platinum group	340
Nickel	1500

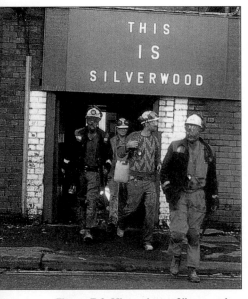

Figure 7.3 Miners leave Silverwood colliery, Yorkshire for the last time, 1992. The pit closed down when diminishing reserves of coal became too expensive to mine.

Renewable resources

We can use a renewable resource over and over again. Soil, water, plants and animals are all renewable (**non-finite**) resources. For example, farmers use the same fields to grow crops year after year. So, in this sense, the land is renewable. Nutrients taken from the soil by plants, are returned as the plants die and decompose. The soil therefore regenerates naturally, provided the land is not used for the same crop for too many years.

However, a resource is only renewable if the rate at which it is used, the rate of depletion, does not exceed the rate at which it can regenerate itself. If a renewable resource is used faster than it can be regenerated, it may be used up or become extinct. Fish, like other animals, are a natural resource. They can be harvested regularly, but if too many are caught and faster than they can reproduce, they may die out (Fig. 7.2).

Resources that, in theory, are renewable are called **flows**, because they are in constant supply. However, as some of these resources are used more quickly than they are being replaced, environmentalists see the need for sustainability. This ensures the use of renewable resources at a rate which allows them to regenerate themselves naturally and successfully.

Non-renewable resources

Non-renewable resources are **finite** as they are limited in quantity and cannot be used more than once. They are also called **stocks**, the opposite of flows. Minerals are the earth's non-renewable resources. These are naturally occurring elements and compounds, usually divided into four groups:

- Metals: copper, bauxite and iron.
- Industrial minerals: lime, soda ash and the by-products of coal and oil.
- Construction materials: sand and gravel.
- Energy minerals: coal, oil and natural gas (fossil fuels) and uranium (the raw material used to produce nuclear energy).

When we refer to non-renewable resources, the term resource means the quantity of a mineral known, or believed to exist, on the surface or in the earth's crust. Mineral resources are 'dynamic', that is, their quantities change as people discover new deposits. However, we call that part of a resource which we know about, and which is available for exploitation, the **reserve** (Fig. 7.3).

Figure 7.4 Landsat satellite image of rock formations in central Utah, USA. The grey/brown oval-shaped feature to the right of centre is the San Rafael Swell, a plateau formed from an eroded dome formation. This is edged at left and top right by shale (blue), with thin golden brown lines indicating sandstone layers. Between this and the deep brown-coloured mountains to the left of centre is a band of the pale blue shales over which alluvial fans (red) have been deposited. The golden yellow area at bottom right is part of the San Rafael Desert. Important uranium deposits are known at the bottom end of the Swell.

?

1 Explain the factors that may influence the life expectancy of a mineral resource (Table 7.1).

2 Discuss the effects of varying 'life spans' of mineral reserves on the economies of those countries dependent on such minerals.

3a Study Figure 7.5 and comment on the consumption of resources as distributed between the richest and poorest nations.
b What are the environmental consequences of these consumption patterns?
c Work in groups. Refer to Malthusian theory (Chapter 5) and discuss the implications of a Malthusian resource crisis for both developed and developing countries.

The life expectancy of a mineral is calculated on its reserves and the current rate of exploitation (Table 7.1). In particular, satellite imagery, also called remote sensing, can reveal an area's geology, often uncovering specific structures that might contain valuable resources. For example, earth observation satellites, such as *Landsat*, have helped discover copper deposits in Pakistan, copper, gold and molybdenum in Mexico, alluvial tin in the Amazon and uranium in the USA and Australia (Fig. 7.4).

Calculations of mineral reserves are, though, made more difficult as scientists discover new reserves through improved research techniques. In addition, more efficient use, recycling possibilities and the discovery of cheaper alternatives, such as ethanol (alcohol fuel for cars made from sugar cane) and orimulsion (liquid coal to generate electricity), all affect the accuracy of attempts to determine the life span of minerals.

Resource use

The distribution of the world's natural resources varies globally, regionally and nationally. Similarly, the use of resources differs, but this depends on how much people need and value them. Population growth and the demands of increasingly high standards of living are two factors increasing the exploitation of natural resources.

On average, more resources are consumed by the rich, developed nations in the North than the developing countries in the poor South (Fig. 7.5). Although three-quarters of the world's population lives in the developing countries, these people consume only one-sixth of the world's resources (Fig. 7.6).

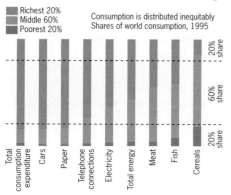

Figure 7.5 Consumption of resources (*Source:* New Internationalist, November 1998)

Figure 7.6 North-South impact (*Source:* New Internationalist, November 1998)

4 Using an atlas, trace the distribution of each of the three main categories of forest. Identify the regions where most of the three forest types are located. (The atlas may include sub-groups of these three categories. Include these in your answer.)

7.3 The distribution and use of forests

There are three main categories of forest type: tropical rainforest, temperate coniferous forest and deciduous woodland forest. Tropical rainforests are much richer in species than the other two types while the temperate vegetation is faster growing. However, many of the tropical tree species take hundreds of years to mature. The rainforest **ecosystem**, or interdependence of species, is fragile and easily disturbed, so this type of forest is more permanently destroyed than the other two.

The importance of tropical rainforests

Tropical rainforests are the richest source of life on earth (Fig. 7.7). They play a vital part in the earth's natural cycles of air, soil and water through photosynthesis, absorbing carbon dioxide and giving out the oxygen which we breathe.

Food
Virtually everything we eat for breakfast (including Rice Krispies, Cornflakes and Coco Pops!) originally came from the rainforests – even eggs. The domestic chicken has been bred from the red jungle fowl of Indian forests. At least 1650 known tropical forest plants have potential as vegetable crops.

Drugs
70% of the 3000 plants identified by the US National Cancer Institute as having anti-cancer properties come from the rainforest. Thanks to the alkaloids yielded by the rosy periwinkle, a child suffering from leukaemia now has an 80% likelihood of survival. One in four household chemicals or medicines contain compounds derived from rainforest species.

Energy
1200 hectares of the fast-growing 'ipilipil' tree could generate the fuel equivalent of 1 million barrels of oil annually. Just 6 Philippine 'petroleum nut' trees can produce 300 litres of oil annually for cooking or lighting – plantations could greatly relieve the fuelwood crisis in the developing world.

Subsistence farming
Rainforests provide food and firewood for local inhabitants.

Commercial agriculture
Over one-quarter of the cleared Amazon rainforest is now used for large-scale cattle ranching. Demand for cheap supplies of animal fodder in developed countries encourages cash crops grown on rainforest land, e.g. Thailand exports cassava to the EU.

Logging
International timber companies fell many tropical trees to find one or two hardwoods for furniture and veneers. Many plantations are also established

Biodiversity
Tropical forests have over half of the world's species in just 7% of land area with highest co-evolution: 155 000 of the known 255 000 plants; 80% of insects and 90% of primates. One hectare had 41 000 tree canopy insects including 12 000 beetles. Tropical forests are 5 to 20 times richer in trees than temperate forests.

Tourism
Rainforests are fast becoming alternative exotic holiday destinations.

Figure 7.7 Tropical rainforests (*After:* Friends of the Earth)

Effects of tropical deforestation

At present, an area of rainforest the size of England, Scotland and Wales is cut down every year (Fig. 7.8). Already this depletion has had serious social, economic and environmental consequences locally, regionally and globally (Fig. 7.9). Intensive cash-crop production in many cleared rainforests has robbed the soil of its nutrients and led to severe land degradation. Similarly, timber and mining concessions, granted to multinationals, mean that much forest is cleared for logging, mines and roads. Landowners and commercial farmers have cleared vast belts of rainforest for large-scale farm production. In the process, they have evicted many smallholders who have then been forced to migrate to the over-crowded cities. Other small-scale farmers have been forced to move on to marginal land with poorer soils.

1950

Other land uses

Temperate and
coniferous forest

Tropical
forest

1975

2000

Figure 7.8 Shrinking forests

5 You are researching wood
energy sources for the Food and
Agriculture Organisation.
a Use Figure 7.10 to describe
regional variations in the
proportions of energy supplied by
fuelwood and charcoal.
b Write an outline plan suggesting
how people dependent on
fuelwood could manage this
resource.
c Assume that your research team
succeeds in developing a
sustainable plan for fuelwood
management. Assess the long-term
benefits of your plan.

6 Which of the environmental
consequences of deforestation is
likely to have the greatest long-
term effects on the global
ecosystem?

**Figure 7.9 Settlers clearing rainforest
to grow crops and grass. Locally: the
soil soon loses its quality and settlers
are forced to abandon the land.
Nationally: loss of rainforest may upset
the water cycle in northern Brazil and
so influence rainfall and human
activities over a much wider area.**

Depletion of temperate forest reserves
Thousands of years ago, much of the earth was covered by forest, but since
people started to cultivate the land, they have used up forest reserves. For
example, the United States has lost one third of its forest cover and 85 per cent
of its primary forest (excluding Alaska). Europe has virtually no primary forest
left, with its remaining forests being managed plantations of just a few commercial tree species. China has lost three-quarters of its forest while most of
the world's remaining temperate forest areas are in Canada and Russia.
Temperate-zone forests are now mostly stable in area, though many of the soil
nutrients in them are declining, together with the wood quality and the
growth rate.

The pressure on temperate-zone forests
Temperate forests are under threat from growing environmental pollution. Air
pollution from industry, energy generation and transport has increased the
concentration of sulphur dioxide and oxides of nitrogen in the atmosphere to
create acid rain. This, in turn, leads to the slow death of vast areas of forest as
trees lose their vegetation and growth is retarded. Also, as soils become more
acidic the forests become less able to regenerate themselves.

To satisfy the demand for increasing amounts of softwood, which is used to
produce paper, many governments in developed countries are actively
encouraging afforestation programmes (replanting trees). For example, the
British government has increased the forested area of Britain from 5 per cent
to 9 per cent by giving tax incentives to those who plant and maintain forested
areas, and by supporting the work of the Forestry Commission.

The link between deforestation and development
Some development experts suggest that there is a close link between
deforestation and growing levels of debt in many developing countries (see
section 2.4). The pressure on many developing countries to increase their
GNPs as quickly as possible, to help pay back their debts, has forced them to
exploit their natural resources, including forests, for export (Fig. 7.10).

Some of those developing countries with large debts and large areas of
tropical rainforest also have high deforestation rates. In fact, the value of
tropical timber from developing countries has increased enormously during the
last few decades, rising from US$500 million per annum in 1960 to an
estimated US$20 000 million per annum in 1994. In spite of this huge increase
in the value of tropical rainforest products, a high percentage of the export
earnings for many developing countries is still used to service their debts and
gain valued foreign currency.

The demand for hardwood production is growing rapidly. Some pressure to increase logging comes from the main importers in the North, but timber is also in demand in the South e.g. India produces 243m³ for domestic fuelwood.

In developing countries, it is mostly women who collect firewood. This is usually free, but in parts of India landowners forbid the collection of wood without payment, either as labour or as a percentage of crops.

Proportion of energy supplied by fuelwood and charcoal (%)
- >90
- 60 – 89.9
- 30 – 59.9
- 5 – 29.9
- <5

1.0 → Hardwood exports (million m³)

North
South
Peters projection

Figure 7.10 Where the wood goes

?

7 Study Table 7.2. Using an economic atlas, identify the countries with the largest deposits of those minerals listed.

8a Find out how much the earnings from these minerals contribute to each country's GDP.
b Which of these countries are developing?
c Discuss the economic results for a developing country which gains large export earnings from mineral deposits.

9a List some of the economically important uses of the minerals in Table 7.2.
b Identify four or five household items which contain some of the metals listed in Table 7.2.
c Suggest reasons why those countries depending heavily on mineral exports have low GDPs.

10 How much are developed countries dependent on mineral exporting countries for the production of consumer goods?

Fuelwood

Natural vegetation, especially wood, is the oldest resource to be exploited by people. In fact, in the year 2000 wood is still the single most important source of energy for many developing countries (Fig. 7.10). It accounts for up to 60 per cent of energy consumption in Africa, and for a global energy average of about 6 per cent. However, in many parts of the world, the exploitation of firewood far exceeds its regeneration. As a result, the depletion of fuelwood in developing countries is as serious an energy crisis as the dwindling of fossil fuel reserves for developed countries.

7.4 The distribution and use of minerals

Minerals are naturally occurring inorganic substances. A mineral resource, or deposit, exists when there is a concentration of minerals which would be economically profitable for people to mine (Fig. 7.11).

Non-fuel minerals

The distribution of minerals is spread unevenly throughout the world. Some countries have a lot of valuable minerals which, with metals, they are dependent on for over 50 per cent of their exports. For example, Zambia is a major world supplier of copper and cobalt. These two minerals earn at least 85 per cent of the country's annual foreign exchange, along with lead, zinc, gold, tin and coal. Although Zaire is the world's largest producer of cobalt and industrial diamonds, copper is its most valuable exported mineral giving 55 per cent of Zaire's export earnings. It also exports uranium, tin, gold, silver, zinc, manganese, tungsten and cadmium.

An ore is a metal-bearing rock which occurs naturally in the earth's crust. Table 7.2 lists the economically most important metallic ores. Different rocks have varying degrees of concentration of metal. Where there is a particularly low percentage of metal in the ore, it becomes uneconomic to mine the rock for its

The developed countries consume well over half the world's oil. About three-quarters of the world's total energy produced in 1990 was consumed by America, Europe, Russia and Japan.

Ore production (%)
- Zinc
- Lead
- Copper
- Iron ore
- Bauxite

Fuel production (%)
- Uranium
- Coal
- Gas
- → Oil trade (approx. 20 m tonnes)
- Oil producing countries

Winkel projection

Figure 7.11 World ore and fuel production

metal content. The cut-off grade is the lowest concentration of metal necessary to make the ore worth mining. If more efficient methods of extracting minerals were invented or if the price of a mineral rises, then the cut-off grade may go down.

Table 7.2 Economically important minerals (*Source:* Meadows, Meadows, Randers, *Beyond the Limits*, Earthscan, 1992)

Element	Percentage of the earth's crust	Cut-off grade as a percentage of the resource
Mercury	0.000 008 9	0.1
Tungsten	0.000 11	0.45
Lead	0.001 2	4
Chromium	0.011	23
Tin	0.000 17	0.35
Silver	0.000 007 5	0.01
Gold	0.000 000 35	0.000 35
Molybdenum	0.000 13	0.1
Zinc	0.009 4	3.5
Manganese	0.13	25
Nickel	0.008 9	0.9
Cobalt	0.002 5	0.2
Phosphorus	0.12	8.8
Copper	0.006 3	0.35
Titanium	0.64	10
Iron	5.820	20
Aluminium	8.3	18.5

11 Study Figure 7.11 and describe the major oil-source regions and the major oil-receiving regions.

12 What does the world's flow of oil tell you about the varying levels of industrial activities in different regions of the world?

13 To what extent is the Middle East strategically important to the world's energy supply (Fig. 7.13)?

14 In what ways could: • the supply of oil and • the prices of oil, be affected by political instability in this region?

15 Comment on the distribution of uranium deposits in relation to the **North/South divide**.

Fuels

The Industrial Revolution, which took place in the developed countries from 1750 to the late 1800s, was based largely on the supply of non-renewable sources of energy. Even today, industrialised countries consume large and increasing quantities of non-renewable fossil fuels such as oil, coal and gas (Table 7.3, Fig. 7.11). Forecasts suggest that the global demand for oil will continue to increase into the 21st century (Fig. 7.12). At the same time, oil

Figure 7.12 Oil supply profiles 1996–2030 (*Source: The Journal of European Environmental Policy*, Vol. 9 no. 4, July–Aug 1999)

supplies are expected to decline steadily which has led to current initiatives to develop alternative energy supplies (see Section 7.6).

Table 7.3 Fuel resources

Resource	Locational examples	Uses	Problems
Oil	Middle East: more than half the world's oil reserves are in Saudi Arabia, Iraq, Kuwait and Abu Dhabi USA: 6 per cent	Petrol, aviation fuel, diesel oil, chemical industries, gases, asphalt, domestic heat	Oil spillage e.g. Exxon Valdez, 1978; Ogoni Land, Nigeria; effluents affect vegetation, marine life; cause of international conflict, e.g. Gulf War, 1991
Natural gas	Canada, North Sea, former USSR	Chemical industries, fuels	Transported by pipeline; impact on natural environment; leakage.
Uranium	Australia, Africa, North America; Canada is the world's leading producer since it exploited a rich vein averaging 2% uranium at Key Lake in Saskatchewan	Nuclear power for electricity	Threat of radiation leaks, e.g. Chernobyl, April 1986
Coal	USA, Canada, W & E Europe, former USSR, Australasia and China	Thermal power for electricity, coal by-products used in chemical industry	Emissions of SO_2 contributes to acid rain

Figure 7.13 Oil prices in the twentieth century

Exploitation of natural resources in Venezuela

Venezuela is one of the wealthiest nations in South America with one of the world's fastest growing economies (Table 7.4). It owes its wealth to the mineral and energy resources of many kinds throughout the country (Figs 7.15–7.16). However, although Venezuela has vast mineral resources, non-oil mining contributes less than one per cent towards the country's GDP.

Coal

Venezuela has huge reserves of coal, estimated at over 2 billion tonnes, much of which are in the Guasare open-cast mine in the western state of Zulia. There are plans to invest in a port-and-rail infrastructure to transport the coal, which should help make it possible to increase production to 20 million tonnes per annum by the end of the 1990s. In eastern Venezuela, the Fila

Maestra mine, which produced 0.3 million tonnes in 1992, is part-owned by the Japanese **transnational corporation** (**TNC**) Mitsubishi. Most of Venezuela's coal is exported with 1.85 million tonnes sold to the EU, Scandinavia, the USA and the Caribbean in 1991.

?

16 Use Table 7.4 to make some comparisons of Venezuela with other South American countries and the UK.

17a Use Table 7.4 and Figure 7.15 to identify problems faced by Venezuela.
b Suggest how Venezuela's use of resources can help with these problems.

Table 7.4 Venezuela: basic and comparative data (1999) (*Sources*: Population Reference Bureau, World Population Data Sheet; The World Bank Group, World Development Indicators 1999, Human Development Report 1998)

Country	Area (thousand sq. km)	Population (millions) 1999	Population growth (%) 1999	Urban population (%)	Life expectancy 1999	Infant mortality 1999 (per 1000 births)	GNP per capita (US$) 1997	Inflation (1995) (%)
Venezuela	912	23.7	2.0	86	73	21.0	3 480	50.1
Colombia	1139	38.6	2.0	71	69	28	2 180	21.1
Argentina	2780	36.6	1.2	89	73	21.8	8 950	4.5
UK	245	59.4	0.2	89	77	5.9	20 870	2.8

Deforestation rate
1% net annual
Mining/quarrying
Diamonds: 219 000 carats
Iron ore: 11 770 000 metric tons
Phosphate rock: 100 000 metric tons
Gold: 4 670 kilograms
Oil industry
• production peaked in 1970
• nationalised in 1975
• reserves of heavy and medium crudes estimated at 64 billion barrels (largest in the western hemisphere)
• 1993 accounts for: 23% GDP; 74% export earnings; 61% central government revenues (1993)

Figure 7.15 Venezuela

Figure 7.14 Iron ore mining, Cerro Rico, Venezuela

Bauxite

The Venezuelan government owns a bauxite mine in south-east Venezuela. Aluminium is the country's second most important export commodity after oil and the largest alumina factory in South America is located at Puerto Ordaz on the River Orinoco. In 1990, 0.6 million tonnes of aluminium were produced and the government plans to increase this output to 2 million by the year 2000. Cheap hydro-electric power (HEP) has enabled Venezuela to become the world's lowest-cost producer of aluminium. This is because the production of aluminium from bauxite requires vast amounts of electricity.

Gold

Gold has been mined for many years in Venezuela, although much of the output is produced illegally by unofficial or 'wildcat' miners known as *garimpeiros*. The use of mercury for the extraction of gold has led to serious environmental degradation in many parts of eastern Venezuela.

Oil

Thirteen per cent of Venezuela's GDP comes from oil exports. Venezuela is in fact the world's ninth largest producer of oil and was a founder member of OPEC (Organisation of Petroleum Exporting Countries) in 1960 (see Fig. 7.13). The country's oil industry was nationalised in 1975. However, Venezuela's 1992 oil production levels were lower than those of the early 1970s because of quotas imposed by OPEC to avoid a fall in the price of oil on world markets (Fig. 7.15). None the less, new oil discoveries continue to be made and export revenues reached US$8.8 billion in 1996.

Figure 7.16 Venezuela: oil production

Natural gas

Venezuela has huge reserves of natural gas. In 1992, 31 million tonnes of coal equivalent were produced. The government is trying to increase demand by laying pipelines from the gas fields in the Paria Peninsula to the industrial towns in the central and western parts of the country.

Electricity

HEP produces the largest percentage of electricity in Venezuela. The Guri hydro-electric complex in the Guyana region (south of Cuidad Guayana) is one of world's largest and has a capacity of 1000 megawatts. Other HEP plants are under construction. Small oil-fired power stations are also being converted to burn natural gas or orimulsion (a new 'liquid coal' developed jointly by British Petroleum and Venezuela's national oil company).

Economic outlook

For most of the 20th century the economy of Venezuela has been based on the exploitation of petroleum and petroleum products. Before then, the country's economy was based on agricultural exports, in particular coffee and cocoa. Investment of the proceeds of the oil industry gave Venezuela high rates of growth and rising standards of living in those years when demand for oil was steady and the international price was rising.

The international recession of 1979–81 led to a slump in demand for oil and collapse in prices which seriously affected Venezuela's economy. Since then the country has tried to diversify its economic base by encouraging other sectors of the economy, for example exploiting rich deposits of other minerals and by developing manufacturing industries and services, including tourism (Figs 7.17–7.18).

In 1995, Venezuela's economic policy was concentrated on dealing with the combined effects of recession, the large budget deficit and high inflation (Table 7.5). Economic growth contracted by 3.3 per cent in 1994, compared with just –0.4 in 1993. In fact, it was only a strong performance by the oil sector which prevented Venezuela's economy from worsening further, as the non-oil sector had contracted by 5.3 per cent.

In spite of the increasing revenue from oil, the external debt problem in Venezuela remains. It was hoped that huge reserves of oil would guard against deficits, but the drop in oil prices in the late 1970s and early 1980s, caused Venezuela to fall into debt. In 1996, Venezuela's debt had grown to US$35.3 billion, that is 51 per cent of the country's GNP. Venezuela's economic growth and future thus depends very heavily on a stable international oil price.

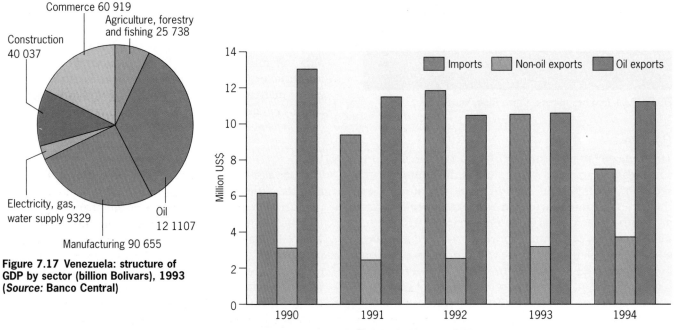

Figure 7.17 Venezuela: structure of GDP by sector (billion Bolivars), 1993 (*Source:* Banco Central)

Figure 7.18 Venezuela: external trade (*Source:* IMF)

Table 7.5 Venezuela: growth indicators (*Source:* IMF; Dun & Bradstreet's International Risk & Payment Review)

	1989	1990	1991	1992	1993	1994
Real GDP growth (%)	8.3	4.5	10.4	7.3	−0.4	−3.3
Oil production (%)	6.8	5.3	10.3	−0.3	3.4	5.7
Inflation (%)	—	—	31	31.9	45.9	70.8
Unemployment (% of workforce)	—	—	8.9	7.9	6.6	8.7

7.5 Over-exploitation of resources

Resource consumption patterns show that the developed countries use an unequal share of the earth's resources (Fig. 7.5). As the developing countries also try to industrialise, following the rich North's example, they too cling to the idea that economic growth is the key to employment, social mobility and technological advance. Consequently, as the supply of natural resources lessens, both the developed and the developing countries must consider how best to conserve these resources. At the same time, they will continue trying to raise the standard of living for their populations although the world's increasing population means that more resources are used (Fig. 7.19).

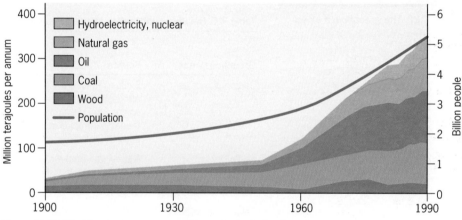

Figure 7.19 World resource consumption and population growth

Environmental, social and economic effects
The high rate of exploitation and depletion of the earth's natural resources has serious social and economic implications for both the developed and developing countries.

Declining fisheries
Both pollution and over-harvesting of the world's fishery resources have resulted in a steep decline in fish catches and the near extinction of some species of fish (see Fig. 7.2). For example, of the 30 species that once supported commercial fisheries in the Black Sea, only five remained by the mid-1990s. The Black Sea is a dumping ground for chemical and organic pollutants from countries around its shores. As a result of pollution and over-harvesting during the last decade, the total fish catch in the Black Sea has fallen from 700 000 to 100 000 tonnes. Similarly, we can see declining fish resources in other world fishing regions, such as in the north-west Atlantic where the catch has fallen by 42 per cent in twenty years and in the north-west Pacific where it fell by 10 per cent between 1988 and 1992.

Burning fossil fuels
When fossil fuels burn, waste gases are released. Large quantities of these gases can be toxic and this therefore affects both our health and pollutes the environment.

Global warming and the greenhouse effect

One of the main waste gases emitted by burning fossil fuels is carbon dioxide (CO_2). CO_2 is also one of several greenhouse gases (Table 7.6). These are important for trapping some of the sun's heat in our atmosphere and so maintaining temperatures (Fig. 7.20). Without this **greenhouse effect**, temperatures on earth would fall at least 30 °C and so life could not exist. However, an accumulation of greenhouse gases is also harmful to life. This is because the more gases there are in the atmosphere, the more heat is trapped at the earth's surface. Scientists blame the large-scale consumption of fossil fuels, especially by the developed industrial nations (Fig. 7.20), for the increasing CO_2 in the atmosphere. In turn, scientists consider this CO_2 to be responsible for **global warming,** or raising the temperature of the earth's atmosphere. There are national and regional variations in carbon dioxide emissions as shown in Figure 7.23. The industrial countries generate the vast majority of carbon dioxide emissions which are partly blamed for increasing global temperature (Fig. 7.22).

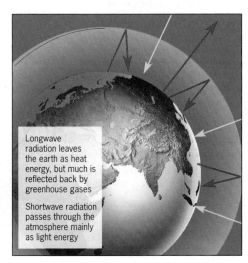

Longwave radiation leaves the earth as heat energy, but much is reflected back by greenhouse gases

Shortwave radiation passes through the atmosphere mainly as light energy

Figure 7.20 The greenhouse effect

Table 7.6 Relative contribution to the greenhouse effect of various greenhouse gases

Greenhouse gas	Source	Approximate relative greenhouse effect per molecule	Current rate of increase (% pa)
Carbon dioxide (CO_2)	Exchanged naturally between the atmosphere, oceans and the living world. The burning of fossil fuels and the loss of tropical rainforests adds to the normal amount.	1	0.5
Methane (CH_4)	Natural gas from rocks, swamps, rice fields and animals.	21	0.9
Nitrous oxide (N_2O)		290	0.25
Chlorofluorocarbons (CFCs)			
CFC11 }	Aerosols, fridges, blown	3 500	4
CFC12 }	plastic, packaging.	7 300	4

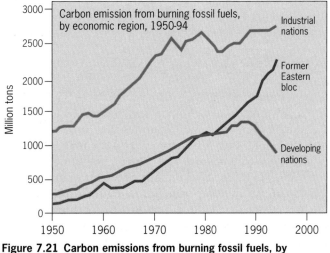

Figure 7.21 Carbon emissions from burning fossil fuels, by economic region, 1950–94

Figure 7.22 Global average temperature at the Earth's surface in degrees Celsius, 1965–95

?

20 Work in groups.
a Suggest ways of reducing gas emissions.
b Which of your suggestions: • can individuals do, • need government involvement?

21 You have been approached by the United Nations Environment Programme (UNEP) to join an international group examining the greenhouse effect. Your task is to write a report on the greenhouse effect for presentation at a UN conference. Your report should comment on the following:
• evidence for the greenhouse effect.
• the implications of the greenhouse effect.
• the political options for limiting social and economic damage.

loping countries 16.3%
st of Asia 1.5%
Brazil 0.6%
Rest of Latin America 3.2%
North Africa and Middle East 2.2%
Rest of Africa 1.6%
India 1.6%
China 5.5%

Australia/ New Zealand 1.1%
Japan 3.7%
Eastern Europe 5.5%
Former USSR 14.1%

stern ope 26.1%

trial countries 83.7%

North America 33.2%

Figure 7.23 National and regional contributions to global increases of carbon dioxide in the atmosphere

Acid rain
Burning coal also produces sulphur dioxide (SO_2), or acid gas. In turn, sulphur dioxide combines with water vapour to form **acid rain**. Acid rain upsets the chemical balance of the soil, making it difficult for plants to absorb nutrients (Fig. 7.22), while the chemicals in acid rain are also dangerous to marine life.

Cars and aircraft run on oil-based products that emit nitrogen oxides (NO_x), gases which contribute to the formation of acid rain. Hydrocarbons, either from car exhausts or from industrial activities, usually react with ultra-violet radiation from the sun to produce photochemical smog near the ground. The resultant poor air quality irritates the eyes and lungs and, for some people, causes asthma.

Ozone
Ozone (O_3) in the ozone layer filters out ultra-violet short-wave radiation from the sun. Since the 1970s, scientists have observed that the ozone layer above both the Arctic and Antarctic has thinned. Many people believe the cause of this depletion is human interference with the atmosphere, particularly by the use of chlorofluorocarbons (CFCs). CFCs release chlorine into the atmosphere and this eventually breaks down ozone. In addition, vehicle and aircraft exhausts react with ultra-violet radiation to produce nitrogen oxides which also destroy ozone. Ultimately, destruction of the ozone layer means that harmful ultra-violet radiation can reach the earth's surface. Some scientists link this radiation to increases in skin cancer and cataracts in humans and a reduction of growth and photosynthesis in plants.

Green economics
As people become more concerned over the global environmental and health problems caused by burning fossil fuels, they have developed measures to reduce greenhouse gases (Table 7.7). In addition, while much of the cause and effects of pollution are seen in the developed North, there is a need for international co-operation. Some pollution-control economists suggest tradable

?

22a Give a Malthusian explanation for the environmental problem of acid rain and the theoretical catastrophe of global warming.
b Write an environmentalist's response to these issues to prevent them getting worse.
(For a and b, see section 5.2.)

Table 7.7 Measures to reduce greenhouse gases

Measure	Example
Changing use of fossil fuels	Change from the heavy use of coal to oil and gas
Alternative energy sources	• Renewable energy sources, e.g. HEP, tidal, wave, solar, and wind power, would reduce CO_2 output • Burning methane (a potent greenhouse gas) at landfill waste sites • An increase in nuclear power
Energy pricing and efficiency	• Increasing the fuel efficiency of buildings • Increasing the fuel efficiency of transport • Global energy pricing strategy that involves pricing fuels to reflect their environmental costs
Control of deforestation	• Provision of constructive advice on forest management
Programmes to replant trees (afforestation)	• Alternative uses like tourism could help to conserve these resources

• Each country prepares a budget of greenhouse gas emissions to set against the size of its population and its carbon 'sinks', i.e. vegetation, soil and the earth's total cleaning capacity.

• Each country's share of the oceanic and atmospheric sinks is calculated.

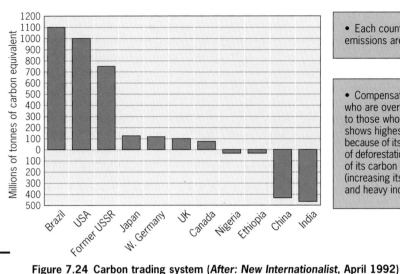

Figure 7.24 Carbon trading system (*After: New Internationalist*, April 1992)

• Each country's permissible emissions are worked out.

• Compensation is paid by those who are over the permitted level to those who are under. Brazil shows highest above quota because of its unique combination of deforestation (reducing the size of its carbon sink), forest burning (increasing its carbon emissions) and heavy industrial pollution.

?

23 Study Figure 7.23 and discuss the potential for tradable emission quotas to reduce global carbon dioxide emissions.

24 What practical problems might arise if the tradable emission quotas system were adopted?

emission quotas for each country (Fig. 7.23). This proposes that total carbon emissions should equal the earth's capacity to absorb them (earth's natural sinks). Countries with unused emissions quotas, mostly in the developing countries, could then sell them to high-level carbon producing nations at fixed rates. This system is part of a global strategy to unite environmentally damaging production methods with national income. The term for such policies is **green economics**. In June 1997, at an Earth Summit in New York, representatives of 160 countries expressed concern at the continuing deterioration of the environment. Since greenhouse emissions have continued to grow, the European nations proposed at the Earth Summit that all industrialised countries reduce their carbon dioxide emissions to 85 per cent of 1990 levels by 2010.

Petroleum exploration and the environment, Nigeria

Figure 7.25 Nigeria

Oil was first discovered in Nigeria (Fig. 7.25) in the late 1950s. Ever since, it has been the major source of foreign exchange for this country. Nigerian oil production has fluctuated since the early 1970s reflecting changes in oil prices in the world market (see Fig. 7.13). In the mid-1990s, 95 per cent of Nigeria's foreign earnings were from petroleum. The environmental costs of producing oil have been enormous especially to the local communities.

Shell oil company

Shell, an Anglo-Dutch oil company, is one of the world's largest oil TNCs in the Niger Delta. The company accounts for over 50 per cent of Nigeria's daily oil production. Shell found oil in Rivers state in 1958 and established six oil fields in this highly productive agricultural area. Shell has operated in the area ever since, and has been the target of considerable criticism about the recurrent environmental problems related to drilling.

The Ogonis

The Ogoni region is one of the most densely populated areas in Africa with about 600 people per square kilometre (see section 1.4). The Ogoni people, who have lived in this fertile area for centuries, depended on fishing and farming for their livelihood. In fact, they used to supply most of the food needs of the urban population of Nigeria's south-east.

Effects of oil explorations on the local community

Since 1958, farmers in Ogoni have had to compete with oil companies operating in their area. The powerful influence of Shell and other TNCs in the region has meant that valuable farmland is lost to oil operations. Although traditionally the Ogonis were major food exporters to other parts of Nigeria, they now have to depend on food imports to feed themselves.

Oil spillage and pollution

Oil spillage has been frequent with serious environmental and health consequences for the local community (Fig. 7.26). Between 1976 and 1991, 2976 oil spills amounting to 2.1 million barrels of oil were reported in the Niger Delta area, an average of four spills a week. The Nigerian Ministry of Petroleum attributes most spills to equipment failures and corrosion but the results involve enormous damage to both land and water resources. In 1970, a Shell pipeline carrying crude oil spilled into Ogoni farmland. As a clean-up measure, the leaked fuel was burnt – leaving a semi-solid crust about five metres thick and useless agricultural land. Losses to the local farmers are considerable. In June 1993, a pipe from Shell's Korokoro pumping station burst. Palm oil trees were covered in an oily sheen stopping tappers from collecting any palm oil, chickens and goats died while fish stocks and vegetation were stunted.

Impoverishment and health hazards
While the local economy of the Ogoni people has been devastated by the operations of the oil companies, the people benefit very little from the oil revenue. Although Ogoni land has produced US$30 billion in oil revenue for Shell and the Nigerian government, most Ogonis remain poor. The government has used the oil wealth to develop urban areas such as Lagos, Kaduna, Kano and the new Federal Capital of Abuja (see Fig. 3.1).

Apart from the obvious environmental damage caused by oil spillage, oil exploration also poses serious health hazards to the local community. At Shell's Korokoro flowstation, a large quantity of poisonous gases is constantly released into the atmosphere through gas flaring. There are reports that hydro-carbons are affecting the health of the local population. Oil also bubbles into local water supplies and diarrhoea and vomiting are treated as regular complaints.

The Ogoni response
The people of the Niger Delta area have expressed their anger against the Shell operations in largely peaceful demonstrations, although there have been occasions when the local Ogoni people clashed with the Nigerian military police. In October 1990, the village community at Umuchen, 15 kilometres from Ogoni, organised a peaceful protest against Shell. In the course of this protest, the heavily-armed Nigerian mobile police took part, resulting in the death of 80 villagers and the

Figure 7.26 Crude oil leak, Korokoro, Niger Delta

destruction of about five hundred houses. The Ogoni people of Nigeria are still seeking compensation for the damage caused to them and their environment through oil prospecting (Fig. 7.26).

?

25 In what ways can local people, such as the Ogonis in the Niger Delta, benefit from the exploitation of natural resources on their land?

26 List, in detail, the possible conflicts of interest over the need to exploit natural resources for national development and the needs of the local communities where such resources are located.

27a As an external investigator, write a report summarising the problems in Rivers state.
b Evaluate the arguments of both the Ogoni people and Shell.
c Give brief suggestions for future development in the area, clearly indicating your priorities.

Figure 7.27 Letter from Ken Saro-Wiwa seeking support against the activites of Shell on Ogoni land, Nigeria. Saro-Wiwa and the Ogoni community have been campaigning against environmental damage and inadequate compensation for destruction of land and crops by oil companies operating in Ogoni land (*Source: The Guardian*, 24 August 1995). Nigeria's military dictatorship executed Saro-Wiwa on 12 November 1995.

ALL letters of support are welcome; except that my predicament, and that of the Ogoni people, require just a little more urgency.

At the root of my travails lies Shell, which has exploited, traduced and driven the Ogoni people to extinction in the last three decades. The company has taken over $30 billion out of the Ogoni and has left a completely devastated environment and a trail of human misery.

When I organised the Ogoni people to protest peacefully against Shell's ecological war, the company invited the Nigerian military to intervene. Lethal arms supplied by the British government were used on unarmed Ogoni people while they were sleeping in their beds. Thousands have been murdered, hundreds of thousands driven into the bush and tens of villages flattened.

The World Bank, after studying the Niger delta, has warned that 'an urgent need exists to implement mechanisms to protect the life and health of the region's inhabitants and its ecological systems from further deterioration'. Shell has not faced the consequences of its ecological war on the delta... Help save life and the environment of the Niger delta.

7.6 Alternative energy resources

Because of the problems caused by conventional energy production, people recognise the need for more sustainable methods (Figs 7.27–7.31). These alternative, or renewable, sources of energy tend to use natural resource flows, rather than stock resources (see Fig. 7.1).

Hydro-electric power (HEP)

Water under high pressure is used to drive a turbine linked to an electricity-producing generator. HEP produces one quarter of the total energy generated worldwide and is growing in importance: Norway receives 99 per cent of its electricity from HEP, Zaire 97 per cent and Brazil 96 per cent.

Transport costs, from the production areas mostly in mountains, are high e.g. about 70% of China's HEP capacity is in the south-west, but less than 10% is harnessed because of the cost of transporting it to more populated areas. However, China is building the large-scale Three Gorges HEP Project on the Yangtse River. Financed by the USA and Canada, it has the world's largest volume concrete dam. Elsewhere, parts of China depend on small-scale HEP plants with capacities of between one kilowatt and one megawatt. These supply just over 2% of China's energy needs.

Solar power

The sun's rays are concentrated by reflectors (heliostats), heating fluid which drives a turbine for generating electricity or for heating. Because plants need the sun to grow, fuelwood, agricultural waste and animal dung, collectively known as **biomass**, are also classified as solar energy.

Wave and tidal power

After tides rise behind the barrage (13.5 m at Rance), water is gradually released turning turbines to generate electricity. This is a cheap form of generating electricity but building costs are high.

?

28 You work for the Department of Energy.

a Gather information about the varieties of renewable energy in order to assess their development in the UK (Figures 7.28–7.32).

b For each renewable energy source, list the possibilities and limitations of its development.

c Would you recommend the Department of Energy to invest in renewable resources? If so, which three should be encouraged? Give your reasons.

Figure 7.28 Itaipu plant on the Paraná River, between Brazil and Paraguay, has the largest HEP-generating capacity in the world of 12 600 megawatts

Geothermal power

Geothermal energy is derived from steam trapped deep in the earth which, when brought to the surface, drives a turbine. Theoretically, this source of subterranean energy is limitless, but in most habitable areas of the earth the hot rocks lie so deep that drilling is too expensive.

Figure 7.29 Geothermal power complex using hot springs, Iceland

Figure 7.30 Basin of solar generating screens, California, USA

Figure 7.31 Tidal barrage across the Rance estuary, France (1966)

Wind power

Wind pushes three spinning rotor blades which drive a turbine to generate electricity. The electrical energy produced from a turbine is proportional to the windspeed. Thus, a 10m/s wind will produce 8 times more electricity than a 5m/s wind.

Figure 7.32 World solar and wind energy capacity in megawatts, 1980–95

Energy resources mix in India

Commercial energy consumption

In India (Fig. 7.32), industry is by far the largest consumer of commercial forms of energy, with transport being the second largest. Commercial energy sources include coal, gas, oil, hydro-electric and nuclear. Coal is the main source of commercial energy and India is, in fact, one of the world's leading coal producers. Oil and gas supply just under half the country's commercial needs, while HEP is also important, although only 20 per cent of the country's potential has been tapped.

India also has large reserves of thorium. Thorium is a fuel similar to uranium and is used in nuclear reactors. Partly because of this, India is one of the relatively few developing countries which has its own nuclear power industry (Fig. 7.34). Approximately three per cent of India's electricity comes from nuclear power and there are ambitious plans for a ten-fold expansion by the end of the century.

Traditional sources of energy

Over 40 per cent of the total energy used in India comes from non-commercial, renewable sources. Non-commercial energy is mostly used in rural areas where 72 per cent of the population lives. A majority of these people depend on fuelwood, agricultural waste and animal dung.

Inadequate electricity facilities in many villages and limited use of kerosene for cooking, mean that biomass provides the cooking fuel for many rural households. A large programme of rural electrification has brought electricity to two out of three of India's 500 000 villages, but only about eight per cent of rural homes are connected to the electricity grid. The electricity in

Figure 7.33 India

these areas is used mainly for irrigation pumps to bring water to farmland.

Forests cover nearly a quarter of India, but there is an acute shortage of fuelwood in many areas (Fig. 7.35, see Fig. 7.10). The amount of fuelwood burned annually far exceeds India's afforestation programme (Fig. 7.35).

Figure 7.35 India: supply and demand for fuelwood (*Source:* M Raw, *Resources and Environment*, Unwin Hyman, 1989)

This results in soil erosion and a shortage of fuelwood, so people are forced to burn animal dung which could otherwise fertilise the crops and so increase food production. Ultimately, this creates a **poverty trap**, the effects of which are difficult to reverse once set in motion.

The problem of energy shortage in rural areas in India, as in many developing countries, can only be solved through the expansion of the non-commercial sector. The greatest demand for energy in Indian rural areas is for cooking. However, the traditional stove, the *chullah*, is extremely inefficient, although it burns firewood, agricultural waste and dung. The introduction of improved *chullahs* is already proving effective and it is hoped that eventually the new-version chullah will help save up to 17 million tonnes of firewood a year (Fig. 7.35).

Figure 7.34 Commercial energy: nuclear power station, Bombay where the production of nuclear energy is important for India's industrialisation

Figure 7.36 The local hope for India's energy future?

Biogas

Another solution is the production of biogas. This is made by placing animal dung, other farm wastes and vegetation in sealed concrete and steel containers. The sun's heat then helps bacteria to decompose these natural materials rapidly and, during the process, methane gas is produced. The methane is stored and used for cooking and lighting, either by individuals or by whole communities. In addition, farmers can use residue from the sealed containers as fertiliser. The Indian government is keen to promote such community energy projects which also help improve the output of small-scale farmers. In light of the global fuelwood crisis (see Fig. 7.8) such schemes can also help to save valuable wood.

Trombe walls

A more 'alternative' approach to saving energy is at Leh, in Northern India. Trombe walls absorb heat by day and let it out at night by working on the same principle as a conservatory. A thermally blackened wall is placed behind glass on the south-facing side of a dwelling. The air in the living space is then warmed by natural or forced convection through a system of ducts. Heat loss may be minimised at night or there may be vents to allow for cooling on hot days. Alternatively, the trombe wall can be filled with water and the structure relocated on the roof provided that the load can be supported by the building.

29 As an expert for the United Nations Development Programme (UNDP) you have to recommend alternative strategies for energy production to the Indian government.
a Assess the advantages and disadvantages of: • high-tech commercial energy production (Fig. 7.34); • low-tech small-scale production (Fig. 7.35).
b Compare the different approaches and for each suggest: • who is likely to benefit; • the sustainability of the strategy.

30 Considering the estimated reserves and current consumption rates of non-renewable resources (see Tables 7.1 and 7.2), how might countries benefit in the long term from the use of renewable flows of energy?

Summary

- Resources are vital for successful economic development.
- The types of resources are broadly categorised into renewable and non-renewable.
- Renewable resources, known as flows, are capable of being used over and over again. Non-renewable resources, known as stocks, are finite.
- The depletion of the tropical rainforests has serious social, environmental and economic consequences, not only for local areas but for the whole world.
- High rates of deforestation in the developing countries have led to a large-scale fuelwood crisis as many people depend on this primary source of energy.
- Although the distribution of the world's natural resources varies widely, the developed countries consume the most.
- Exploitation of renewable resources must not go beyond their ability to regenerate. If it does, then the use of the resource is considered non-sustainable.
- The high use of non-renewable resources means a global reduction of stocks.
- Heavy reliance on fossil fuels has resulted in serious environmental pollution. This has serious consequences for both developed and developing countries.
- Alternative, sustainable supplies of energy are being developed in response to the loss of non-renewable resources.

8 World trade, commodities and communications

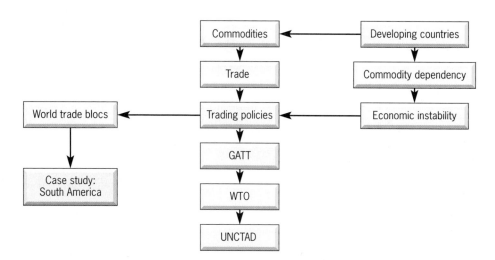

Commodities ← Developing countries

Trade → Commodity dependency

World trade blocs ← Trading policies ← Economic instability

Case study: South America

GATT

WTO

UNCTAD

8.1 Introduction

Trade is the exchange of goods and services. In this chapter we examine world trade with special reference to commodities. Commodities are goods for sale, either raw materials or manufactured goods. However, the term is most commonly used for raw materials, like coal, cotton, tin and bananas, as it will be in this chapter. Trade is the major force behind economic relations between nations, with some countries benefiting more than others (Fig. 8.1). This follows the concept of **comparative advantage** (see section 6.7). We discuss the reasons why many developing countries receive low returns from international trade and examine the issue of dependency on exports of primary commodities.

8.2 The history of trade between developed and developing countries

There has been trade of commodities and manufactured goods between nations for thousands of years. One early example is the Egyptians who, four thousand years ago, exported gold and wine to the area we know as Syria, in exchange for wood and pottery. During the colonial period, from the 16th to the 19th centuries, the 'triangular trade' between Europe, Africa and the Americas flourished (see Fig. 2.5).

The natural resources of the world are unevenly distributed (see Figs 7.10, 7.11). For instance, Europe has few **reserves** of minerals compared with Africa, and it does not have the climate to grow cotton or coffee. Over the past five hundred years, the more powerful nations have imported raw materials as cheaply as possible to manufacture into goods for export. In return, they sold their finished goods back to the colonies – as expensively as possible. This pattern fits the economic theory of **mercantilism**. Mercantilism relates to trade during the seventeenth and eighteenth centuries. It suggests that the wealth of a nation is dependent on gaining natural resources through foreign trade.

This pattern of world trade persists today and results in a division between the industrialised **developed countries** of the North, and the **developing countries** of the South (See Fig. 1.1). In addition, some developing countries have industrialised to become **newly industrialising countries** (**NIC**s, see

Figure 8.1 Trading floor of the New York Stock Exchange. The Stock Exchange is a financial market where investments in industrial and commercial corporations are bought and sold. Commodity trading, which occurs at a separate commodity exchange, is the buying and selling of natural products.

section 6.7). However, most developing countries today lack the basic skills, infrastructure, technology and finance to establish a significant industrial base. At the same time, many of their commodities are still in demand by the developed countries. This dependence of developed and developing countries on one another ultimately causes problems for both, although mostly for the developing countries.

8.3 Problems for developing countries dependent on commodity exports

The main problem for countries which depend on the export of primary commodities (Fig. 8.2) is economic instability. This is especially so for countries which depend on the export of just one primary product (Fig. 8.3). Even a small change in the price of the commodity exported can affect a country's economy drastically. For example, world demand for copper fell heavily as factory-made fibre optics replaced copper telephone wires. As a result, the price of copper also fell and Zambia's national income was greatly reduced.

?

1a Study Figure 8.2 and describe the regional variations in commodity dependence throughout Africa.
b Select four countries in Africa which depend heavily on commodity exports (other than those listed in Fig. 8.3). Find out which commodities are associated with each country.

2a On a base map of Africa, shade the countries you selected in **1b** and those in Figure 8.3 which depend heavily on a single export commodity.
b Find out to where each of these products is mostly exported.
c Find out what other commodities each of these countries produce on a commercial scale.
d Write a paragraph to explain the importance of trade in commodities for Africa.

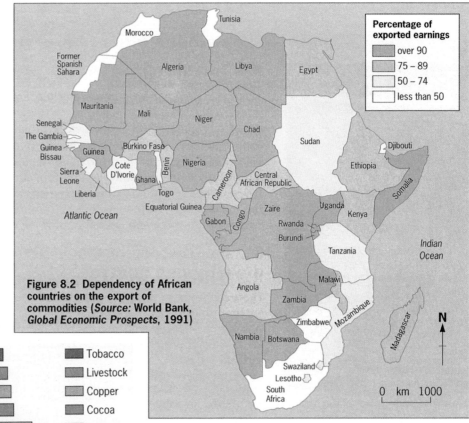

Figure 8.2 Dependency of African countries on the export of commodities (*Source:* World Bank, *Global Economic Prospects*, 1991)

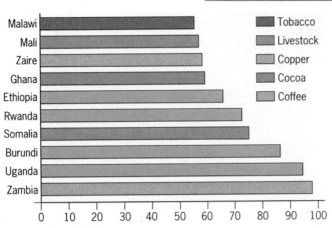

Figure 8.3 Dependency of Sub-Saharan African countries on the export of one commodity as a percentage of their exports (*Source:* Oxfam, *The Trade Trap*)

1970s debt crisis

The debt crisis of the 1970s hit the developing countries hard. At that time, the Middle East countries put up the price of oil (see Fig. 7.13). They then invested much of their income in European and US banks. In order to pay interest to their Middle Eastern investors, the banks encouraged developing countries to take out loans. In turn, to raise money to pay their interest, the developing countries had to export more commodities. This, of course, pushed down prices resulting in a reduction in developing countries' income.

An attempt to maintain and stabilise commodity prices in the 1970s was the International Commodity Agreements (ICAs). However, many of these agreements encouraged nations to increase their production so much that it led to oversupply. For example, too much coffee caused the International Coffee Agreement to collapse in 1989 after the market price of coffee fell from US$1.4 to US$0.70 per pound in just four months. This had an enormous impact on countries which relied heavily on coffee exports. In El Salvador, the value of coffee exports fell from US$700 million in 1988 to US$500 million in 1989.

Oversupply and changing demand

Oversupply affects the price of commodities. For example, many developing countries grow coffee (Fig. 8.4). If there is a good harvest the result is a coffee glut on world markets as supply exceeds demand. This forces prices down. After severe frost in Brazil in 1974 (Fig. 8.5), fungi in Colombia and Mexico in 1976, drought in the Ivory Coast and war in Angola, world coffee stockpiles ran out. Prices rocketed and farmers therefore planted more and more coffee bushes. As these additional bushes contributed to regular production, oversupply took place and so, since the 1980s, coffee prices have gradually dropped off (Table 8.1).

Commodities are also prone to 'boom-bust' cycles. In some years, profits from commodity sales are high, so countries accumulate wealth. However, during 'bust' periods, business slows as demand falls, profits go down, unemployment rises and the economy enters recession. These bust periods may even be the result of fashion, as tastes and styles change. Thus demand for primary products such as cocoa, coffee, sugar and tobacco will fluctuate as people's attitudes to consumption changes. Another set-back is caused by recession in the North. If factories in developed countries close, the producer of their raw materials will no longer have a market. Ultimately, unemployment in the North means increased poverty in the South.

Commodity substitutes

Developed countries now manufacture cheaper, artificial alternatives for certain natural products. The results of this engineering and biotechnology include synthetic cocoa butter, vanilla flavouring and food sweeteners. The long-term effect of such artificial production is to reduce demand for natural goods, which results in a decline in prices. We are all familiar with the substitution of polyester for cotton. In addition, since the early 1980s, US food manufacturers have used maize-based sweeteners instead of sugar. These now make up 60 per cent of the US sweetener market. At the same time, Europeans have increased their sugar-beet production from which they also manufacture sugar products. These changes, and the development of other artificial sweeteners, have led to a fall in the demand for sugar cane from developing countries. Because of the decline in US sugar imports, by 1985 a quarter of a million people were without work on the Philippine island of Negros. This was 1.03 per cent of the labour force of about 24 000 000.

Non-agricultural raw materials have also suffered from synthetic alternatives. Until the mid-1980s, Bolivia's economy was dependent on the export of tin. In the late 1970s, 79 per cent of the country's exports were tin, while it ranked ninth in world production (4 per cent). However, technological advances mean

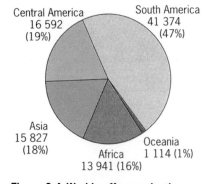

Central America
16 592
(19%)

South America
41 374
(47%)

Asia
15 827
(18%)

Oceania
1 114 (1%)

Africa
13 941 (16%)

Figure 8.4 World coffee production (*Source: New Internationalist*, Sept. 1994)

Table 8.1 The changing price of coffee, 1975–93

1975	144	1982	309	1989	240
1976	315	1983	290	1990	150
1977	517	1984	327	1991	135
1978	359	1985	330	1992	135
1979	382	1985	330	1993	145
1980	344	1986	440	US cents per Kg	
1981	282	1987	258		

Figure 8.5 Brazilian coffee crop destroyed by frost

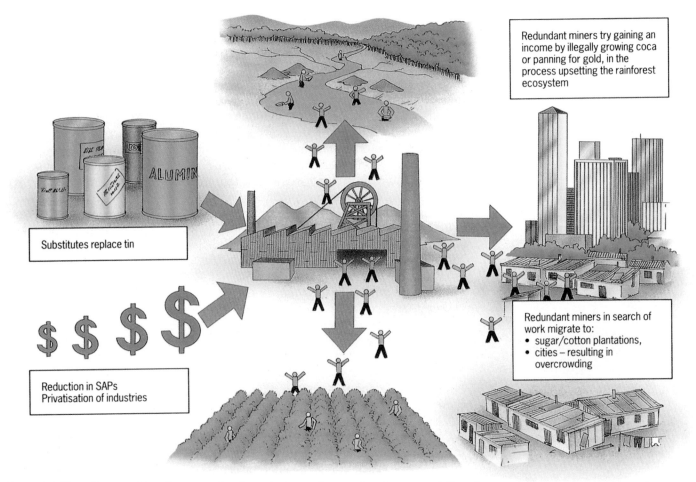

Redundant miners try gaining an income by illegally growing coca or panning for gold, in the process upsetting the rainforest ecosystem

Substitutes replace tin

Reduction in SAPs
Privatisation of industries

Redundant miners in search of work migrate to:
• sugar/cotton plantations,
• cities – resulting in overcrowding

Figure 8.6 Tin collapse and its effects in Bolivia

that less tin is used to make tin cans while other types of container have also been invented. In October 1985 the price of tin fell from UK£8000 to UK£4000 per tonne, halving the Bolivian revenue and leaving thousands of miners without work (Fig. 8.6).

Weather

All countries dependent on crops are at the mercy of the weather. Tropical countries, in particular, are threatened by powerful storm systems, such as hurricanes. These sweep through the Caribbean every year and can devastate whole crops. Plants are also vulnerable to frost, drought and disease (see Fig. 8.5). Thus, a country dependent on the export of its crops will be damaged financially if the crop fails. In addition, any farmer who tries changing his crop, has the expense of changing production systems and waiting for the new plants to mature. For example, a coffee bush will only be productive after four years' growth.

Trading policies

Traditionally, it was the developed countries who established and gained most from international trading policies. We can see the effects of this control in the form of **tariffs**. Tariffs are taxes added to the cost of goods at different stages of production. Thus raw materials tend to have much smaller tariffs than manufactured goods. This means that it is relatively cheap for a manufacturing country to import the raw materials it needs for production, but it would be expensive for that country to import the equivalent finished product made from those raw materials (Figs 8.7–8.8).

?

3 In what ways can the market collapse of a commodity lead to poverty in the producing region (Fig. 8.6)?

4 Discuss the potential problems of biotechnology on: • countries that depend on primary commodities and • on the consumers of such manufactured products.

5 Some development experts have expressed concern over the effects of biotechnology on the developing nations, believing it is 'biological colonialism'. Do you agree? Explain, giving reasons.

?

6 Use Figures 8.7 and 8.8 to complete a matrix showing the advantages and disadvantages of tariffs for both developed and developing countries.

7a Using Figure 8.9, describe the trends in commodity prices during the 1980s.
b Suggest the impact of such changes on countries supplying commodities.

8 Use the information in section 8.3 to draw an annotated flow diagram summarising the factors which can lead to changes in the price of primary commodities. Your diagram should show factors originating in both developed and developing countries.

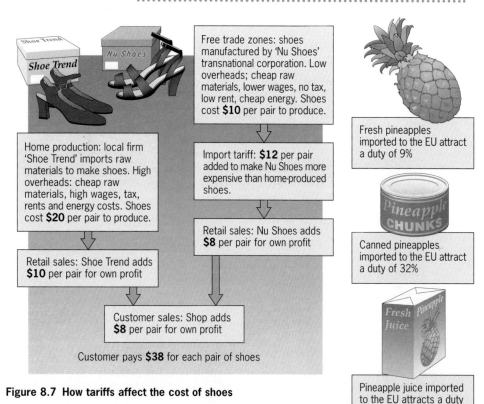

Figure 8.7 **How tariffs affect the cost of shoes**

Figure 8.8 **Tariff escalation: the more processed a product, the higher the tariff** (*Source: A Raw Deal*, Christian Aid, 1992)

Figure 8.9 **Commodity price decline, 1980–92** (*After: The Economist*)

A combination of these problems has led to a long-term, steady decline in the price of commodities (Fig. 8.9). In relation to the price of manufactured goods, this commodity price decline means that in 1975 farmers in Africa could buy a tractor for the equivalent of 8 tonnes of their coffee, but in 1992 a tractor cost them 40 tonnes of coffee.

8.4 World trading blocs

An essential feature of world trade and economic co-operation between nations today is transnational trade organisations or trading blocs (Fig. 8.10). Countries which share geographical, political, historical or economic characteristics often form such blocs to strengthen their trade links.

Types of integration
There are different types of economic and political integration. For co-operation between nations we can use the terms transnational or supranational. In either case, such national relationships are based on either formal or informal agreements. An informal integration is 'loose' and unregulated, for example, a group of developing countries voting along a common line in a UN ballot.

Political collaboration
Some agreements involve political links between nation states, for example, the Organisation of African Unity (OAU), British Commonwealth Association and the North Atlantic Treaty Organisation (NATO). Under these arrangements, the sovereignty of each member state is maintained.

Economic collaboration
The main motive for many agreements between countries is economic. Examples include the European Union (EU), United Nations Organisation and General Agreement on Tariffs and Trade (GATT, see section 8.5).

?

9 Use Figure 8.10 to comment on the location of trading blocs. Suggest why few blocs cross the **North-South divide**.

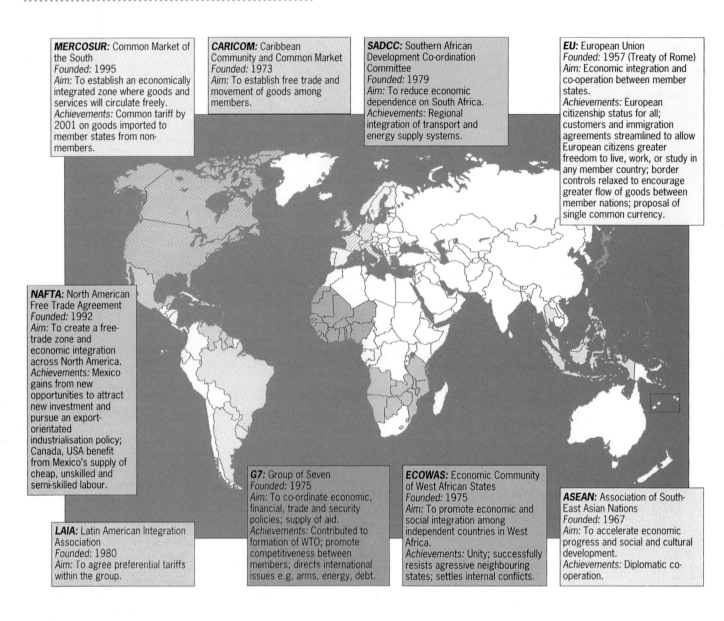

MERCOSUR: Common Market of the South
Founded: 1995
Aim: To establish an economically integrated zone where goods and services will circulate freely.
Achievements: Common tariff by 2001 on goods imported to member states from non-members.

CARICOM: Caribbean Community and Common Market
Founded: 1973
Aim: To establish free trade and movement of goods among members.

SADCC: Southern African Development Co-ordination Committee
Founded: 1979
Aim: To reduce economic dependence on South Africa.
Achievements: Regional integration of transport and energy supply systems.

EU: European Union
Founded: 1957 (Treaty of Rome)
Aim: Economic integration and co-operation between member states.
Achievements: European citizenship status for all; customers and immigration agreements streamlined to allow European citizens greater freedom to live, work, or study in any member country; border controls relaxed to encourage greater flow of goods between member nations; proposal of single common currency.

NAFTA: North American Free Trade Agreement
Founded: 1992
Aim: To create a free-trade zone and economic integration across North America.
Achievements: Mexico gains from new opportunities to attract new investment and pursue an export-orientated industrialisation policy; Canada, USA benefit from Mexico's supply of cheap, unskilled and semi-skilled labour.

LAIA: Latin American Integration Association
Founded: 1980
Aim: To agree preferential tariffs within the group.

G7: Group of Seven
Founded: 1975
Aim: To co-ordinate economic, financial, trade and security policies; supply of aid.
Achievements: Contributed to formation of WTO; promote competitiveness between members; directs international issues e.g. arms, energy, debt.

ECOWAS: Economic Community of West African States
Founded: 1975
Aim: To promote economic and social integration among independent countries in West Africa.
Achievements: Unity; successfully resists agressive neighbouring states; settles internal conflicts.

ASEAN: Association of South-East Asian Nations
Founded: 1967
Aim: To accelerate economic progress and social and cultural development.
Achievements: Diplomatic co-operation.

Figure 8.10 Organisations of state and economic integration

Trade blocs in South and Central America

Bananas are a tropical crop, produced mainly in the developing world. Asia is the world's main banana growing region, but Latin America is the biggest exporter. Between 1988 and 1997 the world's exports of bananas were just over 12 million tons. Ecuador, with 4.4 million tons in 1997, is the world's largest exporter, followed by Costa Rica (1.8 million tons), the Philippines (1.6 million tons) and Colombia (1.5 million tons). While many developing countries depend on fruit for much of their export income (Table 8.2), world fruit markets are dominated by a few **transnational corporations** (**TNCs**) which control transportation, storage and marketing (Fig. 8.11).

People in developed countries are consuming ever-increasing quantities of bananas. New Zealand (Aotearoa) imports the highest per capita amount of bananas in the world at 20.4 kg per year, closely followed by Malta at 19.6 kg. Bananas account for a quarter of the fresh fruit consumed by Americans each year, while trade with the Eastern European countries has also grown. Bananas come fifth in terms of world trade in agricultural produce, after cereals, sugar, coffee and cocoa. As with most commodities produced in developing countries and consumed in the developed countries, more than 90 per cent of the price paid by the consumer never reaches the producer. Most of the risks producing perishable fruit are, however, borne by

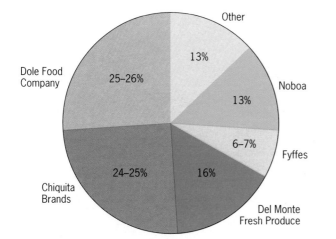

Figure 8.11 Bananas: main companies, percentage share of world production, 1997

Table 8.2 Fruit as a percentage of selected countries' exports (*Source:* UNCTAD, 1990)

Chile	9
New Zealand	5
Kenya	5
Philippines	5
Turkey	7
Spain	5
Israel	3
St Lucia	54
Guadeloupe	42
Costa Rica	33
Greece	5
Dominica	73
Jamaica	3
Martinique	49
Honduras	46
Belize	25

Volume of world trade

Retailer 40%

Importer/wholesaler 20%

Shipping costs 10%

Export charges and handling 5%

Warehouse and packaging 15%

Picker/ grower 10%

Figure 8.12 Total value of world trade in bananas

Figure 8.13 Banana producing countries in Central America

Five Island Group

UBEP

183 Banana production, 1990 (000) tonnes

the producer, while profits are shared between the transnational companies and the retailers – mostly the dominant supermarkets and chain stores (Fig. 8.12).

UBEP in South America

Between 1970 and 1974, some Central American producers (Fig. 8.13) tried to raise the export taxes paid by the TNCs. However, the corporations resisted strongly, setting off the 'Banana War' of price bargaining and searching for new banana growers. In response to this, the Central American countries gave in to the TNCs and dropped their taxes. Collectively, they lost millions of dollars of revenue from their banana exports each year.

In 1974 a group of South American producers formed the Union of Banana Exporting Countries (UBEP). UBEP's original members were Guatemala, Nicaragua,

Colombia, Costa Rica and Panama. These countries were joined later by the Dominican Republic (1976) and Honduras (1979) and together, inspired by the successes of OPEC (Fig. 7.12 and 7.13), they hope to use their group's power to secure prices and guarantee markets.

Overall, UBEP's share of the world banana market is almost 70 per cent. Were this to increase, UBEP would hold considerable power over the large fruit corporations and consumer nations. In such a position, UBEP could seek the abolition of the 20 per cent European Union (EU) import tariff on Central American bananas. This tariff alone costs Central America around US$1.5 billion every year.

Caribbean co-operation

In the same way that the South American countries grouped together for economic protection, so some Caribbean countries grouped to protect the interests of their banana growers (Fig. 8.14). Historically, these countries were colonies tied into trade agreements to supply particular products for their European colonisers.

Since independence, St. Lucia, the other Windward Islands, Jamaica, Guadeloupe and Martinique have kept close links with their former colonisers, the UK and France. They also formed the Five Islands Group to maintain banana prices, give the growers a steady income and keep jobs on the family-owned fruit farms. In fact, we can see these countries' past colonial ties in

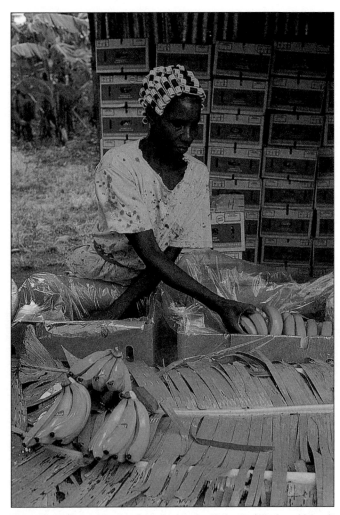

Figure 8.14 Preparing bananas for export, St Lucia, Windward Islands

Figure 8.15 UK banana imports, 1991

Table 8.3 Banana differences

Five Island bananas	Dollar bananas
• higher risk of crop damage from hurricanes	• production areas outside the world's hurricane zones
• mainly grown on family-run small farms	• mainly grown on plantations owned by transnational companies
• family workers sharing wages and profits	• low wages and often poor living conditions, with a ban on trade unions
• high proportion of manual work	• high degree of mechanisation
• softer, browner-skinned bananas, variable in size	• larger bananas, more uniform size, often yellow/green skins

?

10 Banana sales to the UK make up 70 per cent of Dominica's export earnings. These bananas are usually grown by poor farmers who get only 1.5 per cent of the sale value. Comment on the impact of: • past colonial relations, • TNCs, • tariffs and • trade blocs on both Caribbean and South American growers.

11 Assess the dangers of over-reliance on the commodities exports for the developing countries.

the UK's banana purchases (Fig. 8.15). While France and the UK buy bananas from their former colonies, other countries, such as Germany, prefer to 'shop' for cheaper bananas. These are known as 'Dollar bananas'.

Recently, the USA called for a lifting of the preferential treatment some EU countries give to the Caribbean banana producers and demanded that a free trade system prevail. It was through the Lome Treaty first signed in 1975, that some European countries (such as France and the UK), agreed to import bananas from the Caribbean at the same time as imposing import duties on bananas entering Europe from elsewhere. All the bananas exported by Dominica, Grenada, St Lucia and St Vincent enter Europe under this existing agreement. The big banana producing companies have complained that the agreement is unfair. For example, Chiquita claims to have lost £400 million between 1996 and 1999 because of the trade agreements between Europe and the Caribbean producers. As the dispute continues and since the Lome Treaty is up for renewal in 2000, most experts believe that the Caribbean will inevitably lose its preferential treatment and that market forces will prevail. If this is the case, the small farmers in the producing areas will be the losers while the big producers will be the main beneficiaries.

Table 8.4 GATT and changes to trade with WTO (*Source: Financial Times*, 16 Dec. 1993)

GATT	Changes with WTO	Impact
Industrial tariffs About 5% in rich countries (was 40% in 1940s)	• Tariffs on industrial goods cut by rich countries by more than 33% • 40% of imports enter duty free • Main traders scrap duties on pharmaceuticals, construction equipment, medical equipment, steel, beer, furniture, farm equipment, spirits, wood, paper and toys	• Easier access to world markets for exporters of industrial goods • Lower prices for consumers • Higher-paying jobs as industries become more competitive
Agriculture High subsidies and protected markets in Europe and USA lead to over-production e.g. 1992 OECD grants at $354bn and dumping of surpluses	• Subsidies cut • Farm grants cut 20% • Import barriers converted to tariffs and cut 36% • Japan's and S Korea's closed rice markets opened • Tariffs on tropical products cut 40%	• Lower food prices for consumers • Better sales opportunites for producers • Special treatment for developing countries
Services No international rules covering services, e.g. banking, insurance, transport, tourism, telecommunications, so much protectionism	• Rules for fair trade established • Markets to open between individual countries	• Trade in services boosted
Intellectual property Trade friction with no standard of protection for patents, copyrights or trademarks; much trade in counterfeit goods	• International agreement on patents, copyright and trademarks • Extra time for developing countries to put rules in place	• Boost for foreign investment and technology transfer • Poor countries fear higher prices patents, for drugs and seeds
Textiles and clothing Imports to rich countries restricted; high tariffs; protection raises prices but fails to protect jobs	• Tariffs reduced by both developed and developing countries • Quotas dismantled	• Developing countries able to sell more textiles and clothing abroad • Reduced prices for consumers worldwide

12 Several **non-governmental organisations** (**NGOs**), such as Christian Aid, Traidcraft and World Development Movement, are campaigning for fairer trade terms in developing countries (see section 11.3). You are the publicity officer for one of these NGOs. Write an article for your magazine outlining the reasons for your charity's work.

13 Discuss the possible effects of a reduction in government subsidies to farmers in the European Union.

8.5 General Agreement on Tariffs and Trade

The General Agreement on Tariffs and Trade (GATT) is an international organisation set up in 1947 to encourage open economies and free trade among all nations. GATT was one result of the Bretton Woods conference, held in 1944, to discuss world economic problems following World War 2 (see section 2.3). Together with the World Bank and International Monetary Fund (IMF), GATT was established to help control the world economy and to promote global competition and corporate enterprises. In 1994, over 100 nations were signatories of the agreement.

The underlying principle of GATT is that free movement of all goods and capital will ultimately lead to rapid global economic development. Since its creation, GATT has played a major part in world trade and commodity pricing. However, the goal of global development failed to materialise. As we are aware, the economic gap between developed and developing countries has in fact widened (see Fig. 1.1).

GATT and the developing countries
Economists in both developed and developing countries blame the failure of GATT for some problems of developing countries. These include:

- Growing debts (60 per cent of GDP for some countries in 1992), due in part to unfavourable terms of trade under GATT.
- Budget and trade deficits, particularly for countries that rely on a single commodity.
- Discriminatory tariffs: i.e., low tariffs on commodities and high tariffs on semi-finished and finished products which discriminate against developing countries (see Fig. 8.8).

?

14 How would you structure international trade? Do you think it needs to reduce the bias towards the developed countries, or not? Give your reasons.

15 Discuss the ways in which trading has led to increasing economic dependency of the developing countries on the developed nations, since the end of the colonial period.

16 Essay: Attempts to improve the bargaining position of the developing countries and reduce world poverty can only succeed with the support and co-operation of the developed countries. Discuss.

8.6 World Trade Organisation

The World Trade Organisation (WTO) began on 1 January 1995, replacing GATT (Table 8.4). It was formed following the eighth round of multilateral negotiations of GATT and GATT's member states signed the new agreement on 15 April 1994 in Marrakech, Morocco.

The major issues covered by the new WTO are outlined as follows:

- Reduction of tariffs and opening up of markets: e.g. the European agricultural market will be opened up with a 30 per cent cut in farm subsidies; protective barriers against imports of textiles will be reduced.
- General agreement on trade of services: the aim is to open up world markets and promote international financial and insurance services.
- Trade-Related Intellectual Property Rights (TRIPS): TRIPS protects patents by individuals or companies, giving legal protection against piracy or theft.

WTO and developing countries

The new WTO scheme gives developed countries control over many of the economic policies of developing countries. For example, while TRIPS covers agricultural products, medicines and other primary products, it is still the developed countries who control much of their development and production. Transnational companies who manufacture pharmaceutical products, genetically engineered agricultural seeds and artificial fertilisers will thus enjoy new patent rights, giving them greater control over the goods. This makes competition by local industries illegal.

As a result of WTO, the developing nations which export much of their agricultural produce are now forced to open up their markets. This is in contrast with the developed countries, especially the USA and members of the European Union, who refuse to remove trade barriers against imports from the developing countries.

Many development experts believe that WTO, just as GATT, is biased towards the richer nations. WTO considers the corporate business interests of the developed nations while paying little attention to the needs of, and the growing poverty, in many developing nations.

The advent of the knowledge-based society opens up a promising path to dematerialisation, making intensive use of information and skills, rather than natural resources.

A knowledge-based society, emphasising creativity and diversity, can enlarge human choices. Although knowledge is created by private individuals, knowledge is a public good because we can share it without diminishing. Three important issues:

- A knowledge-based society is more than a service economy. In a knowledge-based society typical workers are highly skilled, and their knowledge resides in their brains and life experience, rather than in the machines that they operate.
- Any restriction on the sharing of knowledge is inefficient, because knowledge can be shared at no cost and can make others better off. But without some restrictions, there may be no incentive to create new knowledge. Solving this paradox of knowledge may require new institutions.
- A knowledge-based society is also an information society. An information society requires information infrastructure, encompassing such modes of telecommunications as cable and satellite coverage and telephone lines; computer infrastructure, such as personal computers and the Internet; and social infrastructure, such as educated people and an open society that allows information to flow freely within a society and to and from the rest of the world.

Source: Human Development Report, 1998

Figure 8.16 Potential share of knowledge-based society

Figure 8.17 Top Internet countries

8.7 Communications and development

Economic development that depends essentially on the use of natural resources is becoming a thing of the past. Future development is likely to be linked to new patterns of consumption, new technologies and greater efficiency in resource use (Fig. 8.16).

Access to information and communication facilities is an essential aspect of the development process. Communication technologies comprising computers, fibre-optics and satellite systems have all changed the amount and speed at which information can be stored, transmitted and exchanged. In recent times, the development of the Internet and World Wide Web has had significant impacts on the way we work, live and play (Fig. 8.17). Just like the Industrial Revolution in Europe during the eighteenth century when the use of machines became popular in industry and commerce, computers became a dominant feature of the 1990s. This has become known as the information highway phenomenon. In 1995, the worldwide sale of computer chips was more than US$150 billion. Currently, the number of Internet users is put at 50 million worldwide, while about 10 000 new computer hosts (computers through which users connect to the network) are added every day.

However, as with other resources covered in this book, there is a huge gap in the telecommunications infrastructure between the developed and developing worlds. About 80 per cent of the world's population still lacks the most basic communications technologies on which the modern economic activities depend. Over 90 per cent of internet hosts are in North America and Western Europe (Fig. 8.18) and access by poor countries to global high-tech communications is very limited (Fig. 8.19).

Apart from the uneven distribution of information technologies, some critics have expressed concern over the negative effects of computerisation, especially in the workplace. The widespread use of computers means most activities can be automated with fewer people required to perform certain tasks. This trend has been blamed for the growing rates of unemployment in Europe and North America. Between 1983 and 1993, banks in the US replaced 37 per cent of their workforce with automated banking machines (ATMs) and by the year 2001, it is estimated that 30–40 per cent of jobs in banking and finance will be eliminated. The International Metalworkers Federation in Geneva predicts that by 2025, only 2 per cent of the current global labour force will be needed to produce all the goods necessary for total consumption.

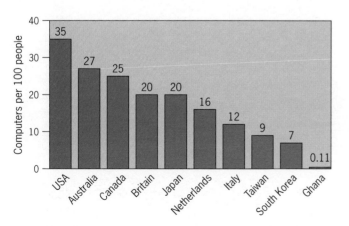

Figure 8.18 Computers per 100 people

Region by income	Population (millions)	GDP per capita (per 100 people)	Phone line (per 100 people)	Personal computers (per 100 people)
Low	3147	$415	1.5	0.14
Lower middle	1111	$1529	8.4	0.72
Upper middle	508	$4515	14.4	2.68
High	839	$22 621	51.9	18.26

Figure 8.19 Basic telecommunications infrastructure

?

17a In what ways has the spread of information technology affected the way people live in your community?
b What are the potential social and economic problems associated with the widespread use of these technologies?
c Suggest ways in which the information gap between the developed and developing countries can be reduced.

Summary

- The structure of world trade today has its origins in the colonial period.

- Much of the wealth of the industrialised nations was founded on the supply of commodities from the colonies.

- Most developing countries still depend on the export of commodities.

- While the volume of trade of commodities has increased in the last two decades, the value of such products has declined significantly.

- The dependency on commodity exports by many developing countries makes them vulnerable to outside influences.

- Attempts by some developing countries to stabilise primary commodities prices, by forming trade groups, have largely failed.

- Some countries have organised trading blocs to protect their economies with tariff barriers.

- Many developing countries face discrimination by high tariffs on the import of manufactured goods.

- The international trade organisations have failed to address the disadvantaged position of many developing countries in international trade.

- Future development is likely to be linked to access to the new information technologies.

9 Regional development policies

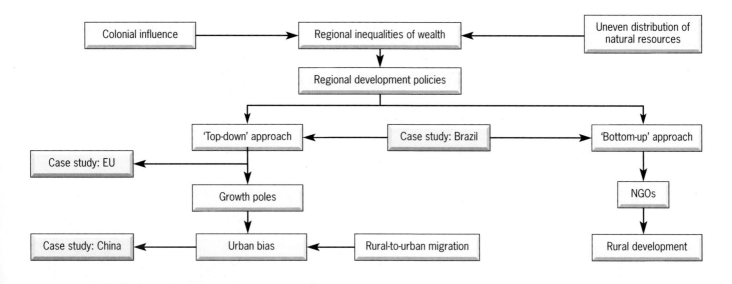

9.1 Introduction

Just as we have seen inequalities of wealth on a world scale, so we can see such divisions on a regional scale. Most governments face the challenge of how best to spread wealth and economic opportunity evenly across their country. In this chapter we discuss approaches to addressing this problem in both **developed** and **developing countries**.

9.2 Reasons for regional disparities of wealth

As we have seen, natural resources are never distributed evenly (see Fig. 7.11). Areas rich in natural resources are at an advantage and frequently develop into **core areas**, while the relatively poorer areas remain on the **periphery** (see section 1.4). The terms core and periphery refer to richer and poorer areas of a country respectively. In Friedmann's model (see Fig. 1.17) those in between are 'upward/downward transitional areas' or 'resource frontiers'.

All countries also vary in climate, soils and altitude. These variations can give one area excellent opportunities for agriculture, for example, whilst in another, even **subsistence** farming is difficult.

Additionally, variations in development may have their roots in a country's past. For example, we can partly explain the core and peripheral regions in Brazil by its colonial history. Brazil became a Portuguese colony in 1500. It was governed directly by Portugal until 1822. During this time, the Portuguese exploited the country as a source of commodities for export. Gold, silver, diamonds, timber, sugar and coffee were produced, principally from the south-east of the country and exported to an expanding Europe (Fig. 9.1).

The Portuguese made the south-east of the country their centre for trade and commerce (though they had at first preferred the north-east, where sugar-cane was the primary resource). Ports on the Atlantic coast, such as Rio de Janeiro, Salvador, Fortaleza, Recife and Santos, grew up to export raw materials from Brazil and to import finished products from Europe (see Fig. 9.11). The Portuguese discouraged manufacturing in Brazil throughout the 18th century to prevent competition with their own goods imported from Portugal.

Figure 9.1 São Paolo: statue of the *Bandeirantes*, **Portuguese pioneers who explored Brazil in their search for gold and diamonds.**

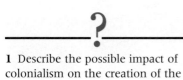

1 Describe the possible impact of colonialism on the creation of the rich core and the poor peripheral areas of a country (see also section 2.2).

2 Study Figures 9.2 and 9.3.
a What are the objectives in the creation of growth 'poles'?
b How does the creation of growth poles benefit: • cities, • rural areas?
c Why might large distances between major urban centres and remote peripheral areas make the creation of growth-poles difficult?

3 Using a base map of the UK, identify the major economic growth poles.

9.3 Two approaches to regional development

Regional policies aim to spread economic wealth and development evenly across a country and so reduce differences between regions. There are two approaches to regional policies.

The 'top-down' approach

The government makes decisions about development of regions without the involvement of local people. These 'interventionist' policies tend to concentrate on investment in industry in urban areas, based on the theory that economic growth will spread from large cities to small villages.

Governments therefore often concentrate development resources in **growth poles**, or urban centres. The authorities hope that economic growth will take place and then spread into surrounding areas (Figs 9.2–9.3).

Governments may also designate **growth corridors**, or axes, to encourage industrial investment. Such corridors are usually along major roads which provide good access and so connect large urban centres (Figs 9.4–9.5).

Myrdal's model (see section 1.4) suggests that the spread of development will occur naturally, but most governments favour this interventionist approach.

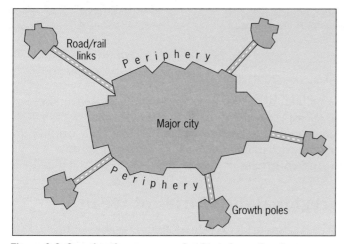

Figure 9.2 Growth poles: an example of top-down planning. Governments direct development funds to specific towns away from a major city. Good road and rail links are an important part of this strategy.

Figure 9.3 Greenfield growth pole in Wales: the UK government gave Sony huge financial incentives to build their new factory on a greenfield site at Pencoed in South Wales, adjacent to the M4 motorway and main railway lines

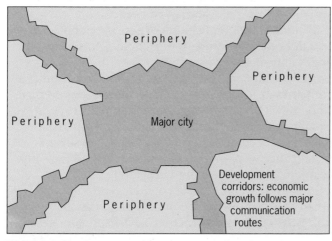

Figure 9.4 Development corridors: an example of top-down planning. Governments direct development funds to development axes along major roads spreading from a core city into the periphery.

Figure 9.5 Development corridor in the south of England: industrial and business park next to the A329 motorway off the M4, Winnersh, Reading

Figure 9.6 Bottom-up approach: women from Saidpur area constructing embankments to prevent flooding, Bangladesh

?

4a Explain how the development of growth 'corridors' could reduce the size of the periphery and so improve living standards across a region/country (Figs 9.4–9.5).
b Describe why growth corridors may develop automatically, without government assistance.
c Suggest reasons why some countries, such as the UK, make deliberate attempts to control the spread of growth corridors along major routeways.

5a What methods has your government used to encourage economic growth in depressed areas?
b How could you measure whether such policies have been successful?

6 You are a Christian Aid representative for Uganda. Explain to members of a remote rural village what advantages they might receive from a bottom-up approach to regional planning.

7 Do you think a bottom-up approach would also work for regional planning in developed countries? Give reasons for your answer.

The 'bottom-up' approach

The 'bottom-up' approach is people-centred, concentrating on helping people to help themselves. It involves local people being involved in making decisions about how their region is managed. As such, local communities, especially those in rural areas, are consulted when their government is planning the best method to provide them with food, safe drinking water, shelter, hygiene, health care and education.

Non-governmental organisations (**NGOs**) often give financial aid and technical expertise to help with community-based development strategies (see section 2.5). The projects the NGOs promote are generally small-scale so that groups of people can use relevant technology and local resources. Success of these projects, however, depends on the local people being actively involved and taking control from the beginning, even when outside expertise is involved (see sections 11.2, 11.3).

In bringing development to rural areas, many local projects also provide permanent work and prevent migration to the cities. For example, local people may work to reclaim land by building flood defences and then, once built, the project allows farmers to use their land productively (Fig. 9.6). Without fertile land, farmers could not earn an income, and so would have to leave area, perhaps for a city where they may be unable to find work.

Small-scale local development projects aim to be self-sufficient, but most experts believe that integration with larger-scale national development policies is important. Thus, good transport and communication systems between smaller communities and larger centres are essential.

9.4 Regional development policies in the developed countries

In most developed countries, regional development strategies focus on the promotion of industry and job creation. These policies aim to improve people's standard of living, particularly in areas of industrial decline and in times of recession. Regional policies in developed countries tend to follow the top-down approach.

European Union regional policy

There are large variations in the levels of economic development within the European Union (EU). Parts of the EU are very prosperous, while others are under-developed (Table 9.1, Figs 9.7–9.8).

One of the aims of the European Commission is to reduce inequalities of wealth and to raise the standard of living in all regions of the EU. A purpose, therefore, of the single market, established in 1993, was to make it easier for industry to invest anywhere in Europe. This was in response to growing fears that the core (see Fig. 1.10) would continue to attract industry at the expense of the periphery, for example Spain and Greece. This would widen the gap between rich and poor areas.

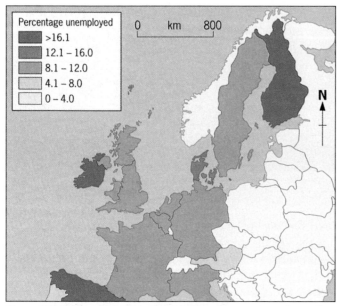

Figure 9.7 Regional unemployment in Europe as a percentage of the working population (Source: Geography Review 1998)

Table 9.1 GNP per capita for European Union countries, 1992–97 (*Source:* World Development Report 1998/99)

Country	US$ (1992)	US$ (1997)
Greece	7 290	13 080
Portugal	7 450	13 840
Ireland	12 210	16 740
Spain	13 970	15 720
UK	17 790	20 520
Italy	20 460	20 060
Netherlands	20 480	21 340
Belgium	20 880	22 370
Finland	21 970	18 980
France	22 260	21 860
Austria	22 380	21 980
Luxembourg	22 600	45 330
Germany	23 030	21 300
Denmark	26 000	22 740
Sweden	27 010	19 030

?

8 Using a base map of Europe, devise a suitable scale and map the data in Table 9.1.

9 Study Figures 9.7 to 9.10. With reference to Figure 1.10, describe some of the main features of the European core and periphery.

Approximately 9% of Structural Funds are reserved for Community Initiatives or areas with special needs, for example:

- Telematique: promotes advanced telecommunications in Objective 1 regions.
- Regen: promotes the construction of gas and electricity distribution networks in Objective 1 regions.
- Rechar: assists areas suffering from colliery closures
- Interreg: assists areas close to national borders disadvantaged by their peripheral location.

Figure 9.8 Regions in the European Union eligible for structural funds (*Source: Geography Review,* 1998)

Structural Funds amount to less than 0.5% of the total GDP of all the member countries.

A technology park has been created in Malaga and parts of Seville's Expo '92 site are being offered for high-tech research and development.

Regional GDPs vary from 83% higher than the European average in Hamburg to 61% lower than the average in Voreio Algaio in Greece.

The 'high-accessibility' belt between London and Milan has become a **megalopolis** of 80 million people.

The Highlands and Islands of Scotland has one of the most advanced telecommunications networks in Europe. This gives small businesses in the region the ability to link instantly to major centres of commerce and industry.

There is evidence that poorer and less successful cities, dominated by traditional industries, are slipping behind other cities which can attract tertiary and quarternary industries e.g. Greater London has 116 head offices, Helsinki has 12, Copenhagen has 5.

Figure 9.9 Observations about EU regional development policies

Financial assistance

All disadvantaged regions receive financial assistance from the EU's Structural Funds. There are three main categories of funding:
1 European Regional Development Fund (ERDF) is for disadvantaged regions.
2 European Social Fund (ESF) provides training and employment for the unemployed and, in some areas, helps small and medium-sized businesses to train their workforces.
3 European Agricultural Guidance and Guarantee Fund (EAGGF) supplies monies to the Common Agricultural Policy (CAP). All regions in the EU receive support from EAGGF.

The main objectives of these Funds are:
Objective One The provision of improved infra-structure and new industries in regions with a GDP per capita less than 70 per cent of the EU average and any other region where economic growth is slight. Objective One regions are a priority and received approximately 70 per cent of the Structural Funds between 1994 and 1999 (Table 9.2).

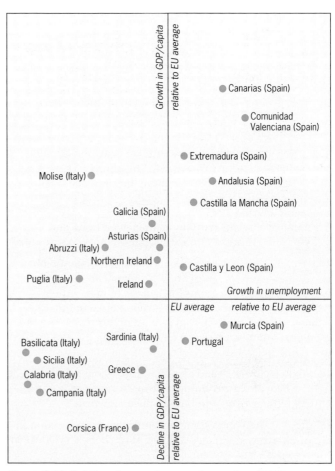

Figure 9.10 Relative changes in unemployment and GDP per capita in Objective One regions during the 1980s (*Source: Drake, 1994*)

Table 9.2 Allocation of Structural Funds by country

Country	Allocation 1989–93	Country	Allocation 1989–93
Spain	£12 000 million	Germany	£5 500 million
Italy	£9 000 million	Ireland	£3 500 million
Portugal	£6 500 million	Belgium	£800 million
Greece	£6 500 million	Netherlands	£700 million
France	£5 500 million	Denmark	£300 million
UK	£5 500 million	Luxembourg	£60 million

Objective Two The promotion of economic development by encouraging economic diversification in regions suffering from decline and high unemployment. More recently, there has been a tendency to focus support on small- to medium-sized enterprises and on 'soft' infrastructure in the residents' capacities and skills within these regions to enable them to participate in development projects (i.e. a bottom-up approach).
Objective Three The promotion of new economic activities, such as small-scale industry or tourism, in rural areas.

Governments and the European Commission decide jointly how much money will be donated to each region, but the region's national government decides

?

10a Using Table 9.2, draw a choropleth map to show the allocation of Structural Funds throughout the EU by 1993.
b How has the allocation of Funds 1989–93 influenced the changes in GNPs for 1997?

11 Describe how closely the distribution of funds reflects the core/periphery pattern which you described in 9, and as shown in Figure 1.10.

12a Referring to Tables 9.1 and 9.2, use Spearman's rank correlation to test the following null hypothesis: There was no statistically significant relationship between the wealth of a country and the size of the Structural Funds allocation between 1989 and 1993.
b Comment on your result by stating: • the trend and stength of the relationship; • the significance of your result.

13a Explain how European policy makes sure that national governments cannot ignore their peripheral areas.
b Categorise the statements in Figure 9.10 into: • those which believe that convergence is taking place in Europe; • those which do not see convergence occurring.
c Suggest other ways in which European funds could be used to help peripheral areas.

14 Study Figure 9.10 and identify those regions which appear to have benefited from European assistance in terms of the growth of their GDPs and rates of unemployment.

15 Collect information from daily newspapers concerning the use of EU Structural Funds. Do you think there is evidence of convergence?

16 With reference to the UK, explain how the EU regional development policy has influenced the location of economic activities in the peripheral regions.

how the money is spent. To stop governments cutting their own spending in the disadvantaged regions, any EU grant must be matched by national government funds. This is the principle of additionality. In fact, there is evidence which suggests that the opportunity to obtain EU funds actually encourages national governments to spend more on disadvantaged regions.

European regional development: success or failure?
It is difficult to assess the success or failure of these regional policies (Fig. 9.9). Many of the countries that have joined the EU in recent years have a low GDP per capita, so it is hard to calculate the effect of EU aid after only a short time. Politicians speak of 'convergence', with the reduction in the gap between the rich and poor regions in Europe, but opinion varies. Globalisation is also influencing development in peripheral areas.

9.5 Regional policies in developing countries

Regional policies in developing countries have tended to copy those in the developed, industrialised countries by using top-down strategies. As a result, most investment is in capital-intensive modern industry. However, the demand for labour by these industries can be relatively small. The factories are usually located in urban, core, areas to make the best use of the concentration of facilities, such as financial and insurance services, skilled labour with managerial skills and high-tech methods of production. As a consequence, the more remote, rural areas receive little investment or support.

Regional development in Brazil

Brazil is the fifth most populated country in the world with 159 million people in 1994. It is the largest country in South America, of 8.5 million square kilometres, and has a wide variety of geographical and climatic regions (Fig. 9.11). Brazil is classified as a **newly industrialising country** (**NIC**) (see section 6.7) and has one of the largest economies in the world. However, the wealth of the country is not distributed evenly (Table 9.3, see Fig. 4.3).

Post-colonial development
In the post-colonial period, after 1822, Brazilian exports, dominated by tobacco and coffee, were produced on plantations mainly in the south-east of the country. The income from the coffee plantations helped fund the first stage of industrialisation in Brazil (Fig. 9.12). As the main industries grew up in the south-east, so the regional imbalances of wealth, previously established by the Portuguese, continued to develop.

Table 9.3 Brazil: selected indicators of development compared with the USA, 1999 (Sources: Population Reference Bureau, World population Data Sheet 1999, Human Development Report 1998.

Country	Population, 1999 (millions)	Population growth (%)	Urban population (%)	Infant mortality (per 100 births)	GNP per capita, 1997 (US$)	Unemployment 1995 (%)	External debt, 1996 (million US$)
Brazil	168.0	1.5	78	41	4 790	4.3	179 047
USA	272.5	0.6	75	7.0	29 080	0.5	—

- Ports established by the Portuguese for the export of raw materials
— Main road
— Railway

Climate zones
- Hot, wet/Tropical
- Semi-arid
- Semi-tropical
- Sub-tropical/Temperate

When the Portuguese arrived in Brazil they thought they had found a paradise of untold wealth. They called it El Dorado, the land of gold.
Natural resources include:

- Iron ore
- Gold
- Salt
- Manganese
- Diamonds and gemstones
- Bauxite
- Lead
- Chromium
- Tin
- Copper
- Nickel

Figure 9.11 Brazil: climate, states and communications

Figure 9.12 Brazilians continued development after Portuguese influence diminished: improving the railway network, São Paulo, c.1900

Industrial growth

During the 1940s Brazil's dependence on coffee lessened with the development of food and textile industries, mainly in the south-east. The government also invested, with foreign companies, in the manufacture of motor vehicles and components, the production of iron, steel and chemicals and engineering industries.

However, Brazil has limited reserves of fossil fuels and has to import three-quarters of its oil requirements. The main oil refineries are close to Rio de Janeiro, Belo Horizonte and the São Paulo area in the south-east (Fig. 9.13). The first regions to supply hydro-electric power (HEP) were also in São Paulo and the Minas Gerais areas. HEP now produces 90 per cent of the country's electrical energy supply. For these two reasons, industry continues to locate in the south-east, although successive governments have tried to reduce the regional inequalities resulting from this concentration of industry. Governments have encouraged transnational corporations to establish plants in areas outside the industrial 'triangle' by stressing the lower labour costs elsewhere. None the less, the superior facilities and infrastructure of the south-east still remain attractive.

Regional policy in Brazil

There have been different approaches to regional policy in Brazil. Some are based on top-down methods, as used in developed countries, and others on the bottom-up approach.

Brazil's own schemes

In 1956 the Brazilians built a new administrative capital, Brasilia (Fig. 9.11). They hoped the new city would integrate the country more fully and focus development resources on the interior. One aspect of this was the construction workers who built the new capital. They came from the north-east where unemployment levels were high.

In another effort at integration, governments have tried to attract modern industries to the north-east of the country around Recife and Salvador. Brazil considers these cities to be important growth poles with great economic potential (Fig. 9.13). In addition, engineers have built modern irrigation systems to boost the area's traditional agricultural income which, in the past, has suffered from drought.

Since the world-wide increase in oil prices after the 1973 crisis (see Fig. 7.13), the Brazilians have adopted strategies for conserving energy as well as developing a fuel derived from sugar-cane. This has stimulated growth, especially in the north-east where suger-cane grows, and has reduced Brazil's dependence on imported oil.

A top-down plan with the World Bank

In 1982 Brazil started the Polonoroeste Project (Fig. 9.14). The World Bank lent Brazil US$443 million for the project.

A bottom-up regional development approach in Brazil

In 1988 four rural workers' unions founded the Agrarian Foundation of Tochantins-Agraguaia (FATA) in the northern province of Pará. With the support of Christian Aid (an NGO), FATA is funding **sustainable** development for the 60 000–70 000 small-scale farmers devoted to growing rice and sugar-cane in the area.

Between 12 000 and 15 000 peasant families directly benefit from the project. Collectively, the farmers decide which types of crop they will grow and the scale of production. To help them, FATA has created a small farmers' co-operative where the farmers develop strategies for marketing rice and avoid any costly middle sales person. This means that the farmers receive most of the profit from the sale of their crops. In addition, FATA has built a

Figure 9.13 Economic growth centres in Brazil

?

17 Use Figure 9.13 to draw the country's core and peripheral regions on a base map of Brazil. With reference to Friedmann's model (see section 1.4) label the: • core areas; • upward transitional areas; • downward transitional areas; • resource frontiers.

18 Compare and comment on Brazil's regional development policies.

Scheme:
• aimed to ease population pressure in Brazil's crowded south-east.
• aimed to provide land for migrants from the south who had lost their jobs as a result of agricultural mechanisation.
• involved a major national advertising programme to attract Brazilians to this new frontier.
• Involved building a 1500km highway and access roads through the heart of the Amazon Basin.
• Involved landowners buying massive areas of deforested land from migrants and converting them for commercial agriculture e.g. cattle pastures; sugar-cane plantations for Gasohol programme.
• TNCs building new factories e.g. Goodyear; Volkswagen; Nestlé; Nixdorf computer.
• released new resources and minerals e.g. copper, bauxite, zinc; timber, rubber.

Figure 9.14 Aerial view of part of the Polonoroeste Project, Rondonia State, Brazil. This part of the Amazon Basin was virgin rainforest in the early 1970s. By the late 1970s the Brazilian government had designated the area as a resettlement region for people from the drought-prone north-east and urban south. The region, equal to 80% of the size of France, now shows extensive deforestation along roads and rivers.

Problems:
• migrants found the lands to be unsuitable for settlement and agriculture because even after one harvest the delicate Amazon soils became unproductive. Only rainforest agriculture, or shifting cultivation, is sustainable because it allows the rainforest time to restore itself.
• many migrants were therefore forced to sell their land and return to the cities looking for work.
• thousands of people were forced to find waged labour in local factories or on cattle ranches.
• 34 indigenous tribes in the area have been threatened by exposure to disease and the loss of their traditional lifestyles
• hundreds of plant and animal species unique to the rich rainforest ecosystem are at risk of extinction.

research and training complex where courses are held on relevant topics for small-scale farmers. The success of FATA shows that large-scale and export-orientated agriculture is not the only way to improve living standards. This bottom-up approach provides an alternative way forward in which the poor are involved and traditional skills are valued and shared for the benefit of all.

In conclusion, despite government attempts to reduce regional inequalities, the development problems of Brazil persist. We saw the extent of these problems in the scale of Brazilian debt and the poverty felt by the majority of the Brazilian population (see Table 9.3).

9.6 Problems in developing countries

Export-led growth drives many development strategies in the developing countries but it favours metropolitan core regions. For example, large areas of farmland devoted to growing export crops on plantations in Brazil left little land to produce goods for local or national consumption. As a result, subsistence farmers lost their land (see Fig. 4.3), while jobs on the plantations were insecure because of the fluctuations in demand for primary products (see Chapter 8).

In some developing countries, governments enforce national policies for development. These, though, tend to ignore specific regional conditions, local needs and may not be appropriate for the local economy. In response to these problems, therefore, people now view the smaller-scale, 'bottom-up' policies as more appropriate for both local and national needs in the developing countries.

Regional development policies in China

In both developing and developed countries, regional planning tends to have an urban bias (see Figs 9.2–9.5). China is no exception. In 1979, the Chinese government established four small areas along its coast as Special Economic Zones (SEZs). These were open to the rest of the world for trade and investment. By 1984, several other urban areas were declared 'open cities', also to encourage foreign trade (Fig. 9.15).

These 'open' areas are particularly remarkable because China has a communist government which is politically opposed to capitalism and **free trade**. In the past, the government supported all industry, which meant that there was little competition or motive for local management to make a profit. However, the Chinese are now keen to learn new management and manufacturing skills to improve efficiency and make industry more profitable.

There are now 288 open cities, mainly along the coast, with a total population of 160 million people. To encourage foreign trade and investment here, the Chinese government offers a variety of incentives:

- special tax rates at 80 per cent of industrial taxes
- capital, equipment and raw materials imported into China to produce goods for export free from custom duties, VAT and import taxes
- exports, except oil and oil products, free from taxes

Figure 9.15 China's special economic zones and open cities

- high-tech industrial investment of US$30 billion subject to only 15 per cent income tax
- local control allows each city to manage its own affairs with little direction from Beijing.

China sees its low-wage-cost workers as its main asset. It hopes this cheap workforce, alongside the incentives of the SEZs, will attract foreign investors to build factories. These factories will then produce goods which China can export for hard currency. In the immediate areas surrounding these prosperous towns, China plans to improve agricultural production to feed the growing city populations and to keep the rural dwellers in work (see Fig. 4.10).

Guangdong province

One of the areas for this new economic activity is the province of Guangdong (Figs 9.16–9.17), with its capital Guangzhou, which aims to copy the commercial success of Hong Kong.

Plans to spread wealth to rural areas

The Chinese government recognises the problems of core areas prospering along a relatively narrow coastal zone (Table 9.4) at the expense of peripheral rural areas (Fig. 9.18). The government has therefore allowed individual ownership of workshops and factories in an effort to spread wealth out from the SEZs into township enterprise schemes. Such schemes include food processing and handicraft industries and are aimed at rural people who cannot find work on the land. In 1987, 23 per cent (88 million people) of the rural workforce were employed in such schemes in areas relatively close to the coastal SEZs. None the less, this government initiative has created work in construction, farm tools, cement manufacturing, coal mining and power generation.

Guangdong province:
- Six-lane motorway recently built to link Guangzhou with Hong Kong.
- Shenzhen SEZ grew rapidly from a small market town of 30 000 people in 1979 to an industrial centre of 600 000 people in 1989 with 15 000 factories.
- Exports to Europe include jackets, trainers, toys, children's clothing and electronics.
- Guangdong's export income rose from £2.3 billion to £6 billion in 5 years

Figure 9.16 Guangdong province

?

19 With reference to Figures 9.17–9.19, compare the main features of life in the remote parts of rural China with life in the coastal cities.

20 If present regional development policies go unchanged, suggest what problems there might be in the future for the Chinese government and for young people living in the peripheral parts of China.

21 You are a regional policy advisor to the Chinese government. Your brief is to reduce the economic gap between rich coastal and poor rural areas. Write a report outlining your suggestions to spread wealth and opportunity more evenly across the whole of China.

Figure 9.17 Urban China: Central Guangzhou

Figure 9.18 Rural China: village life, Dali, Yunnan Province

Table 9.4 China: average annual income per head, yuan (*Source: The Economist*, 6 June 1992)

District	yuan
Beijing	2040
Shanghai	2334
Xiamen	2737
Shenzen	4205
Guangzhou	2906
Haikou	2295
Rural China	710

Figure 9.19 China's peasants hold the seeds of discontent (*Source:* Ian Johnson, *The Guardian*, 24 Sept. 1994)

Poverty is absolute for forgotten majority

FAR away from China's boom towns is Hu Banjing, an intense girl aged 12, who lives alone in a small hut with two pigs. Her goal is to be a primary school teacher.

In this remote part of China's rugged south-west, poverty is absolute. Many people wonder how they will feed themselves, and up to 30 per cent of children do not attend school, some because their families cannot afford to clothe them.

Here the average farmer earns just over £46 a year. About 10 million of 33 million people in Guizhou province are classified as poor, meaning they earn less than £12 a year.

This is part of China often overlooked by its government. While many envision a China pulled into the future by its prosperous cities and coastal regions, the hundreds of millions inland may have more impact than the wealthy few.

Indeed the inland's widening gap with the prosperous coast worries China's rulers. With at least 80 million Chinese unable to feed or clothe themselves, the potential for instability is enormous.

Many are not bothering to stick around. About 300000 people have moved to other parts of China, according to a local official.

This flood of the economically disadvantaged is what concerns Beijing.

When China's overheated economy eventually cools, they will stop sending money back to their poor relatives and return to swell the unemployment lines there. Already, they form part of China's 'floating population' of 50 million who roam the countryside looking for work.

Summary

- Every country, whether developed or developing, has regional variations in wealth.

- Current inequalities in the distribution of wealth of developing countries may result from strategies adopted by former colonial governments.

- Regional development policies aim for a relatively even spread of wealth and development across the whole of a national territory.

- The 'top-down' approach to regional development has governments making decisions with relatively little participation from people in the region.

- 'Top-down' policies tend to concentrate development resources in a few major urban centres (growth poles) with the hope that economic development will 'trickle down', or spread, to neighbouring, economically backward areas.

- Other government interventionist approaches include policies to encourage investment in the run-down areas, mostly rural and semi-rural.

- Globalisation is leading to the location of industry in some peripheral areas.

- The 'bottom-up' approach encourages the involvement of local people in the planning and development of projects which will benefit people at the local level.

- In many developing countries, NGOs are actively involved in community-based, bottom-up development strategies.

10 Tourism as a development strategy

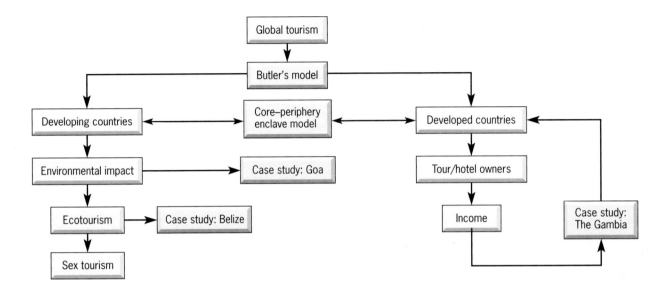

10.1 Introduction

Over the last two decades, tourism has become an important industry in both **developed** and **developing countries**. Every year, an increasing number of people travel as tourists either within their own country or abroad. In this chapter, we examine the economic, social, cultural and environmental impact of this growing industry and its role in development.

10.2 Trends in world tourism

Tourism is the world's largest growth industry. In 1950, about 25 million people travelled as tourists; by 1996 this figure had reached 529 million. Revenue from tourism in the same year reached US$423 billion, outstripping both the oil and arms trades. Most of the tourists travel from one developed country to another, but there is a growing demand for holiday destinations in the developing countries (Fig. 10.2).

1 Use Figure 10.1 to comment on the links between tourist arrivals, income from tourism and the world's economy.

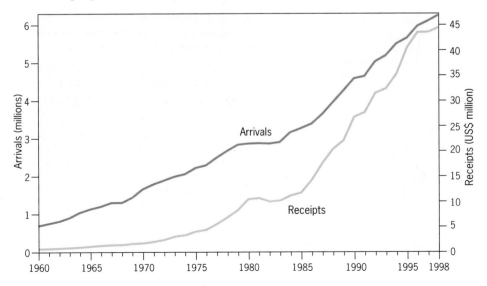

Figure 10.1 World total tourist arrivals and receipts, 1960–98 (*Source:* World Tourism Organisation, 1999)

?

2a For each world region shown in Figure 10.2, calculate the percentage rise in the number of tourist arrivals between 1980 and 1997.
b Which regions show the highest percentage growth rates?

3a With reference to Tables 10.1 and 10.2 draw two graphs to illustrate the changes in the number of tourists arriving in Africa and South Asia from the different regions of departure.
b Using the statistics provided, draw two Lorenz curves on the same graph to compare the origins of tourists visiting South Asia and Africa (see Appendix A4).

4 Summarise the changes in world tourism patterns since 1950 and suggest reasons for them.

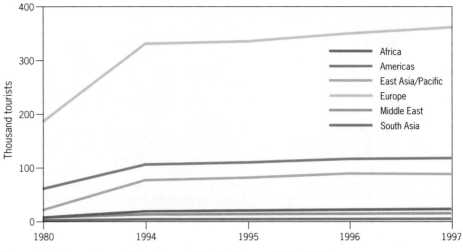

Figure 10.2 Growth in world tourism, 1980–97 (*Source*: WTO, 1999)

Table 10.1 International tourist arrivals in Africa (*Source*: WTO 1999)

	1993	1994	1995	1996	1997
Total (thousands)	18 544	19 092	2357	21 824	23 157
of which from					
Africa (%)	45.86	44.59	43.38	43.07	41.50
Americas (%)	2.92	3.06	3.30	3.42	3.74
Europe (%)	32.80	33.97	33.57	34.20	36.68
East Asia and the Pacific (%)	1.49	1.63	2.33	2.31	2.35
Middle East (%)	3.80	3.67	3.90	3.27	3.51
South Asia (%)	0.32	0.29	0.33	0.42	0.42

Table 10.2 International tourist arrivals in South Asia (*Source*: WTO 1999)

	1993	1994	1995	1996	1997
Total (thousands)	3511	3866	4200	4434	4830
of which from					
Africa (%)	2.28	2.33	2.52	2.53	2.57
Americas (%)	9.29	9.47	9.76	10.01	9.73
Europe (%)	45.17	45.81	44.69	43.48	45.34
East Asia and the Pacific (%)	12.50	12.62	12.98	13.78	13.48
Middle East (%)	5.47	4.84	4.55	4.53	4.16
South Asia (%)	25.01	24.73	25.38	25.42	24.60

10.3 The role of tourism in development

Many countries now include tourism in their development strategy. It is a valuable source of foreign currency which, in turn, stimulates economic growth. However, there are people, notably environmentalists (see Table 5.1), who are unsure of the benefits of tourism, particularly for developing countries. They feel that the social, cultural and environmental impact of tourism outweighs any economic gain. For example:

- people leave their homes and families to work in tourist resorts
- local culture becomes a spectacle for tourists
- land is taken for building hotels
- less food is grown locally and more is imported
- too much money is spent on tourist facilities
- too little money is spent on improving health, education and housing for the local population.

The core-periphery enclave model

The core-periphery enclave model (Fig. 10.3) explains the complex social influences of tourism on the developing nations and the role of tourism in economic development. It was developed by Stephen Britton in 1981, and is based on the idea of the **core** and **periphery** (see section 1.4).

Britton's model states that there is a flow of tourists from the developed countries (core) in the 'North', especially Western Europe, North America and Japan, into the developing countries (peripheral) such as The Gambia, India and the Caribbean. However, the tour operators, airlines and owners of hotels in the developing countries tend to be located in the core, so it is those developed countries that control the tourist industry.

Colonial domination and dependency has, to a very large extent, determined which countries are developed and which are developing nations (see section 2.2). Tourism has tended to continue this unequal relationship, with tourists travelling from the core countries to the periphery.

This model also states that there are tourist 'enclaves'. An enclave is an area within a developing country especially designated for tourism. Tourist facilities, such as hotels, restaurants, recreational activities and utilities (e.g. gas, water and electricity) are readily available within these enclaves. As a result, and as the model indicates, these enclaves make sure that tourists have very little contact with local residents and so rarely experience the reality of life in the host community.

?

5a Use a selection of holiday brochures to make a list of popular destinations in developing countries.
b For each country listed, identify the main resort enclaves and locate these on a base map of the country.
c Are there any common features of the enclaves you have identified?

6a To what extent do you agree with the model that the creation of resort enclaves reduces the contact between tourists and locals?
b Suggest what effects such minimal contact may have on:
• the local economy; • the visitors?

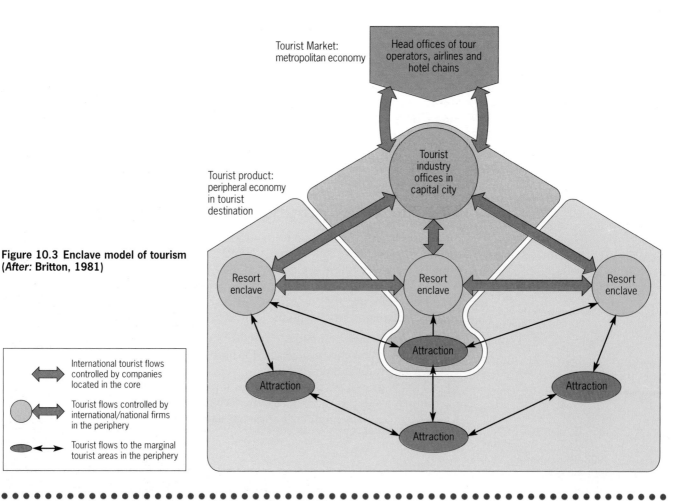

Figure 10.3 Enclave model of tourism (*After:* Britton, 1981)

International tourist flows controlled by companies located in the core

Tourist flows controlled by international/national firms in the periphery

Tourist flows to the marginal tourist areas in the periphery

The development of tourism in Goa

Goa is a small state on the west coast of India (Fig. 10.4) with a population of 1.16 million. It was a Portuguese colony for 300 years (1440–1740) although the Portugese influence was restricted to the coastal areas. We can see this particularly well in the 'Old Conquest' area, which is the part of Goa most popular with European tourists (Fig. 10.5). In contrast, Indian tourists tend to visit areas further inland which have Hindu temples, such as Ponda.

The tourist boom began in the 1960s when young people, rejecting conventional society of the developed countries, travelled to Goa. They brought 'hippie' tourism to this part of India and even in 1995 all foreign tourists in Goa are known locally as 'hippies'.

The government's plan for tourism

In the mid-1980s, the Indian Government drew up a Tourist Development Plan designating Goa as a tourist development area (Fig. 10.4). It also decided that the beaches in the states of Kerala, Orissa and Malbahlipuram should be developed for tourism. The plan proposed a wide range of tourist facilities with large five-star hotels as well as smaller, cheaper hotels.

Five-star tourism and environmental concerns

Two pressure groups emerged at this time, though, concerned that an influx of foreign tourists would cause environmental damage unless there was sensitive planning. The Goan Foundation and the Tourist Development Corporation aim to persuade the government to restrict their ambitious plans for tourism in the state of Goa. They are particularly concerned about the following issues.

Building close to the shore line

Many of these new buildings are five-star hotels, owned by foreign companies or companies from other parts of India. Until 1991 no building was allowed within 500 metres of the beaches in Goa. However, the law was then changed permitting hotel companies to build as close as 200 metres to the beaches.

Increasing numbers of high-rise buildings

The most intensive tourist development has been in Calangute (Fig. 10.4). Originally, the legal limit for the height of buildings across all of Goa was two storeys, so that no building should be higher than the palm trees, which are an impressive feature of the Goan coast. However, pressure from hotel developers has meant a change in building regulations so that there are now three- and four-storey hotels along Calangute's main road.

Wildlife visible in all the sancturies:
Monkey, bison, lepoards, panthers and tigers.
There are a variety of birds including: green bee-eaters, shrikes, large pied-wagtails, black-headed seagulls, priah kites, sparrowhawks and kestrels.

Figure 10.4 Goa

Figure 10.5 Colonial church, Old Conquest area, Goa

Water supply and the sewerage system

During the peak season, between October and May, there is a massive influx of tourists to Goa. However, there is no adequate sewerage system to cope with the increase in numbers of people. Most hotels, therefore, discharge their wastes directly into the sea. Obviously, this has serious environmental consequences threatening the coastal ecosystem.

The hotels in Goa require enormous quantities of fresh water for washing, swimming pools and the irrigation of gardens. In fact, clean drinking water is piped directly to some hotels, while many local people do not even have water on tap in their homes. However, as wells are sunk within the 500-metre limit from the high-tide line, environmentalists fear that salt water may leak into the local supplies of drinking water (Fig. 10.6).

Waste disposal

This is a relatively recent problem. The hotels, restaurants and shops buy food packed in plastic containers which soon litter the streets. At present, there is no co-ordinated refuse collection or waste management in Goa.

Golf courses

In 1993 the Goan government approved the take-over of common land for the development of two golf courses for the five-star hotels at Betul and Verna, in the foothills and on the plateaux of the Western Ghats (Fig. 10.7).

Figure 10.6 The danger of salt in drinking water, Goa

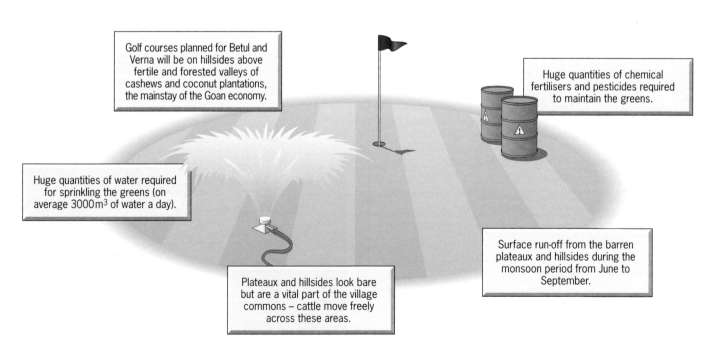

Figure 10.7 The environmental effects of golf courses in Goa

?

7 Use Figure 10.8 and other information in this section to draw a table of the advantages and disadvantages of tourism in Goa under the following headings:
• environment,
• economy,
• social/cultural influences.

8 Relate the enclave model of tourism to the Goan case study by:
a listing the tourist attractions in Goa,
b identifying tourist enclaves within Goa.

9 What do you think are the benefits from tourism to the development of Goa?

THE WORDS and imagery are persuasive: they speak of dream holidays, friendly local people, an unspoilt, palm fringed paradise. But the reality is drug abuse, child prostitution and widespread environmental destruction.

The Indian coastal state of Goa was singled out yesterday as a lesson in how mass tourism to 'exotic' locations has gone badly wrong. According to the pressure group Tourism Concern, Western tour operators are causing much of the damage but are 'washing their hands' of their responsibility.

Goa, which became a Western tourist destination after being discovered by hippies in the 1960s, is now the scene of acid parties, raves and increasing child prostitution.

Tourist buses have been pelted with rotten fish and cow dung, and police mount drives against drug-taking Westerners.

Women protest at their portrayal in tourism literature — at how 'they and events like the local carnival are being commoditised at the expense of their dignity and culture'. Children skip school to peddle drugs to Western tourists, who affront the morality of villagers by sun-bathing in the nude.

Many local groups are also angry at the special treatment tourists receive, according to a Tourism Concern survey. Hotels, many foreign-owned receive subsidised water and electricity. Yet one five-star hotel consumes as much water as five villages and one 'five-star tourist' consumes 28 times more electricity per day than a Goan.

Figure 10.8 Goa's paradise lost (*Source: The Independent*, 27 Jan. 1993)

Effects of tourism on the Goan beaches

The sea and Goa's 105 kilometre coastline are the most valuable source of income to the indigenous Goans. Approximately 50000 people are dependent on fishing mackerel, sardines, kingfish, pomfret and even shark for a living. Problems arise, though, with tourists using motorised pleasure boats which frighten the fishstock away. As a result, both the income of the local people is reduced while the sea is polluted with oil.

The beaches are also central to the livelihood of many Goans (Fig. 10.9). In fact, fishers often cast their nets directly from the beach. However, they are being denied access to some beaches as these are 'fenced off' and reserved for tourists.

The palm trees, which line the coastal fringes, are also a major source of income. 'Toddy tappers' climb the tall coconut palms and extract the sap to make brown sugar, sweets and 'feni', a potent alcoholic drink. Another local custom is for people to congregate under the palms to shelter from the intense heat at midday. Hotel owners, none the less, continue to cut down the coconut palms and replace them with lawns and buildings, thus destroying the authentic Goan environment (Fig. 10.9).

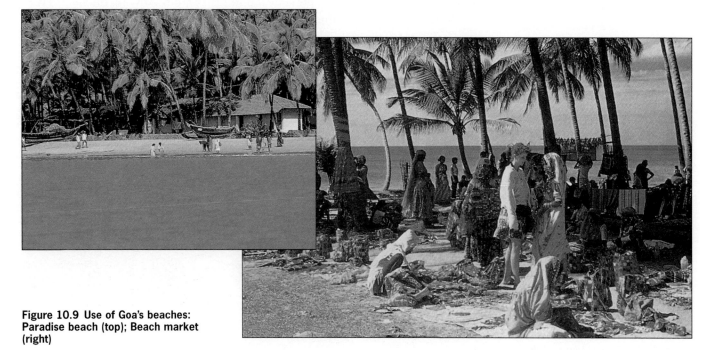

Figure 10.9 Use of Goa's beaches: Paradise beach (top); Beach market (right)

Butler's model of the evolution of tourist areas

This model examines how tourism develops and changes over time. There are six major stages in Butler's evolution theory of tourism in relation to the developing countries (Fig. 10.10).

Exploration: In which a small number of tourists independently explore a new location. The choice of a destination might come from a desire for personal adventure to explore new natural and cultural territory. At this stage, the economic, social and environmental impacts of tourism are minimal.

Involvement: If early tourists are accepted by the local community then the destination becomes increasingly popular. As more people want to explore the area, arrangements for travel, transport and accommodation are improved. This marks the beginning of local people's involvement in the promotion of tourism.

Development: As local people help to encourage and promote tourism, more outsiders are attracted to the area which leads to a well-defined tourist market. At this stage, tourist firms, mostly from the core countries in the North, take control of the management and organisation of tourism to the area. Package holidays now become commonplace and with them, the loss of local involvement.

Consolidation: Tourism now becomes an important social and economic activity in the country. The extensive development of tourism, through marketing and advertising, affects local communities. Large areas of agricultural land are bought for hotels and other tourist facilities while local people may be forbidden to use beaches reserved for tourists. This causes resentment from local people who do not see how tourism directly benefits them. During this period, the total number of tourists may increase, but the rate of increase in the numbers of tourists begins to decline.

Stagnation: The growing opposition to tourism from the local people and the increasing awareness of the economic, social and environmental problems associated with tourism may prevent the industry from growing further. Fewer new tourists visit, suggesting that the original cultural and physical attractiveness of the destination has gone.

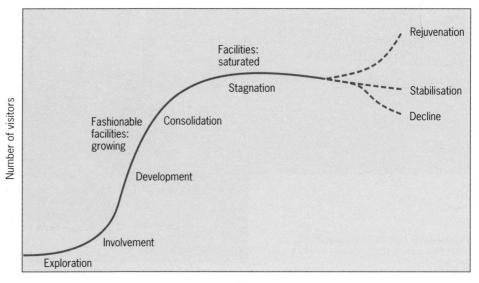

Figure 10.10 Butler's model of the evolution of tourist areas

?

10 Read Figure 10.11.
a According to Butler's model, at which stage of tourism development is South Africa?
b In what ways do you think the government should contribute to the development of tourism here?
c Assess how much the development of tourism in South Africa could stimulate economic and social development in the country as well as in the rest of southern Africa.

11 Design a questionnaire (see Appendix A2) and conduct a survey in your local community to find out:
a who has been on holiday abroad,
b the country(ies) they visited,
c their reasons for choosing such destinations,
d how long they stayed,
e the time of the year they travelled.

12 Based on the information you collect, write a report for a tour operator on holiday destination preferences by people in your community.

Decline: As the destination loses its appeal, tourism will decline. As a result, other destinations become more attractive. Because international tourist firms and operators move out, local involvement may increase for a while. However, as local investors are unable to provide the same services as the foreign tourist companies, the area will eventually lose its tourist industry.

Although the model suggests that the decline stage is reached eventually, it also recognises that it is possible for tourist areas to be rejuvenated. They do this by changing to meet new demand or by sustaining tourist interest. This has happened in Turkey and The Gambia where foreign investment in tourism is creating new resorts and recreating the old ones previously neglected.

South African job hopes ride on tourism

Passport Control at Johannesburg International Airport is overstretched, the new terminals under construction can hardly keep pace, but nobody is complaining. South Africa's tourism boom is well under way and with it the opportunity for enormous economic growth.

After decades in the wilderness, South Africa is not prepared for the onslaught. Hotels are packed, the game reserves are booked up months in advance, and there are not enough flights to meet demand. By the end of June, the number of visitors was already up 52% on the whole of last year, although this rise is expected to tail off by the year-end. For the full year 1 million foreign visitors are expected, against 700 000 in 1994.

But therein lies the new government's dilemma: if the potential of tourism is to be realised and momentum maintained, large-scale investment is vital. This year, tourist's contribution to gross domestic product is set to reach 3.6%, against 2% in 1994, but even that figure is risible against a world average of 7%–10%.

International and local hotel groups are stepping into the breach. Inter-Continental has linked up with Southern Sun to run jointly three five-star hotels in Johannesburg, Cape Town and Durban; Hilton is planning a R200m (£35m) hotel in Sandton, Johannesburg, and the Hyatt hotel also in Sandton is virtually complete. Such is the scramble for prime sites that land prices are soaring and the building cost per room has soared from R250 000 to R450 000.

But while most new hotels are in the top price bracket, two- and three-star hotels are in short supply. The next step in

'Tourism this year will account for 3.6% of GDP in South Africa. The world average is more than twice as much'

expanding tourism as a growth market is package holidays but at present they are pitched too high for the mass market. And capacity constraints are being experienced across the board.

Satour sees small hotels and bed-and-breakfast outlets as a big growth area, playing an important role in the government's strategy to integrate tourism into the wider community. In line with the RDP's aim of boosting jobs and rural welfare, game farms for instance, are widening their buying net, taking handicrafts and fresh produce from local villages. This in turn stems the flow of job seekers to the towns and encourages ecologically-sound management, reducing poaching and heightening awareness of tourism's rewards.

Figure 10.11 A new booming industry for South Africa (*Source: Madeleine Wakemagel, The Sunday Times, 8 Oct. 1995) © Times Newspapers Ltd 1995

Tourism and development in The Gambia

Figure 10.12 The Gambia

The climate, environment, flora and fauna, clean beaches and culture of The Gambia in West Africa (Fig. 10.12) attract foreign tourists. The Gambia first emerged as a tourist resort in 1965, but since then its tourist industry has grown considerably (Fig. 10.13) with the support of the United Nations Development Programme (UNDP) and the International Development Agency (IDA). Most tourists come from Northern Europe, with 57 per cent from Britain and 13 per cent from Sweden in 1989–90. In addition, the number of tourists from France, Italy and Germany is growing.

Tourism and foreign investment

Tourism contributes a significant amount to The Gambia's **GNP** (Fig. 10.14). This success is largely due to foreign investment in the industry (Fig. 10.15).

Figure 10.13 Tourist arrivals in The Gambia

For example, the Scandinavian Vingressor Group and the UK Copthorne Hotels (formerly British Caledonian Hotels) play a significant role in hotel development. The government also encourages foreign invesment with incentives of duty-free concessions, tax breaks and preferential land allocations to foreign investors.

However, most tourists in The Gambia book their holidays through a foreign tour operator, use foreign air lines and stay in foreign-owned hotels. In fact, much of the price they pay for their holiday ends up as profit which stays in the developed country where the tour company is based. Some tourism analysts suggest that only 23 per cent of the price of a package holiday to The Gambia reaches the country. Overall, The Gambia is particularly dependent on the British package-holiday market. In 1993–94, of a total of 89 000 air-charter arrivals, 61 000 were from the UK.

Tourism as an employer

Despite foreign operations, tourism does provide employment which benefits the country's economy. In 1989, more than 7000 Gambians, out of a population of one million, **formally** worked in the tourist, or its related, industries. Most of these jobs were direct employment in hotels, restaurants, tour operators and transport. In addition, there are **informal** tourist-related activities, such as manufacturing local handicrafts and supplying fruit and vegetables to hotels. About 3000 people are employed in this indirect way. Unfortunately, though, some hotels close down during the low season from April to October. This means that most workers are **under-employed** (see section 6.2) and are laid off or paid lower wages.

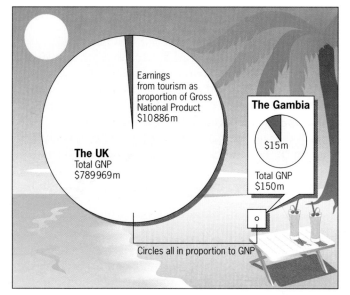

Figure 10.14 Tourism's economic importance to The Gambia (*Source: The Guardian*, 7 May 1991)

Figure 10.15 How much foreign exchange will this hotel really earn for The Gambia?

Growth of tourism and provision of tourist facilities

Tourists are usually attracted to areas where there are hotels, clean beaches and other tourist facilites. As in many countries, tourism in The Gambia is concentrated where these facilities are available, in a relatively small area near Banjul. Here, there are about 17 standard hotels with 5000 beds.

The impact of tourism on farming and regional development

Such a concentration of facilities results in wide inequalities, with the Banjul area attracting development while the 'up-country' area remains stagnant. Any further development therefore needs to ensure an even geographic distribution of tourist facilities to attract people into less developed parts of the country.

A major problem associated with tourism is that it takes labour away from farming (Fig. 10.16). As a result, the diversion of labour and investment from agriculture into tourism has resulted in an increase of food imports. In 1988, 30 per cent of food consumed in The Gambia was imported at a cost of US$105.2million.

?

13a Use Figure 10.15 to help you estimate how much international tourism expenditure reaches the local people in The Gambia.
b Discuss what might restrict the distribution of tourists' spending to local people.

14a Assess the extent of The Gambia's dependence on international tourism.
b Explain the implications of this for the country's overall economic development.

15 In what ways can a developing country, such as The Gambia, maximise economic advantages from tourism and have greater control over the industry?

Figure 10.16 Effects of tourism on agriculture

All schools and cinemas in New Delhi closed until 15 October after 18 out of 47 suspected plague cases confirmed. Some cases suspected in Rajasthan, Madhya Pradesh and Uttar Pradesh.

Forty-eight deaths from plague in India: one in Maharashtra, the rest in Surat, Gujarat. Total suspected cases: 1500: 483 in Maharashtra and 871 in Gujarat.

Figure 10.17 Keeping the tourists away (*Source: The Guardian*, 30 Sept. 1994)

Table 10.3 World's top 10 tourist destinations. (*Source:* World Tourist Organisation, *Yearbook of Tourism Statistics*, 1999)

Rank	Country	Tourist Arrivals*	World share of arrivals (%)
1	France	66 864	10.95
2	USA	47 754	7.82
3	Spain	43 403	7.11
4	Italy	34 087	5.58
5	UK	25 515	4.18
6	China	23 770	3.89
7	Poland	19 520	3.20
8	Mexico	19 351	3.17
9	Canada	17 285	2.83
10	Hungary	17 248	2.82

*in thousands

?

16 Study Tables 10.3 and 10.4.
a Suggest two reasons why so many of the top-ten countries are European.
b Using a suitable graphical technique, illustrate the world ranking of countries which are the top-ten earners and spenders on tourism.
c Identify those countries which are not *both* top-ten earners and spenders.
d Suggest reasons why the countries identified in **c** are not top tourist spenders.

10.4 Vulnerability of the tourist industry

Tourism is a fluctuating industry. Essentially, this is because of peak and low seasons, which are usually determined by the weather. However, there can also be other factors which affect tourism and its income. These include political instability, inflation, fashion and even the outbreak of disease. Personal safety therefore has a strong influence on people's choice of holiday destination. For example, the failed coup attempt in The Gambia in 1981, and the military takeover there in 1994, meant that people cancelled their package holidays. Similarly, income from tourism slumped in northern India when bubonic plague broke out in 1994 (Fig. 10.17). In fact, many developed countries now issue advice to tourists on personal safety, health and the political situation in certain holiday destinations.

10.5 Tourism in the developed countries

The growth of tourism is not just limited to the developing countries (Tables 10.3 and 10.4). In fact, political instability in some holiday destinations, in countries such as in the former Yugoslavia, The Gambia, Egypt and in the Middle East, means many tourists prefer to visit developed countries – which are probably more peaceful. One clear example of this occurred in the first year after the ceasefire in Northern Ireland. The number of visitors to the province rose by 48 per cent.

Table 10.4 World's top 10 tourist earners and spenders (*Source:* WTO, 1999)

Tourism earners				Tourism spenders		
Rank	Country	Tourism receipts (US$ million)	World share of receipts (%)	Rank	Tourism expenditure (US$ million)	World share of expenditure (%)
1	USA	73 268	16.81	1	51 220	13.56
2	Italy	29 714	6.82	5	16 631	4.40
3	France	28 009	6.42	6	16 576	4.39
4	Spain	26 651	6.11	21	4 467	1.18
5	UK	20 039	4.60	4	27 710	7.34
6	Germany	16 509	3.79	2	46 200	12.23
7	Austria	12 393	2.84	8	10 992	2.91
8	China	12 074	2.77	10	10 166	2.69
9	Hong Kong	9 242	2.12	—	—	—
10	Australia	9 026	2.07	19	6129	1.62

10.6 Ecotourism

Ecotourism, also referred to as 'rural', 'green' or 'alternative' tourism, is based on the natural environment and wildlife of a country. **Sustainability** is the main feature of ecotourism which has grown in popularity partly because of people's concern with our environment and their recognition for the need to conserve it. In addition, ecotourism provides an alternative to the mass tourism of, for example, the Mediterranean resorts. The main factors of ecotourism to ensure its sustainability include:
1 Planning and control of tourism developments – where they will be located and what they look like; transport routes; regional planning.
2 Increasing involvement and control by local and regional communities.
3 Identification of the type of tourism appropriate to local resources and environment.
4 A balance of conservation and development.

A lot of people are attracted by ecotourism because of its remoteness, the small number of people involved and its less sophisticated facilities. If these features go, then the appeal of ecotourism is lost. Consequently, development must be gradual and limited, although there is an increasing number of tour

17a Explain why some countries are included among the top 10 destinations but not listed as top tourist earners.
b Do you think that tourism has any impact on the economic development of these countries? Give reasons.

18a Research a country or region popular with tourists in either a developed or developing area.
b You are a tourist officer for this region and need to win a government grant for development. The grant is restricted to development that is sustainable. Construct a management plan for your area which combines sustainability with development for locals and tourists.

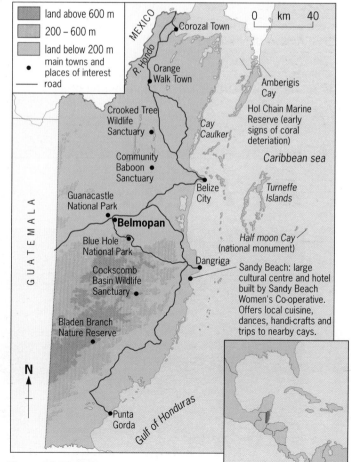

Figure 10.18 Ecotourists: a rainforest experience on a tributary of the River Amazon, Brazil

operators specialising in environmentally sensitive trips to distant and exotic locations (Fig. 10.18).

Ecotourism in Belize

Belize is almost totally undeveloped and only 15 per cent of its land area is cultivated (Fig. 10.19). As a country that recently gained its independence from the British (1981) Belize is now keen to increase its income. In 1992 Belize only had a per capita GNP of US$2200 while 20 per cent of its population of 203 957 were unemployed. The Belize government therefore sees tourism as essential for increasing foreign exchange earnings.

The tourism industry begins
The government of Belize advertises the country as 'friendly and unspoilt', and as 'Belize – so natural' (Fig. 10.20). Although the country is in the early stages of developing its tourist industry, it is keen to avoid the problems associated with mass tourism – pollution; high-rise resorts; crowding; a deteriorating natural environment. Belize therefore promotes small-scale development and tries to foster sustainable tourism.

However, each year increasing numbers of visitors are arriving in Belize. In 1994, tourist arrivals were about 200 000 per annum but the average growth rate stands at 43 per cent. Much of this growth is because of Belize's position close to some of the world's mass tourist resorts. It is only a short trip from the tourist 'crowds' of Miami and New Orleans in the USA, and Cancun in Mexico, to the relative remoteness of Belize.

Sustainable tourism
The government of Belize has designated over 30 per cent of the entire land area as national reserves. As part

Figure 10.19 Belize

of this scheme, farming is banned in the reserves because the government is concerned that both traditional, **subsistence**, 'slash-and-burn' cultivation and more **commercial farming** (see section 5.4) will upset the local ecosystem – and so threaten the country's ecotourism potential.

The government has, though, tried to consider the subsistence farmers living on the reserves. Thus, efforts are being made to incorporate the farmers' needs with the needs of the growing tourist industry. For example, at the Community Baboon Sanctuary, local farmers have agreed to limit their slash-and-burn practices and so protect the habitat of the native howler monkeys. In return, the farmers receive an income from work in tourism as more tourists are attracted to the area.

Development

The challenge for Belize's government is to cope with increasing numbers of tourists while simultaneously protecting the country's fragile ecosystem – including the rare flora and fauna which the tourists want to see. Development, of whatever size, therefore requires careful planning.

Along the coast, development has involved the clearing of mangrove swamps in the north to make room for hotels. However, mangroves perform vital ecological functions without which, the whole coastal area is at risk. Primarily, the mangroves provide rich feeding grounds for fish. Secondly, the swamps protect against coastal erosion. Other environmental problems will also occur as more building takes place. On the island of Caye Caulker, the recent building of an airstrip has destroyed nesting sites. It has also created a lake of stagnant water which may provide a breeding ground for malaria-carrying mosquitoes.

19 According to Butler's model, at what stage of development is tourism in Belize?

20a Use Figure 10.20 to decide whether you would like to visit Belize. List those features that: • attract you, • are not interesting to you.
b Make an assessment of a holiday in Belize according to:
• spending patterns (the proportion you might spend on accommodation, food and drink, souvenirs; who would get your money)
• contact with local people (how and where you would come into contact; whether your contact would help to sustain local communities)
• use of the environment (your impact on the environment; how you would use resources).

21 Write a dialogue between: • Belize's minister for tourism, trying to promote tourism for maximum economic gain, and • the environment minister, trying to minimise the impact of tourism and protect the welfare of local people.
a Consider the tensions and problems these ministers face including: • how tourism might affect the lives of people living in rural Belize; • how increasing numbers of tourists are putting pressure on the government to develop along more commercial lines.
b Try to agree on a plan for the future of tourism in Belize.

A British colony between 1638 and 1981, Belize is a small country on the edge of the Caribbean Sea. Belize particularly welcomes tourists who seek the attractions of a varied, natural, unspoilt environment. You will experience the wilds of over 2000 km² untouched mangrove swamps, wetland savanna, mountain pine forests as well as tropical rain forests. In every area there is a vast mix of wildlife including the jaguar, howler monkey, tapir and manatee. At the coast, we can offer you the longest barrier reef in the western hemisphere – second longest in the world!
You can also see tremendous archaeological sites in Belize. Remains of the Mayan civilisation and the Mundo Maya organisation reveal our rich heritage.

Figure 10.20 What Belize offers the tourist

Figure 10.21 Club, Bangkok, Thailand

?

22 Essay: Tourism's detrimental effects can far outweigh its short-term benefits in developing countries. Discuss.

10.7 Ethical tourism

In the light of the growing awareness of the negative effects tourism can have on the environment, pressure groups such as Tourism Concern are now pushing for a more ethical tourism. This is a kind of tourism that respects the needs of the local community at the same time as protecting the environment.

10.8 Sex tourism

South-East Asia is well known for its links between sex and tourism. In fact, United Nations' estimates suggest that there are 700 000 female prostitutes in Thailand alone, the majority of whom are aged between 17 and 24. The sex-tourism trade relies on poorly educated young women who migrate to the cities for work, especially Bangkok. However, as they are unable to find formal employment, many of them work as prostitutes. The influx of foreign military personnel into Thailand during the Vietnam War in the 1960s is an historical reason for the sex industry in Thailand.

Overall, tourism is Thailand's biggest foreign exchange earner with more than three million people visiting Thailand annually. Male visitors outnumber females by more than two to one and sex-related problems are becoming more and more prominent in the country. One example is the increasing number of AIDs cases where approximately 500000 of Thailand's 59 million people are HIV positive. In the early 1990s the Public Health Committee attempted to force foreign tourists to produce an 'AIDs-free' certificate before entering the country, but the government rejected the idea, fearing the collapse of the tourist trade and loss of valuable income.

However, in 1992 the Thai government tried to improve the country's image and launched a campaign to promote conventional tourist attractions. These included the national parks and the country's heritage, such as the beautiful Buddhist temples in cities such as Bangkok.

Summary

- Tourism is one of the fastest growing industries in many countries throughout the world.

- There are increasing numbers of people travelling both within their own countries and abroad for holidays.

- Many developing countries now promote tourism as a development strategy.

- Although tourism provides substantial foreign exchange for some developing countries, much tourist income 'leaks' back to the developed countries.

- The tourist industry is characterised by seasonal variations and is influenced by changing political and social conditions at both source and destination areas.

- Ecotourism, which is organised around the protection of the natural environment, is an increasingly popular, alternative type of holiday.

- A country's reputation for one type of tourism may change as its government invests in promoting this change.

11 Alternative strategies for development

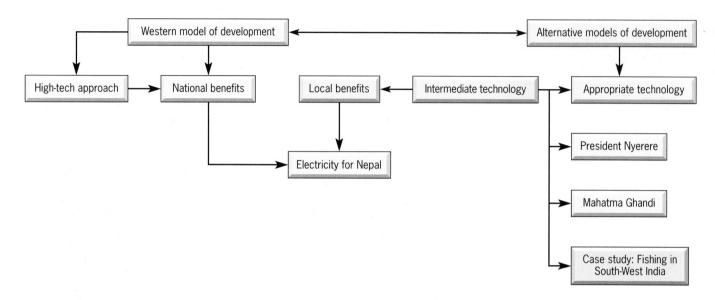

```
Western model of development  ←——————————————→  Alternative models of development
        │    │                                              │
        ▼    ▼                                              ▼
High-tech approach → National benefits    Local benefits ← Intermediate technology    Appropriate technology
                          │                      │                                         │
                          │                      ▼                                         ├──→ President Nyerere
                          └──────────────→ Electricity for Nepal                           │
                                                                                            ├──→ Mahatma Ghandi
                                                                                            │
                                                                                            └──→ Case study: Fishing in
                                                                                                 South-West India
```

11.1 Introduction

Most development strategies since 1945 were designed by experts from **developed** countries. We can see the failure of many of these policies in the increasing economic gap between developed and developing nations (see sections 1.1, 1.3). In the first half of this chapter we examine development strategies proposed mostly by people within the **developing countries**. Because these tend to have different aims and structures from many schemes emerging from developed countries (see section 2.3), we call them 'alternative strategies to development'. The chapter's second half then gives information about energy needs in Nepal which you will assess through a decision-making exercise.

11.2 Development is about people

Generally, alternative strategies encourage self help. Local people, who understand their community's needs, work together to help themselves – often, also, with the support of **non-governmental organisations (NGOs)** (see section 2.5). Because of this local involvement, such strategies are small scale (compare with section 2.3) and often result in **sustainable development** (see Fig. 7.34). Two past political leaders are famous for their support of alternative development, as illustrated below.

Gandhi's approach

Mahatma Gandhi (1869–1948), the first prime minister of India after independence from British rule in 1947, was a social reformer who encouraged rural development (Fig. 11.1). Before independence, British industrial development policy favoured the location and growth of industry in urban areas and so neglected the rural areas.

Conversely, Gandhi stressed that villages should be the basis of development for society. He called this approach *satyagraha* and through it encouraged rural craft, or cottage, industries. So that every village would become self-sufficient, Gandhi developed 'constructive programmes' which he hoped would lead to balanced development across the whole rural area.

Figure 11.1 Mahatma Gandhi spinning his own cloth, Calcutta, India. In 1925 Gandhi objected to British colonial rule, which was epitomised by the cotton industry: raw cotton was exported from India to textile mills in the UK, while finished cloth was then imported back to India. By making his own clothes, Gandhi was boycotting British goods and helping to develop India's village industries.

?

1 Assess how Gandhi's village-based strategy of development could improve the quality of life of Indian people living in:

a villages,

b urban areas.

Gandhi was not totally opposed to the development of industry, but he believed that it should be integrated with agriculture. He thought that industries concentrated in cities lead to increased poverty. In addition, if these industries become too highly mechanised, they cannot employ a large labour force. Similarly, if industries are capital intensive, it is the rich who accumulate wealth because they gain the returns on their capital.

In spite of Gandhi's proposals, development planners in India have continued to pursue policies favouring capital intensive industry in, or for, cities. Rural deprivation and poverty are still widespread in India (see Table 1.5).

Nyerere's Ujamaa concept

President Julius Nyerere of Tanzania believed the poor should be given the freedom to build their own societies as they wished (see Fig. 1.19). 'Growth must come out of our roots, not through the grafting on to those roots of something that is alien to them. It means that our social change will be determined by our own needs, as we see them, and in a direction that we feel to be appropriate for us at any particular time.' (1975)

Nyerere therefore proposed a similar strategy of development to that of Gandhi. Called *Ujamaa* (familyhood) in the Arusha Declaration of 1967, Nyerere's strategy returned to the traditional African way of life where there was no individual ownership of land but it was owned and used by all in the community. In practice this meant that land was not a sellable commodity, so Nyerere was able to establish village co-operatives.

Ujamaa therefore resulted in an economic system that benefited both individuals and households. In conjunction with this, it promoted projects to improve health care, housing, co-operative agriculture and rural crafts. In fact, following Nyerere's reforms, Tanzania boasted one of Africa's best public health services. Additionally, Nyerere believed that African society should rid itself of Western development, which he saw as altering traditional African systems and ultimately creating poverty and misery.

Both Gandhi and Nyerere believed that developing countries themselves should adopt a self-reliant approach. To do so, these countries need to pursue their own appropriate technology and economic principles rather than relying on foreign capital and technology (Fig. 11.2).

Figure 11.2 Imported tractors and trailer being used to harvest sugar cane, Nigeria

?

2 Using Figure 11.3, suggest the impact of the cassava project in Nigeria (Figs 11.4–11.6) on local:
• productivity,
• income,
• control of development.

11.3 Appropriate technology

Appropriate technology includes any technology that makes the most of each local factor of production, i.e. natural resources, capital or labour, and reduces the use of factors which are scarce. By definition therefore, appropriate technology involves projects which local people are able to manage according to their technological expertise (Fig. 11.3) Appropriate technology for developing countries may, however, progress into *intermediate technology*. This occurs when the technology may be more expensive and efficient than traditional methods, but it is still smaller in scale and more labour-intensive than technology transferred from developed countries (see Fig. 11.2).

Figure 11.3 Advantages of using appropriate technology to meet local needs

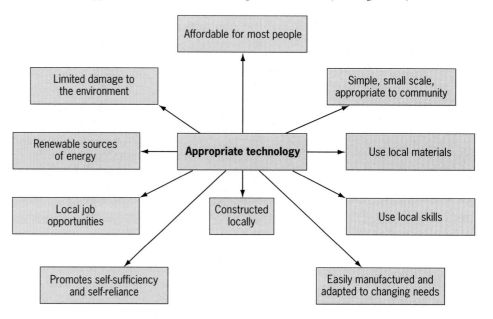

Affordable for most people

Limited damage to the environment

Simple, small scale, appropriate to community

Renewable sources of energy

Appropriate technology

Use local materials

Local job opportunities

Constructed locally

Use local skills

Promotes self-sufficiency and self-reliance

Easily manufactured and adapted to changing needs

Figure 11.4 Cassava-fryer: this new stove has a high burning efficiency and uses much less fuelwood than traditional ovens for drying grated cassava into gari.

Appropriate technology in Nigeria

Gari is a staple food in Nigeria and other countries in West Africa. It is made from the cassava tuber. The traditional method of processing cassava is to peel it, remove its water and then either grate or pound it by hand. This is an extremely time-consuming operation usually done by women. However, several local initiatives have developed simple, low-tech and cheap machines (Figs 11.4–11.6), saving much of the women's working time (see Fig. 6.17).

Figure 11.5 Cassava water-remover: traditionally, boulders are placed on top of bags of grated or fermented cassava to squeeze the water out. This machine is a much neater and faster process.

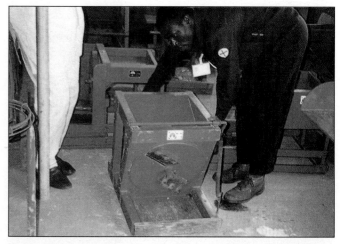

Figure 11.6 Cassava peeler with protected sharp cutting blade: traditionally, cassava is peeled using an open knife or cutlass.

Intermediate technology in India

In 1965, the NGO Intermediate Technology Development Group was set up in the UK to promote small-scale appropriate technology. Now called Intermediate Technology (IT), it seeks to increase the income generating abilities of poor people in rural areas of the developing world. IT is therefore a suitable example showing how local needs are identified and low-cost machinery is produced to meet those needs.

Fishing in South-West India

Villages on the southern tip of India's coastline depend on fishing for much of their income. They are, though, some of the poorest communities in India's rural sector. Along the shores of Kerala and Tamil Nadu, fishers traditionally use either a hollowed-out log (dug-out canoe, Fig. 11.7) or a tied-log raft for fishing (kattumaram). The latter is designed to cope with the fierce South-West monsoon surf conditions common off southern Kerala and Tamil Nadu.

Problems

There are two major problems which have reduced fishing capacity in South-West India. Firstly, as deforestation has increased in the area, so large tree trunks and light wood become more and more difficult to find. As a result, the price of traditional fishing boats has spiralled.

Figure 11.8 Construction of plywood boats using stitch-and-glue method

Secondly, from the mid 1970s to the mid-1980s the catches of traditional fishers declined considerably. Many people blamed the destructive practices of trawlers fishing for prawns in coastal waters. To counteract this threat, local fishers organised themselves into unions to campaign for fairer fishing policies. They also turned to technology and added outboard motors to their fishing boats to help them move out of the trawlers' routes and carry more nets.

Developing appropriate technology

Although the fishing communities saw new technology as the best way to improve their catches, their access to information and funds for development were limited. However, since the 1950s, a number of European agencies have worked with the local fishing communities in South-West India on various development projects. These projects provided new technology options but they were inappropriate for the fishers. Eventually, it was only with the participation and consultation of the local fishers that new technology from the European agencies was successfully transferred to meet the communities' needs. Together, both fishers and agencies assessed that these needs were for new boats which were: • unsinkable, • able to carry engines, • light, • easy to operate from surf-beaten beaches, • built to last about 7–10 years, • more comfortable and with a larger carrying capacity than a boat powered by sail and oar, • within the financial reach of the fishers.

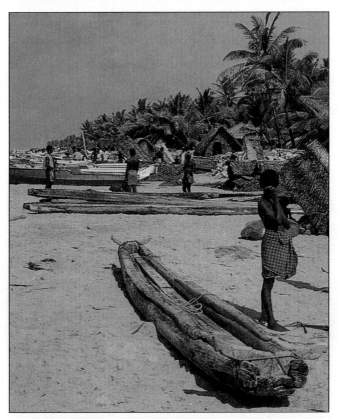

Figure 11.7 Traditional 3-log fishing boat made from mango wood which can only be used once every 3 days

In the early 1980s, the combined efforts of local fishing communities and external agencies had developed a suitable new boat (Fig. 11.8–11.9). While this keeps the centuries-old design of traditional boats, the building technology, known as 'stitch-and-glue', was new to the fishing communities. This technique uses marine plywood and fibreglass, but requires the same carpentry skills of traditional boat-building. The result is easily adapted to several craft designs. Importantly, it is a technology which local industries can adopt and which uses locally available skills.

Following the successful production of the first boat, the local fishers and European agencies developed several other designs. By the end of 1995, there were about 5000 plywood boats in operation. Both the new boat-yards, operated by fishing organisaions, as well as private enterprises were employing local people to build boats and satisfy demand.

?

3 With reference to Figures 11.3 and 11.7–11.9, discuss the effects of small-scale appropriate technology on the economies of developing countries.

Figure 11.9 Plywood fishing boat under sail

Other alternative strategies
Fair trade, ethics, education, participatory rural development and community involvement are all key issues in the alternative thinking on development. Thus, a move away from a wealth-orientated development strategy towards one in which people are at the centre is now considered socially, ethically and environmentally desirable (Figs 11.10–11.11, see sections 9.3, 9.5).

?

4 Use Figures 11.10 and 11.11. Discuss the benefits of adopting a human-based industrial development approach for:
• producers of raw materials,
• firms involved with 'social accounting',
• the employees of these firms.

Figure 11.10 Alternative development: international trade gaining decent wages, worker security and health standards for local producers (*Source:* The Fairtrade Foundation)

Fairtrade

Fairtrade stands for basic human rights for people working in developing countries who produce goods for consumption in developed countries.

Cocoa in Belize
The main source of income for many farmers in Toledo District of Belize is from cocoa beans. Good cocoa prices during the 1980s meant farmers planted new saplings. But within a few years prices for their cocoa on the international market dropped from 50p to 22p per 500g. Farmers were impoverished: many migrated to the cities; others left their fruit on the trees – it wasn't even worth harvesting; the new cocoa growers' co-operative (TCGA) went into debt.

Maya Gold
March 1994: Green and Blacks offered to buy cocoa beans from TCGA. With Fairtrade endorsement for their new product 'Maya Gold' chocolate, Green and Blacks paid well above the market price, at 48p per 500g, and guaranteed to buy all TCGA could produce for the next three years. The Belize cocoa farmers now have the assurance that their work and investment will be rewarded.

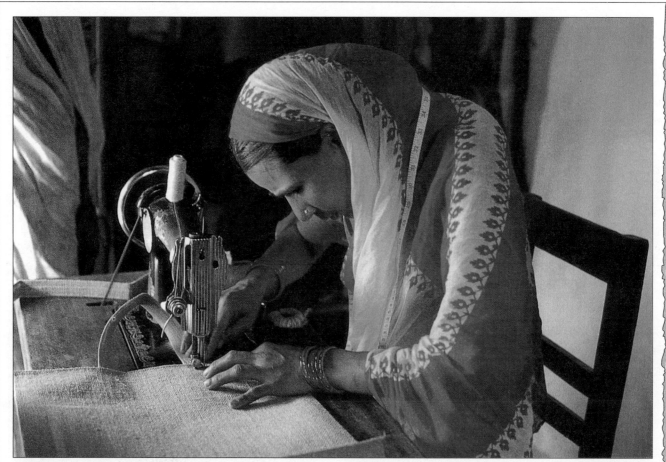

Trade gap: Sadrun earns £28 a month from Action Bag, a supplier to Traidcraft which pioneered social accounting. The Bangladesh worker, who hopes to be elected to the co-operative's management committee, fled her home with her mother during the country's civil war in 1971. Her father and future in-laws were not so lucky. The cash allows her father to eat meat two or three times a month, although she spends most of her income on the education of her four children.

UK firms count the human cost

SOCIAL accounting, by which companies can be assessed against social as well as financial criteria, is about to take off in the UK. At least four major companies are set to publish social accounts detailing how they relate to all their stakeholders — suppliers, employees, customers and shareholders.

Traidcraft, which buys products from more than 100 co-operatives in 26 developing countries and sells them through shops and mail-order catalogues throughout the UK, pioneered social accounting.

According to Richard Evans: 'The prime benefit of social accounting is that it creates a very strong relationship between the stakeholders and the business. For example, last year craft producers noticed that our food side was growing much more

quickly than they were and sought ways to improve their sales.'

Each year Traidcraft focuses on one of its producer countries; this year it was the first and one of the largest suppliers — Bangladesh. This is one of the countries hit by the switch from crafts to foods. Although 21 of the 26 countries saw the value of goods shipped to Traidcraft rise in 1994–95, those from Bangladesh fell by 5 per cent.

Evans visited more than half the 24 producers in the country, all but one of whom expressed confidence in Traidcraft's long-term commitment. The co-operative Action Bag, which makes shopping bags and soft toys, has seen its output double over each of the past two years. But like all suppliers, it demanded more information about the company's marketing

strategies. The social accounts provide at least some of the answers.

The Body Shop and two major financial services groups are social accounting this year.

Allied Dunbar, the insurance giant, is testing the system on its Staff Charity Fund. This will distribute some £35000 to local charities in 1995. According to a spokes-man: 'If we are comfortable with that we may extend it to all our community projects, including the Allied Dunbar Charitable Trust, which spends £2m a year.'

Co-operative Bank is preparing a similar social report on its charitable giving, which will amount to some £1m in 1995. According to spokesman Dave Smith: 'We are putting this together in-house. We see our social responsibilities as closely linked to our ethical investment stance.'

Figure 11.11 Alternative development: social accounting (*Source:* Nick Goodway, *The Observer*, 13 Aug. 1995)

11.4 Energy alternatives for Nepal

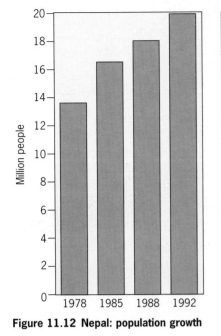

Figure 11.12 Nepal: population growth

Figure 11.13 Nepal

Background information

Nepal is a landlocked, mountainous country with no fossil fuels of its own (Figs 11.12–11.13, Table 11.1, see also Fig. 7.11). People use mostly **biomass** fuels which include firewood (Table 11.2), dung and other combustible natural materials. These account for 90 per cent of the country's energy consumption (Table 11.3). As a result, women spend about a third of their day collecting firewood for fuel. In fact, cooking uses three-quarters of Nepal's household energy (Fig. 11.14). Another source of energy is the *pani ghatta*, a traditional wooden water wheel, which most villagers use to grind grain.

Table 11.1 Economic characteristics of Nepal, 1999 (*Sources:* Human Development Report, 1998; Population Reference Bureau, 1999, World Development Report 1998/99)

GDP	US$ 4.8
Real GDP per capita (PPP*)	US$ 1145
Total external debt	US$ 2.4 billions
Debt service ratio (as % of exports of goods and services)	8%
GNP per capita	US$ 220

*The purchasing power parity of a country's currency is the number of units of that currency required to purchase the same goods and services that a US$ will buy in the USA. The real GDP per capita of a country is the GDP converted into US$ on the basis of the purchasing power parity of the country's currency.

At present, only 10 per cent of Nepal's 19 million people have access to grid electricity. The government recognises the potential of hydro-electricity and is interested in increasing the supply of electricity via the national grid through medium- and large-scale schemes.

Micro- and mini-hydro schemes

Micro-hydro schemes of up to 100 kilowatts (kW) and mini-hydro schemes from 100 to 1000 kW could provide electricity for up to 50 per cent of Nepal's population (Fig. 11.15). These small-scale schemes operate by using fast-flowing rivers in the mountains, so there is no need for the building of large dams.

Table 11.2 Forest resources in Nepal (*Source:* UN Environment Programme: Environment Data Report)

Total forest area	2.1×10^6 ha
Productive forests	1.3×106 ha
Fuelwood production	$12\ 795 \times 10^3$ tonnes 1990
Forest cover of Nepal land area	18%

Table 11.3 Energy potential and consumption in Nepal

- Known exploitable potential of hydro-electricity: 144 000 megawatts (MW)

- Installed capacity: 235 MW

- Traditional fuels consumption, 1971: 96 megajoules (MJ)

- Traditional fuels consumption, 1991: 10 247 MJ

- Commercial energy consumed, 1991: 4 MJ

- Nepal has the potential to generate 30 000 MW of power from its fast flowing rivers from the Himalayas (enough electricity to run Britain's two largest cities, London and Birmingham, with a total population of 8 million).

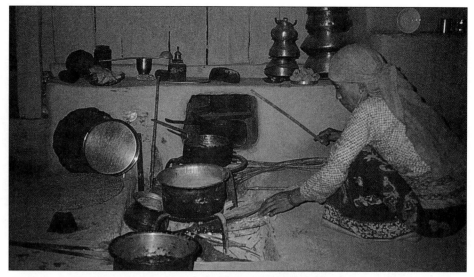

Figure 11.14 Cooking with firewood in a traditional Nepalese kitchen

Figure 11.15 Micro-hydro scheme

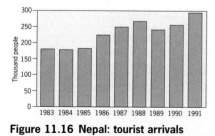

Figure 11.16 Nepal: tourist arrivals

Figure 11.17 Nepal: tourist receipts

In addition to lighting and cooking in homes, people could use this electricity on a commercial basis to mill grain in bakeries and for fruit and vegetable drying.

Proposal for large-scale dam at Ghandruk

The Nepalese government plans to construct a huge dam in the Annapurna region of Nepal. Meanwhile, increasing numbers of tourists are visiting Nepal (Figs. 11.16–11.17), and the Annapurna region is one of the country's most popular tourist areas. In 1993 alone, 7000 tourists visted the village of Ghandruk (Fig. 11.18). Annapurna is also home to endangered species such as the Asiatic black bear, the clouded leopard and the Annamese macaque.

Ghandruk houses about 270 families living in tightly packed, tall stone buildings perched on a steep hillside overlooking the Modi Khola river. Many villagers served in the British and Indian armies in the past as loyal and fearless Gurkha soldiers. Most villagers' livelihoods used to come from farming, but since the 1970s, trekking tourism has provided them with work.

Table 11.4 Deforesation in Nepal, based on all land with about 10% tree crown cover (*Source:* Dr John Soussan, Reading University, 1993)

Year	Million hectares	Area (%)
1965	6.5	45
1980	6.1	43
1985	5.5	37.4

1990s: Deforestation has slowed down, and loss of forest quality is now more of a problem. Deforestation is most noticeable near cities, roads and tourist trekking areas.

Figure 11.18 Ghandruk village, Annapurna region, Nepal

Table 11.5 Advantages of large-scale hydroelectric schemes

1 Developers are familiar with the technology.

2 Running costs are low, the fuel is free and constantly available.

3 Hydro-electricity creates no pollution.

4 HEP schemes are long-lasting.

5 Although an area of forest would be lost with the drowning of the valley, in the long term the pressure on forest resources would diminish as grid electricity becomes more widely available.

6 Additional benefits could include: irrigation, aquaculture, opportunities for recreation and tourism, flood control.

The energy supply in Ghandruk now falls short of demand. There are increasing pressures on forest resources (Table 11.4) and the amount of cattle dung has diminished with the change from an agriculture-based to a tourism-based economy. In fact, the average tourist uses at least three times as much energy as the Nepali householder.

The energy situation has thus reached a crisis. The government's solution is to drown the Modi Khola valley and install a large hydro scheme. The proposed scheme would produce 10 000 MW of power which would supply 10 per cent of the population in Nepal with grid electricity. The government is keen, therefore, to explore the benefits of this scheme for the area and for the country as a whole. This combines with the government's plans to develop the tourist industry and avoid any dependency by Nepal on imported fuels. In an early report, government advisers listed some of the advantages of the proposed scheme (Table 11.5).

Environmental pressure groups

The King Mahendra Trust for Nature Conservation has set up the Annapurna Conservation Area Project (ACAP) to help communities meet the requirements of tourism and development without damaging the environment. From the start, ACAP has stressed community participation. It is involved in forest-

Figure 11.19 Advantages of electric light

?

5 You are assistant to Nepal's government energy adviser. Your task is to prepare a report in which you make recommendations on appropriate energy provision for the Annapurna region.
Although the commercial energy supply in Nepal currently falls short of demand, certain sections of the economy are growing. The demand for energy is therefore increasing. During the general elections in 1991 and 1994 all the major parties included rural electrification as a central issue in their election manifestos. The government is intending to invest heavily in energy production. It is also keen to appear sensitive to environmental considerations because of growing international concern and pressure from environmentalist groups in Nepal. Your report should include:
a Projected population figures for Nepal for the next 50 years, as well as the likely growth in numbers of tourist arrivals.
b A list of the advantages and disadvantages of both the high-tech and low-tech energy schemes proposed.
c A special report on the environmental and social impacts of each of the schemes.
d A detailed account of exactly who would benefit from each scheme and whether benefits would be long- or short-term.
e Using your report, write your formal recommendations in a letter to the Energy Resource Minister for Nepal.

management schemes, reafforestation programmes and a 'kerosene-only' policy for the region near the tourist lodges where fuelwood is severely depleted.

ACAP and Development and Consulting Services (a Nepali non-government organisation) are keen to see the development of micro-hydro schemes (see Fig. 11.15). This would generate 50kW of power by diverting a stream which runs past Ghandruk. With this, every house in the village would receive electric light (Fig. 11.19), all the tourist lodges and 20 per cent of families would be able to cook with electricity.

Key to success of any hydro-electricity scheme

Electricity has to be cheap and affordable for everyone if local communities are to benefit. Similarly, the project will succeed if people are open to new ideas and willing to change to an electric system. In fact, it is mostly the women who dominate domestic affairs in Nepal, and so they will be the ones to learn how to use the new technology. In addition, local people will become aware of the importance of conservation and development issues by supporting the scheme. For example, cooking with electricity means that fuelwood resources will be sustained, so cheap electric cookers should be an affordable alternative even to the poorest of families.

The aims of any hydro scheme are to benefit the local community and improve people's standard of living. Apart from these, no amount of effort, time or money would be worthwhile (Table 11.6).

Table 11.6 Relative costs of hydro-electricity in Nepal
(*Source: Intermediate Technology*, 1994)

- A 50kW micro-hydro would cost rupees 3 590 000 (US$72 000) to build (US$1440 per kW installed).
- Large high-tech hydro-schemes built for the grid cost US$1 billion over 8 years (US$5000 per kW installed).

Summary

- The failures of some large development programmes in many developing countries have prompted a different approach to 'development'.

- Past political leaders have contributed their ideas to 'alternative' development thinking.

- Alternative approaches to development consider local needs and are based on the availability of local resources.

- Such alternative approaches are called development with a 'human face'.

- The technology involved in locally-based strategies is small scale and appropriate to local needs, as well as environmentally more friendly than large-scale, high-tech approaches.

- Small-scale approaches to development can benefit local people and enhance their quality of life.

Appendices

A1 Spearman's rank correlation coefficient

This is a statistical technique used to measure the degree of association (correlation) between two sets of variables. Thus it is assumed that there is a relationship between one variable (x) and another (y). For example, if a country has a high GNP, it is expected that its national energy consumption will also be high. In this case, it is possible to measure the degree of association between GNP and energy consumption by using Spearman's rank correlation method.

The method for calculating the Spearman rank correlation coefficient is as follows:

1 Rank both sets of data (note: highest value is ranked 1).

2 Find the difference between the rank values (d).

3 Square each of the differences (d^2)

4 Find the sum of the squared differences (Σd^2)

5 Multiply the sum of the squared differences by 6 ($6\Sigma d^2$)

6 Divide $6\Sigma d^2$ by ($n^3 - n$), then subtract this total from 1.

Thus the equation for calculating the coefficient is:

$$r_s = 1 - \left[\frac{6\Sigma d^2}{n^3 - n} \right]$$

where d = the difference between the ranked values

d^2 = square of the difference

Σd^2 = total of the squared differences

n = number of paired variables

Once calculated, the value of the coefficient will tell us the strength and direction of the relationship between the two variables. If a perfect positive correlation exists, the coefficient will be +1.0. Conversely, if a perfect negative correlation exists, the coefficient will be −1.0. If there is no relationship whatsoever between the two variables, the coefficient will be 0.

Example

The relationship between Human Development Index (HDI) and literacy rates (*Source: Human Development Report*, 1998)

Serial no	Country	HDI value	HDI rank	Adult literacy rate	Adult literacy rank	d	d^2
1	Mexico	0.855	4	89.6	4	0	0
2	Algeria	0.746	6	61.6	9	3	9
3	Zaire	0.347	13	60.0	10	3	9
4	Niger	0.207	16	13.6	17	1	1
5	Peru	0.729	8	88.7	5	3	9
6	Morocco	0.557	10	43.7	13	3	9
7	Hong Kong	0.909	2	92.2	3	1	1
8	Bangladesh	0.371	12	38.1	15	3	9
9	Haiti	0.340	14	45.0	12	2	4
10	Kuwait	0.848	5	78.6	7	2	4
11	Jamaica	0.735	7	85.0	6	1	1
12	Canada	0.960	1	99.0	1	0	0
13	S. Korea	0.894	3	98.0	2	1	1
14	Sierra Leone	0.185	17	31.4	16	1	1
15	Togo	0.380	11	51.7	11	0	0
16	Gabon	0.568	9	63.2	8	1	1
17	Gambia	0.291	15	38.6	14	1	1

In this example, the Spearman rank correlation coefficient is 0.91. This suggests a strong positive relationship between the HDI and levels of literacy.

Testing the level of significance of the correlation coefficient
Usually, it is necessary to statistically test for the significance of the coefficient. This is to ensure that the nature of the relationship indicated by the coefficient is not due to chance.

The *t*-distribution is normally used for this test of significance. The procedure involves calculating a *t*-value using the formula:

$$t = r_s \sqrt{\frac{n-2}{1-r_s^2}}$$

where n = number of pairs of data

      $(n-2)$ = degrees of freedom

The calculated *t* value obtained from the formula is then compared with the critical value obtained from the *t*-distribution table at the required confidence level and degrees of freedom. If the calculated *t*-value is greater than the table's critical value, it means that the correlation coefficient is statistically significant.

In our example, the calculated *t*-value is 9.31, and the degree of freedom is 18 (i.e. 20 – 2). If we refer to *t*-tables, we find that the critical value at the 0.01 confidence level with degrees of freedom of 18 is 2.88. We can therefore conclude that there is a strong positive association between human development and literacy level and this relationship is statistically significant.

A2 Guide to questionnaires

A questionnaire is a planned collection of questions. It is designed for the purpose of collecting information or particular kinds of data. The basic steps for constructing a questionnaire survey are as follows:

1 State clearly the aims and objectives of the study.

2 Note the critical and essential data required for the study.

3 Know your research methodology and possible alternative strategies of data collection.

4 Understand the central questions you want to ask the respondents. Some questions may be vital for the survey, while others may not be as important.

5 Decide the method of questionnaire administration you will use. This could be respondent's self-administered, researcher's direct interviews of respondents, postal or telephone questionnaires.

6 Understand your target population:
• who they are,
• where they live,
• how and when to contact them,
• when to see them.

7 Think about the possible reactions of respondents to your study. These could be positive, negative, supportive, or argumentative. How people receive your study will determine their co-operation with your questionnaire. Note that some of your respondents could be excited by your questions, some may be unconcerned, while a number may even be cold or aggressive.

8 Decide how many times you want to meet the respondents. Be aware that the first impression is always vital. Most respondents will probably make up their mind on first contact whether or not to support your survey.

9 Determine how large the sample will be, and how best to select the sample. This means you must know the location and distribution of respondents.

The general structure of the questionnaire should consist of:

• a short introductory statement on the survey, or problem, and what the respondents are expected to do,
• respondents socio-economic/demographic background,
• main survey questions,
• other supporting questions.

Sample questionnaire: Holiday experiences in a developing country (survey of British tourists)

This questionnaire is designed to collect information on your most recent holiday experience in a developing country. The survey is intended to examine the social and educational benefits of tourism and to show how tourists' interaction with other cultures can promote better understanding of the world.

This survey is strictly an academic exercise. All information supplied will be used for research and treated in confidence. It is hoped that the study will show how holidays in developing countries can change people's perceptions and attitudes towards such places.

General

1 Estimate the age and sex of the respondent.

	Male	Female
15–25 years	☐	☐
26–40 years	☐	☐
41–60 years	☐	☐
above 60 years	☐	☐

2 To which ethnic group do you belong?

☐ White	☐ Bangladeshi
☐ Black Caribbean	☐ Chinese
☐ Black African	☐ Mixed race
☐ Indian	☐ Other
☐ Pakistani	

3 Name the developing country you have visited

_____

4 What year was your visit? _____

5 How long did you stay? _____

6 What was your major reason for visiting this country?

☐ Holiday

☐ Work/other business

☐ Visiting friends and relatives

☐ Religious pilgrimage

☐ Education (academic/research)

7 Did you travel alone?   Yes ☐   No ☐

If no, who did you travel with?

☐ Family   ☐ Charity organisation

☐ Friend(s)   ☐ Others

8 What type of accommodation did you use?

☐ Hotel   ☐ Bed and breakfast

☐ Homes of family/friends   ☐ Youth hostel

☐ Caravan/camping   ☐ Self-catering

                            ☐ Others (please specify)

9 How would you rate the following facilities in the country?

	Excellent	Good	Average	Poor	Very poor	Don't know
Quality of food	☐	☐	☐	☐	☐	☐
Variety of food	☐	☐	☐	☐	☐	☐
Standard of accommodation	☐	☐	☐	☐	☐	☐
Transport facilities	☐	☐	☐	☐	☐	☐
Leisure facilities	☐	☐	☐	☐	☐	☐

10 Which type of transport did you use most for most travelling within the country?

☐ Train   ☐ Motorcycle

☐ Air   ☐ Bicycle

☐ Car   ☐ Public bus

☐ Boat   ☐ Private coach

                            ☐ Others (please specify)

Choice of destination

11 What were your major considerations when choosing your holiday destination country?

☐ Recreational facilities   ☐ Available tourist facilities

☐ Cultural values   ☐ Safety consideration

☐ Health facilities   ☐ Scenery

☐ Leisure facilities   ☐ Flora and fauna

☐ Religious   ☐ Cost

☐ Good climate and weather conditions

12 Do you feel you really experienced the country's culture?

                            Yes ☐   No ☐

General impressions and experiences

13 Did you do any sightseeing while in the country?

                            Yes ☐   No ☐

If yes, which of these did you visit?

☐ Historical monuments/architecture

                            ☐ Beaches

☐ Art galleries/exhibitions ☐ Landscapes

☐ National parks   ☐ Shrines/holy sites/religious buildings

                            ☐ Others (please specify)

14 Were you concerned about any of the following during your stay in the country?

	Yes	No
Personal safety	☐	☐
Political instability	☐	☐
Begging	☐	☐
Prostitution	☐	☐
Pollution	☐	☐
Food poisoning	☐	☐
Safety of property	☐	☐

15 What are your general impressions of the country you visited?

_____

_____

16 Has your visit given you a better understanding of this country and of the people living there?   Yes ☐   No ☐

17 Do you have any plans/desire to visit again?   Yes ☐   No ☐

Thank you for your help in completing this questionnaire.

A3 Age-dependency ratio

Populations can be divided into three groups.

1 Child dependants, i.e. those aged below 16 years. These young people usually depend on their elders for survival. In some countries, though, children are hardly dependent but actually help to provide an income for their families.

2 Economically active, i.e. those 'productive' members of society who work to provide an income and upon whom the rest of society depend. These people are normally aged between 16 and 65. However, many people classified as 'productive' are unable to provide an income, e.g. students, prisoners, physically and mentally disabled, the terminally ill and the long-term unemployed.

3 Aged dependants, i.e. those at 'retirement age' (usually over 65 years) who depend on others, or state funds (as generated by the economically active), for support. Often, the elderly are dependent more on their own savings, or their children, than financial help from the state.

The relationship between these three population divisions varies from country to country. However, for the purposes of analysing the structure of a population, the following dependency ratio is useful:

$$\text{Child dependency ratio} = \frac{population\ 0-14 \times 100}{population\ 15-64}$$

Example

UK total population = 55.9 million

Population 0–14   = 12.3 million

Population 15–64   = 35.8 million

Child dependency ratio = $\dfrac{12.3 \times 100}{35.8}$ = 34

(i.e., for every person aged 15–64 years, there are 34 children 'dependants'.)

A4 The Lorenz curve

The Lorenz curve is a graph used to show the degree of concentration or diversity of activities within an area (Fig. A4.1). For example, the Lorenz curve may illustrate the concentration or dispersal of immigrants within a city, region or country. It can also illustrate the degree of industrial specialisation or diversification at the same variety of scales.

Example

The purpose of this example is to draw a Lorenz curve based on the data in Tables A4.1 and A4.2. The method for drawing a Lorenz curve is as follows:

a Place your data (column A) in rank order (column B).

b Calculate the total (in this case the total number of tourists visiting both Africa and Asia).

c Convert each value (column A) into a percentage of the total (column C).

d Add these percentages cumulatively (column D).

e To draw the Lorenz curve (Fig. A4.1), plot the rank values (column B) against the cumulative percentages (column D).

Figure A4.1 Lorenz curve: origin of tourists visiting South Asia and Africa, 1991

Table A4.1: Origin and number of tourists in Africa, 1991 (*Source:* World Tourism Organisation, 1993)

Tourist arrivals from:	Column A Thousand tourists	Column B Rank	Column C Percentage	Column D Cumulative percentage
Africa	10 205	1	64.41	64.41
Europe	4 799	2	30.29	94.70
Americas	451	3	2.85	97.55
East Asia and Pacific	221	4	1.40	98.95
Middle East	118	5	0.75	99.70
South Asia	42	6	0.27	100.00
Total	15 836			

Table A4.2 Origin and number of tourists in South Asia, 1991 (*Source:* World Tourism Organisation, 1993)

Tourist arrivals from:	Column A Thousand tourists	Column B Rank	Column C Percentage	Column D Cumulative percentage
Europe	1 238	1	38.17	38.17
South Asia	1 120	2	34.52	72.69
East Asia and Pacific	363	3	11.18	83.87
Americas	257	4	7.90	91.77
Middle East	191	5	5.88	97.65
Africa	75	6	2.32	100.00
Total	3 244			

Developed countries

Developing countries

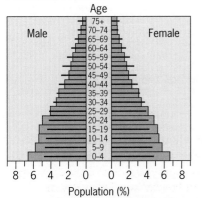

Figure A5.1 Age distribution pyramids (*Source: Philips' Modern School Atlas, 1992, George Philip in Association with Heinemann Educational, London*)

How may the resulting graph be interpreted? If the same number of people were visiting both South Asia and Africa from all the regions listed, the graph would be a straight line (even distribution). The more curved the line, therefore, the greater the degree of concentration. In this case, a high degree of concentration means that the majority of tourists are arriving from relatively few regions of origin. Figure A4.1 shows that South Asia receives a wider range of foreign visitors than Africa.

The Lorenz curve is useful because it reveals a visual impression of concentration. It is especially helpful for comparing several places when their respective Lorenz curves are plotted on one graph (Fig. A4.1). It can also be useful to plot different figures for the same place over several periods in order to illustrate changes over time.

A5 Population pyramids

Age-sex pyramids are bar graphs which illustrate the structure of a population, whether at a regional, national or global scale. A central, vertical, axis is divided into age groups, or cohorts, e.g. 0–4, 5–9, 10–14, 15–19, 20–14 years etc. The horizontal axis represents either the actual number, or the percentage, of people in each of these age groups. The whole graph is then divided into two; males, plotted on the left, and females, plotted on the right.

The typical shape for such population graphs is a pyramid, although this is most usual for developing countries (Fig. A5.1). Developed countries usually have 'mature' population structures which show a more 'balanced' structure. However, the ageing population common to many developed countries gives rise to a more 'top-heavy' pyramid, rather than the wider based pyramid of developing countries.

References

ActionAid (1990), *Common Cause* (Spring edition), Action Aid, Tapstone Road, Somerset.

Agrawal, A N (1994), *Indian Economy, Problems of Development and Planning* (20th Edition), Wishwa Prakashan, a division of Wiley Eastern Ltd., London.

Allen, J E (1992), *UPDATE: Energy resources for a changing world.*, Cambridge University Press.

Archer, M (1991), *Development and health, aspects of applied Geography,* Hodder and Stoughton, London.

Beddis, R (1991), *Third world development and interdependence.* Oxford University Press, London.

Binns, A (1993), 'Nigeria: Africa's Restless Giant', *Teaching Geography*, Vol.18, No.2, 1993, pp50.

Central Intelligence Agency (1992), *The World Factbook,* Central Intelligence Agency, Washington, DC.

Coote, B *(1992), The trade trap: poverty and the global commodity markets,* Oxfam Publications, Oxford.

Department for Economic and Social Information and Policy Analysis, Population Division, (1994): *World Population 1994,* United Nations.

Development Education Centre (1990), Where to draw the line? *Studies in political development for 'A' level geography: Senegambia and Brazil,* Development Education Centre (Birmingham) and Essex.

Drake, G (1994), *Issues in the New Europe,* Hodder and Stoughton, London.

Ecoforum (1993), *Fish curry and rice: a citizens' report on Goan environment.* The Other India Press, Pune, India.

Far Eastern Economic Review, September 30, 1999.

Food and Agricultural Organisation (1991), *FAO Production Yearbook,* New United Nations.

George, S (1990), *The debt boomerang: how third world debt harms us all,* Pluto Press, London, with the Transnational Institute (TNI), Amsterdam.

George, S (1994), *A fate worse than debt: a radical analysis of the third world debt crisis,* Penguin Group, London.

Hall, R (1989), *UPDATE: World population trends,* Cambridge University Press.

Heppel, B (1990), Pacific sunrise, East Asia's newly industrialising countries, *Geography Review,* March 1990.

HMSO (1994), *Social trends,* HMSO Central Statistics Office, Newport, Gwent.

Ho, Mae Wan and Horsch, R. (1999), 'Grains of truth', *Geographical,* October 1999.

Hudson, R. (1998), 'Globalisation and employment in Europe',*Geography Review,* Vol. 11 no. 5, May 1998.

Industrial Relations Employment Review, (IRS) no. 688, September 1999.

Instituto del Tercer Mundo (1997), *The World Guide 1997/98.* Instituto del Tercer Mundo, Uruguay.

Intermediate Technology Group (1994), *Cook electric: the Ghandruk experience,* ITG, Rugby.

John Wiley & Sons Ltd. and ERP Environment (1999), *European Environment,* The Journal of European Environmental Policy, Vol. 9, no. 4, July–August 1999.

Jones, H (1990), *Population geography* (2nd edition), Paul Chapman Publishing Ltd., London.

Jubilee 2000 Coalition (1999): *A Silent war. The Devastating Impact of Debt on the Poor,* at www.oneworld.org/jubilee2000/silent.html

Knox, P and Agnew J (1994), *The geography of the world economy* (2nd edition), Edward Arnold.

Madden, P (1992), *A raw deal* (2nd edition), Christian Aid, London.

Madeley, J, Sullivan, D and Woodroffe, J (1994), *Who runs the world?,* Christian Aid, London.

Marsden, WE and Marsden, VM (1983), *World in change.* Oliver and Boyd, Edinburgh.

Maslen, P (1990), *Tourism: environment and development perspectives,* WWF, Godalming, Surrey.

Meadows, D, Meadows, D and Randers, J (1992), *Beyond the limits,* Earthscan Publications Ltd., London.

Oxfam (UK and Ireland) (1995), *The Oxfam Poverty Report.* An Oxfam Publication.

Pearce, D (1992), 'Economics and environment', *Geography Review,* Vol.6, No.2, November, 1992.

Population Concern (1991), *Population: a comprehensive study,* Population Concern, London.

Population Reference Bureau (1994), *Population today: news, numbers and analysis,* Vol.22, No.5, May 1994, USA.

Population Reference Bureau (1998, 1999), *World population data sheet.* Demographic data and estimates for the countries and regions of the world. USA.

Punnett, N (1993, 1994), 'Nigeria', 'Venezuela', *Geofile, No.216, 243,* Stanley Thornes.

Raw, M (1989), *Resources and environment,* Unwin Hyman.

Robinson, G (1993), 'The world food problem' *Geography Review* Vol.6, No.4, March 1993.

Royle, S (1995) 'Population and resources in Mauritius', *Geography Review,* Vol.8, No.5, May 1995.

Selmes, I (ed.) (1995), *The Geography Collection: World Wide,* Hodder and Stoughton.

Slater, P. (1999), *UK Quality of Life Indicators.* Shell Better Britain Campaign Information sheet No. 168. No.1, Birmingham.

Smith, P. (1999): Poverty in Rural Uganda. *Economic Review,* Vol. 16 No. 4, April 1999.

The African Development Bank Group (1997), *African Development Report 1997.* Oxford University Press, Oxford.

The Economist (1999) *The Shadow over Indonesia.* The Economist, 18–24 September 1999.

The International Bank for Reconstruction and Development/ The World Bank (1999), *World Development Report 1998/99. Knowledge for Development,* Oxford University Press.

The New Internationalist (1996–1999), No.286, 287, 303, 304, 307, 309, 310, 315, 317. New Internationalist Publications, Oxford.

The Stationery Office (1997), *Social Security Statistics – 1997,* the Government Statistical Service, London.

The Stationery Office (1998), *Social Trends 28, 1998 Edition.* Office for National Statistics, London.

The Population Association of America (1986), *Careers in Population,* The Population Association of America, USA.

United Nations Environment Programme (1994), *Environment Data Report 1993–4,* Blackwell.

United Nations Children's Fund (1997), *The State of the World's Children 1997,* Oxford University Press.

United Nations Development Programme (1998), *Human Development Report,* Oxford University Press, New York.

United Nations High Commissioner for Refugees (1999), *Refugees and others of concern to UNCHR – 1998 statistical Overview,* at www.unchr.ch/statist/98oview/tab6-6.htm

Wallis, E (1992), 'Global migration trends 1, 2', *Geofile, No.183, 184,* Stanley Thornes.

Waugh, D (1990), *Geography: An Integrated Approach,* Nelson.

World Bank (1998, 1999), *World Bank Atlas 1898, from the World development Indicators.* The World Bank, USA.

World Bank (1999), *The World Bank Annual Report 1998.* The World Bank, Washington, D.C. 20433, USA.

World Bank Group (1999): *World Development Indicators –1999,* at www.worldbank.org/data/wdi/people.html

World Health Organisation (1998), *The World Health Report,* 1998. Life in the 21st century – A vision for all. WHO, Switzerland.

World Health Organisation (1999), *The World Health Report,* 1999. Making a Difference. WHO, Switzerland.

World Tourism Organisation (1999), *Year book of tourism statistics,* World Tourism Organisation, Vol. 1, 51st edition.

Glossary

Acid rain An increase in the acidity of precipitation because of pollution e.g. the release of sulphur dioxide and nitrogen oxides from, mostly, power stations and vehicle exhausts.

Actual population change The difference between a population's birth rate and death rate, plus the net effects of migration (see **natural population change**).

Asylum seeker A person in need of refuge in a foreign country. This is usually because of their political or religious beliefs which are against those of the government in the origin country.

Backwash effect Exploitation of the peripheral poor areas in order to sustain economic growth in the rich **core**. This often involves a flow of resources and labour from the **periphery** to the core. The long-term effect of such a flow out of the periphery is polarisation, as poor areas continue to get poorer and rich core areas gain more wealth.

Bilateral aid Financial support given by one government directly to another.

Biomass Living organisms. The rotting waste matter from both plants and animals produces methane which can then be collected and used as fuel.

Bush fallow Farming system where land is left uncultivated for about 3–4 years in order to regain its nutrients, following several years of cropping.

Carrying capacity The **optimum** number of people who can be adequately supported by the productive capacity of the land.

Child dependency ratio The number of children in relation to the number of economically active members of a population (usually expressed as a ratio).

Commercial farming Large scale, modernised food production process run on a capitalist system for profit. This usually involves heavy investment with little emphasis on labour (see **subsistence farming**).

Comparative advantage Cost advantages of a country or region for the production of manufactured goods. Such advantages include abundant resources or human skills.

Core area Central, more prosperous area/region, which tends to attract investment and control functions e.g. headquarters of **TNCs**.

Counter-urbanisation Movement of people move away from conurbations to live in smaller cities, towns or villages, mostly in **developed countries**.

Cumulative causation Theoretical process which leads to the formation of **core** and **periphery** areas. New economic development in the core often stimulates local economy and attracts migrants searching for work. The cumulative effects of movements of people and resources increases wealth in the core.

De-industrialisation The process of declining manufacturing industry e.g. 1970s and 1980s in **developed countries**.

Demographic transition stage A country's rate of population growth or decline, as determined by existing birth and death rates. The 'stage' of population change often relates to economic development.

Demography Study of the statistical characteristics of human populations, e.g. total size, age and sex composition, changes over time with variations in birth and death rates.

Desertification Reduction in agricultural capacity as once fertile land degrades into sterile, dry and unproductive land. This often results from overgrazing, overcropping or deforestation.

Developed countries Economically advanced countries characterised by high standards of living, large industrial and service sectors and high **GNPs**.

Developing countries Countries where the **GDP** is inadequate for generating investment in agriculture and industry. Characterised by low standards of living, large primary sectors and low **GNPs**.

Distance decay effect A decrease in numbers of people moving between places A and B as the distance between A and B increases. This suggests greater interaction between places which are closer together.

Downward spiral Process of declining wealth in **peripheral areas** as people and resources move out of the periphery into the richer **core areas**.

Ecological refugee Migrant forced out of his/her normal place of residence because of natural disaster e.g. earthquake, flood, drought. Also includes industrial accidents e.g. oil spillage, chemical/toxic leaks.

Economic gap Differences in levels of economic prosperity between nations, as measured by indices such as **GNP**.

Economic migrant Person leaving her/his native country to seek better economic opportunities and so settle temporarily in another country.

Economies of scale Cost advantages or savings made as a result of large-scale production.

Ecosystem A natural system that shows the relationships between a community of living things (plants and animals) and their non-living environment.

Emigration Movement of people away from their native country to settle permanently in another. (Permanent is defined by the United Nations as a period lasting one year or more).

Fertility gap The difference between the high population growth rates which characterise **developing countries** and the low population growth rates which are typical of the **developed countries**.

Finite resources Resources limited in supply, e.g. fossil fuels (also termed non-renewable or **stocks**).

First World The group of countries mostly located in the Northern and Western Hemispheres which have high standards of living.

Flows Resources which are natural, renewable and in constant supply, e.g. water, air, sun and wind. These resources can be harnessed as renewable energy (compare with **stocks**).

Formal sector Where people work to receive a regular wage and are assured certain rights, e.g. paid holidays, sickness leave. The government recognises work in the formal sector for tax purposes.

Free market economy An economic system where methods of production are privately held by individuals and firms. The market then determines the levels of supply and demand.

Free trade International trade that takes place without trade barriers e.g. **tariffs**, quotas, and so allows the free movement of goods and services between countries.

Global warming Theoretical process by which the earth's average global temperatures are increasing. This is thought to occur because of the release of **greenhouse** gases by e.g. burning fossil fuels.

Green economics Economic activities which seek to conserve the environment.

Greenhouse effect Natural warming of the lower atmosphere as greenhouse gases, e.g. carbon dioxide, sulphur dioxide, nitrous oxide and methane, absorb long-wave radiation emitted from the earth. A build-up of these gases (from pollution) may upset the warming process, causing more heat to be retained in the earth's atmosphere, and so leading to **global warming**.

Gross domestic product (GDP) The total value of all goods and services produced in a country over a period of one year. It is a measure of the wealth of a country and is often expressed as GDP per capita (i.e., the value of the GDP divided by the population total).

Gross national product (GNP) The total value of the GDP plus profits from investments abroad.

Growth corridor/pole An area where governments deliberately encourage investment and resources to stimulate economic development.

Immigration The entry of individuals into a country other than their own, with the intention to stay for at least 12 months.

Import substitution The development of local industries and production to replace imported goods, reduce dependency on imports, conserve foreign exchange and improve the balance of payments of a country.

Informal sector Work done (both paid and unpaid) without the official knowledge of the government and therefore without **formal** control.

Intervening opportunities Alternative places between two locations, A and B, that are attractive to migrants. These places distract migrants from travelling directly from place A to place B.

Law of diminishing returns As inputs are added to the production function, a point is reached beyond which yields do not increase but begin to fall.

Marginal land Land which produces minimal yield and has a low **carrying capacity**. This may be due to poor quality, over-use, or a lack of essential nutrients to support economic agricultural production.

Megalopolis Large city (200 000–500 000 people) which services surrounding area of up to 3m people, and which grows to merge into another large city.

Mercantilism Economic theory prevalent in Europe during the 17th and 18th centuries which stresses the importance of trade and commerce as the source of a nation's wealth. Mercantilism depends on wealth and power through exports and the possession of precious commodities e.g. gold, silver.

Multilateral aid Financial support given through international organisations e.g. World Bank, IMF.

Natural population change Rate of population change calculated from birth and death rates alone. Additional effects of migration are not included

Neo-colonialism Control, by an outside power, of a country that is in theory independent – especially through the domination of its economy.

New world That part of the world discovered since the middle ages. Usually this refers to the Americas (see **old world**).

Newly industrialising country (NIC) A country that has achieved rapid and successful industrialisation and economic development.

Non-governmental organisation (NGO) A voluntary, non-political, non-commercial organisation which seeks to help the less privileged members of society.

North-South divide Term first used in the Brandt report, 1979, to identify the social and economic differences between richer, **developed countries** and poorer, **developing countries**.

Optimum population The number of people who receive the best standards of living when using available resources and technology.

Old world That part of the world that was known before the discovery of the Americas, e.g. Europe, Asia and Africa.

Over-population When a population is so large, in relation to available resources and existing levels of technology, that people do not enjoy decent living standards.

Periphery   Area which is geographically remote from a central **core** area. The periphery often suffers from a lack of resources and wealth and can occur at local, regional, national or global scales (see **cumulative causation**).

Population ceiling   The theoretical maximum number of people who can be supported by the available resources and levels of technology. This is measured according to an area's **carrying capacity**.

Population distribution   The spread of people across the earth.

Population momentum   When current population growth (through increased birth rates) determines future population expansion as new babies reach the child-bearing age.

Reserve   Estimated life-span of a **finite resource** or **stock**.

Shifting cultivation   When farmers clear and burn an area of vegetation to allow them to grow crops for a few years, after which yields decline and they move to a new clearing.

Social forestry   The growing and management of forest resources in a **sustainable** manner.

Spread effects   When benefits from development spread from the **core** to **peripheral** areas. This concept is often associated with the **growth pole** theory.

Stocks   Natural resources which are measurable and limited in supply. The proven quantity of stocks is a **reserve** e.g. coal reserve is the amount of coal known to exist and which remains as yet unexploited.

Structural adjustment programme (SAP)   A set of conditions imposed on countries borrowing money from the World Bank. These often result in the government of the borrowing country having to cut national spending.

Subsistence agriculture   Farming system characterised by simple technology, low capital investment and where most produce is used for domestic consumption (compare with **commercial farming**).

Sustainability   Long-term management of the environment in order to maintain its natural resources.

Tariff   A tax or duty charged by a government on imported goods.

Third World   Group of **developing countries** characterised by low incomes and low levels of social and economic development. These countries are mostly located in Africa, Asia and South America.

Trade bloc   Group of countries united to promote common economic interests.

Transnational corporation (TNC)   Large company corporation, usually based in a **developed country**, which owns businesses in more than one country.

Under-employment   When people do not have full-time, continuous work and are usually only employed temporarily or seasonally.

Under-population   When there are too few people in a given area to fully exploit existing resources with the available technology. As a result, living standards are low. If numbers increased, living standards should improve.

Urbanisation   The process of more and more people living in towns and cities. It is expected that by the year 2000 over half the world's population will live in urban areas.

War refugee   A person displaced from her/his homeland as a result of war, or political disturbance.

Index

Published by Collins Educational
An imprint of HarperCollinsPublishers Ltd
77–85 Fulham Palace Road
London W6 8JB

www.CollinsEducation.co.uk
On-line support for schools and colleges

British Library Cataloguing Data

A catalogue record for this book is available from the British Library.

Editing/Project management: Melanie McRae
Design: Moondisks Ltd, Cambridge
Cover design: Derek Lee
Illustrations: Jerry Fowler
Production: Kathryn Botterill
Printed and bound at Scotprint

You might also like to visit
www.fireandwater.co.uk

Acknowledgements

Every effort has been made to contact the holders of copyright
material, but if any have been inadvertently overlooked, the
publishers will be pleased to make the necessary arrangements at the
first opportunity.

Photographs
Every effort has been made to contact the holders of copyright
material, but if any have been inadvertently overlooked the
publishers will be pleased to make the necessary arrangements at the
first opportunity.

The publishers would like to thank the following for permission to
reproduce photographs (T = Top, B = Bottom, C = Centre, L= Left, R
= Right):

Action Aid/Oxfam/Christian Aid, Fig 2.19;
J H Morris/Axiom, Fig 6.2, Page 38;
Photos from www.JohnBirdsall.co.uk, Fig 3.31;
British Library, London/Bridgeman Art Library, London & New York,
   Fig 2.4;
Rob Nelson/Black Star/Colourific, Fig 5.25;
Prodeepta Das, Fig 2.11;
Mary Evans Picture Library, Figs 2.1, 9.12;
J Sylvester/First Light, Fig 7.2;
Joanne O'Brien/Format Photographers, Fig 5.26;
T Waltham/Geophotos, Figs 9.17, 11.14, 11.18;
Ela Ginalska, Fig 3.16;
Dielenschnieder/Holt Studios International, Fig 3.20;
Hulton Getty Collection, Figs 4.2, 11.1;
Hutchison Library, Figs 3.1, 6.27;
Intermediate Technology/N Cooper, Fig 7.36, I MacWhinnie, Figs
   11.7, 11.8, P Calvert, Fig 11.9;
International Coffee Organization, Fig 8.5;
Francis Jegede, Figs 11.4, 11.5, 11.6;
London Aerial Photo Library, Figs 1.12, 1.16, 9.3, 9.5;
S Franklin/Magnum Photos, Fig 7.14;
Metropolitan Police, Fig 6.1;
Network Photographers/B Lewis, Figs 7.3, 9.18, C Pillitz, Figs 5.1
   (top), 10.21;
Panos Pictures/J Hartley, Fig 1.3, B Tobiasson, Fig 1.4, C Stowers, Fig
   3.15, B Paton, Fig 5.15, R Johnson, Figs 6.34, 10.9, S Leigh-Lewis,
   Fig 7.7, R Giling, Fig 7.34, P Wolmuth, Fig 8.14;
Popperfoto, Fig 1.6;
Robert Prosser, Fig 10.18;
Rex Features Ltd, Figs 4.15, 4.28;
Science Photo Library, Figs 2.9, 7.4, 7.30, 9.14;
South American Pictures, Fig 9.1; Frank Spooner Pictures/G
   Smith/Liaison, Fig 4.18, E Bouvet/Gamma Press, Fig 4.26;
Still Pictures/C Pye-Smith, Fig 2.10, P Harrison, Figs 3.2, 5.16, 6.14, C
   Caldicott, Fig 3.17, M Edwards, Figs 3.18, 3.28, 5.13, J Schytte, Figs
   3.19, 9.6, 11.2, J Maier, Fig 4.3, S Rajkoomar, Fig 5.10, H Netocny,
   Fig 5.1 (bottom), J Echart, Fig 7.28;
Gettyone Stone, Figs 4.13, 5.14, 6.13, 7.9, 7.29, 7.31, 8.1, 10.5,
   10.20;
Traidcraft, Fig 11.11;
Philip Wolmuth, Fig 1.2.

Cover photograph: Gettyone Stone